BILL AND MOYA LEAR

AN UNFORGETTABLE FLIGHT

To Teresa Stupak –

with warm
personal best
wishes –

your friend.

Moya Olsen Lear

9/1/96

Jack Bacon and Company
Reno, Nevada
1996

BILL AND MOYA LEAR

AN UNFORGETTABLE FLIGHT

BY

MOYA OLSEN LEAR

Library of Congress Catalog Card Number: 95-83452

ISBN (limited signed edition): 0-930083-05-9
ISBN (trade edition): 0-930083-06-7

Jack Bacon and Company
8155 South Virginia Street
Reno, Nevada 89511

FIRST EDITION

TO
John, Shanda, David and Tina

Table of Contents

Foreword

What follows is a love story which endured through very thick and very thin.

Taken together, Bill and I have lived for nearly the entire span of the Twentieth Century. If we missed anything, we weren't invited!

An extremely bright teenager in the early teens of this century, Bill was already charging 25 cents to crank recalcitrant engines of bran spanking new motorcars, while I, born in 1915, would grow up backstage, the daughter of "Ole" Olsen of Olsen and Johnson. Our union was an unlikely meld — but sometimes those are the best kind. In our case, it was a million-to-one shot.

By the time we met, in September 1938, at the opening of "Hellzapoppin" — Bill thought he had lived a lifetime. He was a successful inventor who had been married and divorced three times, and was not all that fascinated with getting married again!

I was twenty-three, unmarried, and thought I had lived an entire lifetime, too. Little did I know what life had in store for me!

And now in my eightieth year (Bill's been gone about sixteen years now), I find the job of digging into archives, reading letters, talking to old friends, at once comforting, excruciatingly painful, and illuminating. (For example, sometimes I feel that if I had him back here, I'd punch him right in the nose!)

Among the things we shared were the World War II period, the development of the Automatic Pilot, and the launching of Lear, Inc. on the American Stock Exchange. Then I watched Lear, Inc. become

Lear Siegler as Bill needed the capital for the design and development of the Learjet. About ten years later, we also shared Learstar 600 which became the Challenger. We flew all over the world together: to Nome, Alaska for lunch, to Paris for dinner, to Athens for the weekend, and to Moscow in a Cessna 310 before we had our Learjet.

We still had time to raise four children who've given us twelve grandchildren and a great granddaughter born May 4, 1994.

You're about to read what happened during my lifetime. I could probably write another book on the stuff I've forgotten or about what I didn't know about. And please remember, I loved Bill with an intense, unconditional love which provided a very stable basis for him to accomplish a pretty impressive list of achievements. And his love for me enriched my life to a degree which is hard to imagine in our world today.

I wouldn't change a minute of my life, (well, almost) and so, I present this book to you with my whole beating heart.

Moya Olsen Lear
Reno, Nevada
October, 1995

BOOK ONE

Moya Marie Olsen

(1915–1942)

Chapter One

M arch 27, 1915, a Saturday afternoon, I was born at home at 1429 Marquette Road, Chicago, Illinois. Let's go! I was ready, but Mother wasn't. She hadn't finished painting the bassinet. Daddy ran around the neighborhood looking for a doctor. (See, nothing's changed. You couldn't find a doctor on the weekend in 1915, either!) He ran up and down stairs in the apartment building where we lived, knocked on doors, pleaded frantically on the telephone and finally — triumphantly — appeared with a very uncomfortable gentleman.

"But Mr. Olsen, I'm not an obstetrician!"

"That's all right," Daddy said comfortably. "You're a veterinarian and that's already light years ahead of what I know about the miracle of birth!"

That's the way I came into the world, followed thirteen months later by my brother and inseparable companion — J.C. (John Charles). My birth certificate reads, "Moja Marie Olsen," the original Norwegian spelling of my name, but the kids at school called me "Mo-Ja," and I didn't like that. So we changed the spelling to "Moya." Although I was the oldest child, I was not the first-born.

Mother had had four babies in five years. The first baby they named Martha Jane. They couldn't afford a crib, so they tucked her into their bed and pushed a chair against it so she wouldn't fall out. One night she squirmed around until she smothered in the covers.

Writing about a tragedy like that brings me a stirring mental picture of Mother and Daddy in 1914, in their twenties, suffering and totally devastated, holding on to each other, weeping, trying to comfort each other, yet never quite getting over that loss.

Then J.C. and I were born. Our youngest brother was named Clem, after Mother's family. He died of consumption in 1920 when he was two years old. For years, Mother slept with Clem's little knitted cap under her pillow.

Many years later, Mother and Daddy had another child, who was stillborn. Although infant mortality was more common in those years, I don't believe my parents ever forgot the pain of losing those children, and J.C. and I grew up knowing how much we were loved and wanted and treasured.

□   □   □

My mother's name was Lillian Louise Clem. When she boarded the train in East St. Louis in 1911 to visit relatives in Chicago, she was an elegant, serious and principled young lady of twenty-one. The second of four girls in a fun-loving Irish family, she remembered seeing men staggering drunkenly from the corner saloon with buckets of beer slopping over. Thus she developed a life-long revulsion for drinking or gambling in any form. To her, a glass of wine was "drinking" and there was no compromise. Everything to her was black or white. "Don't come to me with your gray," she used to say, "You know what's right!"

During her teen-years, Mother searched for a religion with substance and meaning. She couldn't believe in a God with a long white beard up in the sky punishing us. She found Christian Science and embraced it fervently for the remainder of her life. She loved good books, good theater, and good music. While in Chicago, she went on a blind date with a charming, fun-loving, dark-haired, dark-eyed young man named John Sigvard Olsen, son of an immigrant Norwegian boilermaker. John had attended Northwestern University, majoring in music; he worked at a steady job as an office boy at Dennison's Manufacturing Company, makers of stationery supplies.

My beautiful, blue-eyed mother had never met anyone like my father who could make her laugh, who sent violets, and wrote songs and poetry for her. On November 17, 1912, they eloped to Crown Point, Indiana. For years, she remained convinced the elopement was neither solid nor legal. In fact, eight years later, with two children (having just lost Clem), she wrote in her diary:

6/5/1920
Met John in Philadelphia today. He goes to Pittsburgh next
week. Wanted him to get married today but he always has some-
thing else to do!

Finally, to her relief, they were re-married on their 25th wedding anniversary in Pacific Palisades, California. J.C. was best man and I was
maid of honor.

In the first years of their marriage, Mother and Daddy lived in
Chicago in the same little apartment where I was born. At the time
there were still three children — me, J.C and Clem. I was almost four,
J.C. almost three, and Clem, a beautiful two-year-old. Every night at
ten o'clock — even when Mother and Daddy entertained — Mother
would get us out of bed and take us to the bathroom. In order to get
to the bathroom, we had to go through the living room. I held
Mother's hand, J.C. held mine and Clem held J.C.'s. As we stumbled
through the guests standing in the livingroom, Daddy called it the
"PEE-RADE!"

By the 1920s, the country had been in and out of the Great War,
seen women inch up their skirts and bob their hair, and discovered the
likes of F. Scott Fitzgerald and Eugene O'Neill. However, J.C. and I
discovered Douglas Fairbanks in the Saturday matinee serials and became Don Q. and Lady Robin Hood in the vacant lots and basements
of our neighborhood. We played hopscotch, jacks and marbles, rode
bicycles and roller-skated; and my skate key was tied securely around
my neck with a blue velvet ribbon — not string (because my Mother
said so!). One afternoon, one of our playmates got hold of some cigarettes and we all had a puff. A neighbor discovered us smoking and
went marching straight to Mother to tell her, "You should keep better
track of your children, they are smoking over in the basement of that
new house across the street." Mother retorted, "You mind your own
business!" We loved her for that.

All in all, in our estimation, it was a fine childhood. Although
Mother didn't always approve, Daddy gave us the best playground of
all — backstage at the theatre.

Mother's life was full. As long as Daddy continued to hold a
steady job as an office boy at Dennison's Manufacturing Company,

she didn't complain too much when he joined a barbershop quartet or took a second job playing the violin for silent movies to make extra money for Sunday dinner. I recall Mother and Daddy playing the violin and piano at home, and it was lovely music. "Oh, I'm Falling In Love With Someone," was one of their favorites.

Mother was always happy at home, keeping track of expenses in a book called "Ins and Outs." She loved the business of keeping a home in order, washing, ironing and cleaning, and she loved her babies. I remember her at her Singer sewing machine. She made our clothes, Daddy's shirts and even his silk robes for his dressing room at the theater, monogramming them "JSO." (Though he was "Ole Olsen" to the theatrical world and the public, he was always — and only — John Olsen to Mother.)

Soon Daddy's extra-curricular activity took on another dimension. Playing the violin for silent movies was steady, but it didn't bring in enough money. And the barbershop quartet? Well, after the piano player quit, Daddy went to look for a replacement and more music at Waterson, Berlin and Snyder, the top music publishers of the day. There, he ran into Harold "Chic" Johnson.

Daddy remembered Chic, with his yellow high-buttoned shoes, from the Chicago Conservatory of Music, where they had been students. So, at Daddy's invitation, Chic joined the quartet, replacing the piano player.

The quartet broke up shortly thereafter, leaving Daddy and Chic to their own unique mischief. Both classically trained, they started playing dinner music in cabarets. They soon got bored, and began to clown in the act, laughing at themselves. It wasn't long before audiences began to love these two boys who made them laugh. That was how Daddy and Chic became Olsen and Johnson about 1917. They kept working in cabarets until they finally got an agent, and then they were on their way to stardom.

In those days, performers traveled by train from town to town, working vaudeville circuits. Among the better-known circuits were Keith's and Albee's, Orpheum and Pantages (better known as Pantime). At the height of vaudeville's popularity, acts worked one-night stands, two-a-days or split-weeks in small theaters where the personalities of the artists could reach over the footlights to touch every member of the audience. Not a word, expression or movement was missed. (An actual year's schedule for Olsen and Johnson can be found in the appendices.)

It was a magic time in the theater. Vaudeville played to audiences of every age and class, in towns big and small, with admission prices ranging from 10 to 60 cents.

Chapter Two

Mother's idea of marriage meant a home in one place, where the father had a respectable career and came home for dinner every night. And that's the sort of man she thought she'd married. Little did she or Daddy know that within just a few years he would abandon his office job and adopt his younger brother's name for the stage, becoming the comic and songwriter "Ole Olsen" of Olsen and Johnson, dedicating his life to making people laugh.

When Daddy's brother got older, he decided to go into show business, too. So because Daddy was already established as Ole Olsen, the young "Ole" became Ole Jr. At one time, there were Ole Olsen (Daddy), Ole Jr. (his brother), J.C. Olsen (my brother) and George Olsen, an orchestra leader (no relation), all staying at the Sherman Hotel in Chicago at the same time! Can you imagine the riot when they had to sort out their laundry when it came back?!

Olsen and Johnson got together around 1917, solidifying a partnership that would span 48 years and earn them distinction as "the oldest theatrical partnership known to man." (To which Daddy would quip: "Not counting Sears & Roebuck!") Their record is unbroken to this day.

Daddy wrote many of their songs and much of their comedic material. And it was always topical. After 1920, when Prohibition took effect, Daddy would invite the audience to "stand and sing our National Anthem!" As they heard a resounding fanfare, everyone obediently and patriotically stood. Then the orchestra would play, "How Dry I Am!" and the laughing audience would fall back into their seats.

Daddy was the straight man, Chic the comic with the infectious laugh. When they could, they would work a recognizable local person into their act. In the sketch "Oh, What A Night," there was a bed in the middle of the stage. There would be a storm, thunder and lightning effects. A girl would come out dressed in a nightgown and say, "Oh, what a night!" and crawl into bed. Then another girl would do the same until there were four girls in the bed. Then Chic (or the mayor or newspaper publisher, etc.) would sit up in the middle of the bed and say, "Oh, My God! What a night!"

Another bit everybody loved in the "Run of the Show" sequence was called "Maniac!" Daddy would run onstage and yell over his shoulder, "Louie, gimme the house lights!" Then he'd lean earnestly over the footlights and say, "Ladies and gentlemen, I have a very serious announcement to make! The manager just called from out front and said there's a maniac in the lobby who's going to shoot the man who's here with somebody else's wife. Now, there's somebody in this audience with somebody else's wife and if he wants to avert a tragedy, he'd better run down the aisle and out the backstage door." At that moment, we'd get 15 or 20 guys to run down the aisle with the "maniac" running after them shooting his gun. The bit was over in about two minutes, but everyone laughed and everybody wanted to be in the "Maniac" bit!

But things weren't so funny at home. Mother was uncomfortable and unhappy with everything that Daddy loved about performing. The constant separations were especially painful for her. Vaudeville performers traveled constantly. In a typical season during the early 1930s, Olsen and Johnson played more than 40 dates (barring canceled bookings, illness or snags such as strikes or costumes not arriving in the right place at the right time), from Cincinnati to Toronto to New York, Seattle, Kansas City, Charlotte, North Carolina — and all points in between. The constant traveling and uncertainty of life on the road bonded vaudeville players into a loosely tied but closely knit fraternity. After a show, players often gathered to swap stories, drink and play poker.

Sometimes, Mother tried to travel with Daddy, leaving us with one of her sisters. However, she disliked being backstage or alone in her hotel room, and hated worse leaving us behind. When she tried to take us along, the business of putting us to bed was a nightmare. The hotels in those days didn't have room service or cribs. Picture this:

I, the oldest, slept in the bathtub; J.C. in a dresser drawer; and Clem was wedged in bed with Mother and Daddy. Mother fed us oatmeal cooked over a can of Sterno. (Boy, it was many years before I was able to eat oatmeal without tasting the smell of Sterno in every bite.)

□   □   □

From Mother's diary entries, it's easy to picture her life with (and without) Daddy:

1/7/17
This is far short of making up for my own flat and my darling babies.

And Daddy's entry in her diary of the same day:

1/7/17
This is proving to be a delightful engagement and the act is a "hit" before a regular audience and consequently I'm happy. Lillian is reveling among "electric lights," real beds, warm room and bath and it looks like I'll have to keep up this "speed" or send Lillian back to the "minors."

1/13/17
Spending Sunday in NY. A grand little hotel, though our room isn't much for $3.00.

3/6/17
Leaving tonight again and everything went wrong with me. first Moya wet all her clothes and after I had changed her throughout and cleaned her all up she upset a cup of cocoa in her lap and there wasn't a square inch of any of her clothes that wasn't dyed in cocoa. After that I was ready to die. But I finally got everything all washed out and hung up to dry — trunk packed and Moya cleaned up again and thought it would be just lovely to have a little supper with John and take a nice walk. So after all my trials and rallying I go down to the theater to have him quickly inform me that he was going over to the hotel to entertain a bunch of officers. Could I be expected to smile after the trying evening? Well I DIDN'T. Moya and I took a walk and I

cried it out to God in the open air of the park. Lovely and cool and dark and a spring flowing and soothing me — a far better soothing syrup in the long run and more dependable than any human help or sympathy.

3/17/18
We went to church today. Moya's first experience and she might have been worse. She whispered loudly "When's the girls gonna dance?" and everyone around us laughed.

Daddy's entries in Mother's diary show a zest for living on the road, and his love for us.

3/27/18
Birthdays are always a big event in a youngsters life. I hope that Moya will always remember her first party which was held in my dressing room of the Palace Theatre in New Orleans. 3 years old, and other little tots at her "party" and candies, rabbits and everything. She's a darling little daughter and 'I LOVE HER TO DEFF!"

3/29/18
Begrimed with dirt, dust and cinders (accumulated in a 319 mile ride on the L & N) we entered Montgomery with murder in our hearts, aches in our bones and coal in our hair — and as the Germans scatter for shelter when a bomb falls so did we scatter for rooms 'ere the evening fell'. Our hotel is called "The Central" inasmuch as you have to call "Central" for a traffic cop to come and guide you into your parking space — otherwise you'd pass it up as a condemned district and in a moment of in-decision you might fall heir to $5 a day rooms at the Exchange.

□   □   □

Eventually, Mother would patch up her sense of humor and find her smile:

4/10/18
Well I cleaned up today and heated the water and cleaned all the babies. Did my first daily washing. Was scolding Moya today — or rather all of them and said "I'm just about to the end of my

string" and Moya chimes in "God is your strength, unfailing quick" (they were the words from a prayer that Mother had taught me that I said every night along with, "Now I Lay Me Down to Sleep").

8/9/18

I am blue tonight. I am beginning to love John Olsen far more than I ever dreamed of and it's because he is so darling and good and I respect him so and trust him and admire him and everything that goes to make a happy marriage. John Lover—I love you tonight.

□   □   □

Mother eventually made beautiful little silk baby caps for newborns and sold them to Marshall Fields for $5 each. She learned how from a woman named Mrs. Harris.

8/20/18

I started to work for Mrs. Harris today at $1.00 a day to learn to make fancy baby things to bring home and work.

8/21/18

Worked today. I love the work and can't imagine ever getting tired of it.

8/30/18

Finished the week and earned $9.62 for the 4-1/2 days.

□   □   □

Mother was elated about our finances improving.

9/8/19

The boys received a beautiful offer to go in a show here in NY $400 a week plus $200 for Ziegfield Frolics. They are contracted though, and of course don't know whether they can accept it or not.

9/20/19

Well my little book — I should write this entry in red ink as I think it will prove the biggest red-letter day in our lives. The boys threw over a 43 weeks route on the National Booking Office at $350 and $300 a week for $450 and $500 a week and a 2 year contract with the producer of Ziegfeld Follies.

10/7/19
 $1000 saved!

12/7/19
Left this a.m. for Dallas. Moya was sick so we took a taxi to the station $1.50!! I'll carry her the next time!

12/25/19
We had a dandy supper on the stage after the show. Then we all went down into the audience to see a film of the San Francisco fire and earthquake. After the film the curtain rose on a living room scene with a big Christmas tree and fireplace. The lights gradually went into a red glow and we heard Santa Claus bells and he came down the chimney and on to the stage. The children were entranced and it was beautiful. On our way back to the hotel J.C. rode his velocipede (tricycle) home and Moya wheeled her doll buggy with three dolls in it. We had all this to take on the train to Sacramento Monday morning.

□   □   □

4/25/21
Used a washing machine for the first time and am tickled to death with it.

8/29/21
Found a love letter of John's from Betty in London. Thank heaven I've been hurt so much that one more hurt doesn't affect me much. It is so disappointing though to believe in John as I have and get such a violent jolt.

When I found entries like this in Mother's diary after her death, my heart ached for her as I realized how she had protected me from my Daddy's infidelities.

11/24/21

**Got another of John's love letters today. I'm getting kind of tired
of this business. Think I'll answer a few of them.**

2/9/22

**Haven't heard from John but I am enjoying being with Aunt
Matte and Uncle John. The peacefulness and orderliness of their
life simply exaggerates the emptiness of my life with John.**

But the storm has passed and I have again that precious "peace that
passeth understanding."

□   □   □

While Mother was struggling with her demons and trying to cope
with her home and marriage, Daddy's days were full of fun and color.
The early '20s were the wonderful heyday of vaudeville. The bright
lights were Sophie Tucker, Fannie Brice, Al Jolson and Eddie Cantor.
In fact, Daddy wrote a song called, "Oh Gee, Oh Gosh, Oh Golly, I'm
in Love!" which Eddie sang in the Ziegfeld Follies.

Fannie Brice was a good friend of Daddy's and was one of the top
comediennes of the era. One day she took my little brother J.C.'s
hand and said to Daddy, "Listen Ole, this little boy's eyes don't need to
be crossed. I'm going to take him to my doctor and have them
straightened." And she did. Daddy gave her a hug and said, "Thank
you, Fannie!" And even Mother thanked Fannie. They hadn't known
you could do anything about crossed eyes except pray.

Another good friend was the legendary Sophie Tucker. She was a
very satisfying correspondent. If you wrote to her, she wrote you
back — in her own handwriting. We loved her. She wrote to Mother
Olsen, my grandmother (who we called Gramonyosing until we were
old enough to vote). For years. J. Edgar Hoover and Eddie Rickenbacker also corresponded with her.

Mother Olsen, Daddy's mother, was a very important part of the
landscape around the theater. She did bits. In one bit, one of the girls
would do an imitation of a baby crying out in the audience. After it
had gone on for some time, Daddy would call from the stage: "Will
somebody please stop that little baby from crying!" But the baby kept
right on crying. "Please, somebody, stop that little baby from crying."
Bam! A gun would go off in the audience. And Daddy would say,

"Thank you," and keep right on talking.

When Mother Olsen would come to visit, they'd give her a bit to do. After the gunshot went off in the baby bit, she'd get out of her seat and start walking up the aisle and Daddy would call from the stage, "Lady, don't leave, we won't shoot any more guns!" She'd keep right on walking. "Lady, please give us another chance!" "That's all right," she'd say, still walking. "But Lady, where're you going?" Daddy'd ask. And Mother Olsen would stop and turn around and say, "Well if it's any of your business, young man, I'm going to the ladies' room!"

Mother Olsen was the first one up with the coffee pot and the newspaper and the last one to bed. She was ready for anything, and considering her hardscrabble upbringing in a log cabin in mid-19th century Peru, Indiana, it was remarkable to have her close to us as long as we did.

When she was convalescing from near-fatal bronchial pneumonia in the early 1950s, she wrote a couple of letters which recalled her childhood as one of eleven children raised in a log cabin. She remembered crawling down an outside ladder from her attic bed in winter, her bare feet on the icy rungs, and walking six miles to and from school. There weren't enough clothes for all the kids in the family to attend at the same time, so she quit after getting her 5th-grade reader so the other kids could go. She also remembered how a woman in Wabash, Indiana, died giving birth to a two-pound baby, and how her own mother wrapped the tiny body in cotton and kept it close to her bosom. After caring for it for three months, the baby not only survived, but lived long enough to become a great-grandmother.

Here are some direct excerpts from my grandmother's letters:

Mother had a bag tied around her waist, in it a series of stockings and, if she just had a minute she would pull one out and put a few stitches on it. We would each get one pair a year and new feet for the old ones. I never remember my mother without that bag around her waist, I thought that was part of her.

Mother made a new asafetida bag (the healer of all ills) every Saturday which we always wore around our necks. And not only that — we had to take a pill of it. It was early America's answer to penicillin. As long as we wore that bag we couldn't be sick.

When I look back, I realize why we couldn't be sick, no disease could penetrate the odor of that asafetida bag! We were mighty healthy in those days.

I spend a lot of time remembering. Old age is like the time after childbirth. The results are so wonderful that you forget the pain that brought it here.

Mother Olsen died in 1958 at almost 100 years of age.

□   □   □

By the mid-'20s, Olsen and Johnson were on their way to becoming headliners, billed as "Likeable Lads Loaded with Laughs." If you got good reviews throughout the country, you were almost automatically promoted from the anonymity of small-time vaudeville circuits to Western Vaudeville and Junior Orpheum, then major Orpheum and on to Keith's big-time circuit.

One of the most coveted bookings in vaudeville was Keith's Theatre in Washington, D.C., where every performance was like opening night. The audiences always sparkled with Congressional VIPs and ambassadorial dignitaries, plus their ladies — all of whom Daddy described as, "be-jeweled, be-medaled, and be-minked!"

One of their most loyal and enthusiastic fans was President Woodrow Wilson, who always occupied the upper left-hand box at Keith's Theatre. He was idolized by performers because he was always ready to laugh and applaud. Sadly, World War I had left him a disappointed and disillusioned man wracked with illness. Daddy once told me a wonderful story about President Wilson, which was also one of the most important events in Olsen and Johnson's career.

The theater had been advised that the President and his party would attend the following night — December 24, 1923. For Daddy, it was an unforgettable night. Everyone backstage was wound up tight! The makeup went on with more care, the costumes were pressed, the sequins carefully sewn on, the props in order.

In happier years, President Wilson had entered jauntily to "Hail to the Chief" and bowed to the enthusiastic applause of the audience. But on this night, there was no gaiety. His arrival in the theater was acknowledged by subdued, respectful applause and — as the concerned audience watched silently and sadly — his wheelchair was pushed down to the front where four rows had been removed so Wilson's aides could maneuver him more easily.

The tension disappeared with the opening fanfare. The lovable brashness of Olsen and Johnson soon prevailed. Wilson and the rest of the audience swelled with holiday exuberance. After a particularly noisy and hilarious bit, a Western Union messenger hurried down the aisle and handed Daddy a telegram. He read it to the orchestral accompaniment of "Jingle Bells":

        OLSEN AND JOHNSON
        KEITH'S THEATRE
        WASHINGTON, DC.

        SANTA CLAUS AND HIS HELPERS JUST
        LEFT TOY LAND AND ARE ALL EQUIPPED TO
        JUMP INTO THE HEARTS AND HOMES OF THEIR
        MILLIONS OF PLAYMATES EVERYWHERE.
        STOP. SHOULD BE IN YOUR VICINITY SOON.
        STOP.

Then as "Jingle Bells" grew louder, the curtain slowly rose to reveal an immense twinkling Christmas tree and a fireplace decked with stockings. Chic, dressed as Santa Claus, burst from the fireplace with a huge bag full of little gifts that he proceeded to throw at an applauding and laughing audience.

A trumpet fanfare interrupted the fun and the orchestra broke into the "Star-Spangled Banner." Down from the flies — where the curtains were rolled up — came a massive picture of President Wilson, entwined with holly and mistletoe. The audience became wildly and warmly demonstrative. Standing in front of the assembled company, Daddy beckoned for quiet and said, "All of the artists here behind the footlights in this make-believe world of ours wish You ... and You ... and You up there ..." (pointing to the orchestra, balcony and gallery) a very Merry Christmas and a Happy New Year."

At that moment, brilliant young vaudeville star Nan Halperin skipped out, climbed a ladder, and fervently kissed President Wilson's picture. The orchestra broke into "Auld Lang Syne" and the performers carried a huge bouquet of roses down the aisle to Mrs. Wilson. The audience and performers wept openly. And then President

Wilson — obviously moved by the heart-felt demonstration of affection — struggled to rise from his wheelchair to acknowledge the pandemonium . . . but sank back, unable to get to his feet. Groping for his handkerchief, he waved his feeble and last goodbye to a vaudeville (and, in fact, to any) audience.

Daddy later wrote: "We were proud of those tears. And we knew, as we dressed slowly, closing up the theater ("Goodnight! Goodnight!") and walked to the hotel, that we had witnessed a tiny slice of history and we were part of it."

□   □   □

By 1928, Olsen and Johnson had reached what they thought was the pinnacle of vaudeville stardom — headlining the Palace Theatre on Broadway and 47th Street. Also on the bill, in small print — was Jack Benny. Olsen and Johnson packed theaters all over the country. Huddling under umbrellas, people lined up around the block in a driving rain to see them. Even during the Depression, people could always find a quarter to go see Olsen and Johnson.

Olsen and Johnson captured the attention of the press for an act that one newspaper labeled "a carnival of the unconventional." Famous for their rapid-fire gags and pranks, Olsen and Johnson regularly bounced their show straight across the footlights into the audience. In a bit called "Hide-n-Seek," Daddy stood and leaned against the proscenium, eyes covered, counting, "five, ten, fifteen, twenty..." while Chic ran out into the audience, yelling, "I'll hide, I'll hide." Chic would sit on some woman's lap and put on her hat! Audiences loved the comic duo and so did the critics:

> **"If you have a fit of the blues and want a good laugh, Olsen and Johnson are good doctors."**

> **"Olsen and Johnson, a pair of boys whose act is so insane, manage to send a house full of Vaudeville fans homeward bound with cracks in the ribs."**

While all this fun was taking place, a wonderful character appeared in the audience: a gentleman who laughed so loudly he kept the audience laughing while Daddy and Chic took a breath. He was so hysterical, Olsen and Johnson were accused of putting a plant in the audience. Well, Daddy wanted to meet this fella and decided that after the next show he'd track him down. He not only met him, but brought him backstage and discovered in the course of conversation that the man was a Catholic priest, Father Wagner, and starved for something to laugh about. Mimicking Father Wagner's laugh, Chic developed his own hysterical giggle, and kept it throughout his career. Father Wagner tried never to miss an Olsen and Johnson show. Matter of fact, whenever he had a sabbatical, he would turn his collar around and find Olsen and Johnson. Their friendship continued for the rest of the priest's life.

Daddy and Chic were out in Hollywood making a movie when they received a telegram from Father Wagner saying he would be arriving at Union Station in Los Angeles, giving them the time and day. Daddy, with his special sense of glee, hauled Chic down to the Western Costume Company and got someone there to dress them as authentic Catholic priests!

Then they went down to Union Station and waited on the platform for Father Wagner's train. It roared in and stopped. Passengers started to get off. Pretty soon they saw Father Wagner, but he didn't see them. Or, not recognizing them, he was anxiously looking right past them for his friends, Ole and Chic. The good priest went about ten feet past them — then stopped suddenly. He turned slowly, not believing what he thought he'd just seen. Daddy and Chic kept playing it absolutely straight. Then the laughter started. Our hero, Father Wagner, wearing slacks and an Hawaiian shirt, pointed at Daddy and Chic, and leaning against a post, laughed that laugh of his. He finally slumped down onto the platform, unable to stand — still pointing at these two uncomfortable "priests," who were looking at him compassionately! For Olsen and Johnson, it was a sight never to be equaled in their memories, as they watched startled passengers trying to walk past the scene. Some of whom, I'm convinced, were sure that orderlies with a straitjacket would appear any minute!

Another funny bit I remember was when Olsen and Johnson were playing the Golden Gate Theatre in San Francisco. It was a show called "Monkey Business," and Daddy wanted to stir up some fun publicity so he got the gang together and they rounded up every organ grinder's monkey in the city (about 20 or 30) and piled them in a panel truck with the names of different critics on tags tied on their collars and drove over to Union Square. Then the door "accidentally" came open, and, you guessed it, the monkeys escaped in every direction all over Union Square to the delight and hilarity of everyone there that afternoon. Finally, after rounding up all the monkeys, Olsen and Johnson were arrested for malicious mischief. Can you imagine trying to pull a stunt like that today?

Chapter Three

If the theater is a fantasy wonderland for adults, imagine what it was like for two children growing up backstage! One of my very first memories was learning how to walk from the hotel to the theater without getting run over. We were taught to get behind a grown-up, and, when the light changed, just follow him across the street.

I loved being backstage, sitting in the chorus girls' dressing room between shows and seeing the costumes and the makeup. I used to stand with my six-year-old mouth open, watching the chorus girls put mascara on by heating it over a can of Sterno, then using a little brush, "beading" their eyelashes again and again.

Daddy never allowed anyone backstage to use vulgar language in front of his children, and people in the company were always very sweet with us. Although I don't remember it, Mother told me that Gracie Allen of Burns and Allen was very fond of me and sometimes looked after me backstage during the show!

J.C. and I were a tiny Lewis and Clark, exploring the silent, empty theaters. What an adventure! One of the spookiest things two children could do was to explore a dark, silent theater at eight o'clock in the morning. With its empty seats and a mute, dimly lit stage. The big shadowy room backstage, where all the props hunched like grotesque giants, was our favorite place to play "Hunchback of Notre Dame." The cavernous, echoing organ loft was another spot we enjoyed. If we were really lucky in our explorations — if there were acrobats on the bill — we'd find a trampoline!

Sometimes during our wanderings we got to be part of the show.

In one scene during the great actor, Walter Huston's dramatic performance, J.C. and I were stuck backstage trying to cross behind the
scenery when we spotted a square of light and crawled through it.
Unfortunately it was just as Mr. Huston reached his most impassioned
climax — and there we were, crawling through the fireplace behind
him! The audience erupted with laughter.

Vaudeville folks loved a good gag, and Daddy was no exception.
Years and years ago, on the bill with Olsen and Johnson was lovely
Irene Castle. She was an elegant dancer and could not understand
how her agent had taken leave of his senses to the extent that he
would put her on the same bill as Olsen and Johnson!

It was all my father needed. He teased her mercilessly. And one
day (it went down in Olsen and Johnson history), he got her good. In
Miss Castle's act, she did a beautiful dance number which pan-
tomimed the allegory of Pandora's Box. There was an antique trunk
on stage and she danced dramatically around it until, at a certain
point, she hesitatingly opened it and jumped back in shock when —
the big dramatic moment of the dance — all the "bad thoughts" flew
out. One matinee, Daddy, full of mischief, stuffed J.C. and me in that
trunk with whispered instructions: "Now, when Miss Castle opens the
chest, just jump out and run offstage!"

Which we did. We jumped out and ran off stage. But no one, not
even Daddy, was prepared for the roar of laughter that exploded in
that theater! Needless to say, Miss Castle (who almost had a heart at-
tack), never spoke to Daddy again. I shouldn't say never, because almost 20 years later a Chicago radio talk-show hostess, Mary Margaret
McBride, brought Irene Castle and Ole Olsen of Olsen and Johnson
together on her show. It showed great character in Miss Castle that
she agreed to do the interview. She was still nervous around Daddy
because he was still winking mischievously at her!

Another time, Daddy became intrigued by the artistry of Owen
McGivney, who was on the bill with Olsen and Johnson for several
seasons. This gifted quick-change artist impersonated Shakespeare,
Dickens characters and even people in the news. He would leave the
stage as one character, and step just inside the proscenium to a chair
where his dresser whipped around him — changing his beard, hat,
cane and coat — so he could step back onstage transformed into a
completely different character.

One night, Daddy nailed Mr. McGivney's boots to the floor just offstage. When he came offstage, he sat in his chair, put his hat and cape on, tucked his feet into his boots and started to return to the stage. But only his head and shoulders made it to the spotlight.

For one of their shows, the marquee spelled out for the world to see: "Olsen and Johnson present the only singing goat in captivity!" There was a big song in those days: "Ma! She's Making Eyes At Me! Ma! She's Got Me Up A Tree!" Eddie Cantor made it very popular. Well, during the show, Daddy and Chic stepped through the curtain holding the goat between them. After a huge fanfare by the orchestra: TAH-DAH! Daddy pinched the goat which let out an eloquent "BAA!" and they sang "She's Making Eyes At Me!" (Another pinch) "BAA!" "She's Got Me Up A Tree!" It was a wonderful bit until the S.P.C.A. caught up with them!

□   □   □

Meanwhile, at home, my wonderful mother tried valiantly to make sure our lives had some discipline, and my fun-loving daddy did his best to make sure there was none, ever. With him, there was always something to laugh about. J.C. and I loved the crazy stuff Daddy brought home: props that had been abandoned, discarded costumes — and all shapes and sizes of dogs.

A white Russian wolfhound Daddy named Ha-Ha came at the same time as a white Pomeranian he named Hee-Hee. My Mother's sense of humor was strained to the limit: she was already steaming about the St. Bernard she had to take care of and feed. This beautiful dog had been given to Daddy by someone in the circus who told him in glowing, extravagant terms what a great "trick dog" he was. He could jump through a hoop in the air, play dead, run in circles, etc. What the man left out was that the dog only responded to German commands. The dog didn't understand English! We were delighted with all the pets but each created just more frustration for my mother.

After weeks and weeks on the road, Daddy would come home, fish us out of school and find the nearest amusement park. With him holding our hands and loving us, we hung onto each other on the "rollie coaster." We loved our daddy and his complete lack of concern about how much anything cost. Then we had to go home and face our mother and her blazing blue Irish eyes.

In her diary she wrote:

8/29/23

Found out tonight that John has bought a home in Malverne, Long Island—Imagine!! Buying a home for ME to live in without me seeing it.

8/31/23

We went out to see the house this morning and I was more disappointed than I dared let John know. I wouldn't even have considered the house for one minute if I had seen it first and it's so far out of town, he's never going to be home. Oh! Such a sick feeling!!

Our home at 50 Roosevelt Ave. in Malverne, Long Island, New York, had a fireplace in the living room that Daddy thought was the centerpiece of the whole house. Mother marched right past his fireplace looking for the closets! They were very few and very skimpy. They'd only hold a few hangers. There was an unfinished basement (no floor) and an unfinished attic. She explored all this, her first home, with something much worse than dismay!

Undaunted, however, she decided that if it was going to be home, then by golly, she was going to make it look like home. So the first thing she did was go to the hardware store, buy some lumber, a hammer and some nails, and she built a table and two benches for the kitchen. We had all our meals on that table for years. When we could afford to buy a "dinette set," we still hung on to Mother's table and benches.

She was strong, independent and knew how to do everything. She drove her car all over the country to meet Daddy when he'd wire her to join him in St. Louis, Chicago, Baltimore or wherever. If she and Daddy were traveling in the car together and they had a flat tire, Daddy would hold the flashlight while she changed the tire! Not because Daddy wouldn't help her, he just didn't know how. She kept the books and took care of the taxes. She taught us economy, tidiness, how to think and act right, and what God and Man are and their relationship to each other. Daddy taught us how to talk to people, how to mix, how to have a good time, how to put people at ease, and, above all, how to laugh.

By the time we were in school and not traveling as often with the show, Mother's diaries (from the later '20s and '30s) don't reflect the aching loneliness of those early years. She was making a life for herself in Malverne. She had her car, she had us, her bridge club, sewing circle — and she had her church.

She always went to church on Sunday and Wednesday nights. Christian Science sustained her through all her difficult years with Daddy; in fact, all her life. She tried long and hard to inspire a similar faith in Daddy. Even though he tried repeatedly to go to church, it just didn't take. Once, we attended a famous church and after the service he said: "Do you know there are 490 lights in that ceiling?" But he was religious about making people laugh.

He was never too busy to do a benefit — he did hundreds. He was never too broke to help out the newsboy or a fellow actor. Everyone around knew what a soft touch he was (to my mother's despair). His motto was, "It's nice to be important, but it's more important to be nice." He and Chic signed off every show saying, "May you live as long as you want to, and may you laugh as long as you live."

When I look at pictures of J.C. and me from those days, I see two skinny, brown-eyed, dark-haired children with mischievous grins — especially if Daddy was in the picture, too. Ours was the house in the neighborhood where all the kids congregated — until Mother sent us to bed at eight o'clock and we had to watch through cracks in the blinds while our friends played out in the street! We knew we were fortunate to be the children of a star, and it was a special treat to be able to take our friends backstage, but we sure wished we could play outside until nine o'clock.

Olsen and Johnson criss-crossed our nation on trains over and over again, month after month. In the club car, poker games went on all the time. During Prohibition, they would buy liquor in Canada, but the only problem was getting it back across the border. They would tie twine around the bottles and hang them out of the train and close the window so when the inspectors came through the train there wasn't a bottle in sight. But one day, the train pulling into the station took a different track and, when an inspector walking along the platform saw all those bottles hanging out the windows, he took his stick and broke every bottle.

I loved the trains. J.C. and I were too fascinated — riding happily in the observation car — to care very much about the dirt and the crowding and the inconvenience that bothered Mother.

Once we were all set to join Daddy on a trip to Sydney, Australia, his agents were going to pay our passage from San Francisco to

Sydney, but not New York to San Francisco. Well, something as trivial as that never stopped my mother when it came to keeping her family together. So, she pawned her jewelry to buy our railroad tickets and off we went!

J.C. and I shared an upper berth and Mother had the lower. In the daytime, there were two seats facing each other. Then, about 5:30 p.m., a man from the dining car would walk sedately through the train ringing his four-tone gong calling, "Dining car to the rear!" And, because we were always ready for the first call, we'd walk as fast as we could through the train to the diner, loving the exciting roar of noise between the Pullman cars. For two children who could remember eating supper on tiny chairs pulled up to Mother's piano bench, the dining car was beautiful, with white table cloths, gleaming silver, fresh flowers and smiling, courteous waiters.

While we were having dinner, the porter made up our berths. When we returned to our seats, the railroad car, which during the day was full of bench seats, had been transformed into a dark green corridor of berths — uppers and lowers. We thought this was magic! We spent many undetected hours scampering up and down those spooky dark green corridors in our bare feet until we encountered the black porter: "You chillun get back in yo berf befo Ah tell yo Mama!" We went.

I remember the sound of the trains at night while speeding through a town in the dark. Approaching a crossing we'd hear DING DING DING DING — then DING DING DING DING as we pressed our noses against the ice cold window, watching the crossing fly by with all the cars snaking through the town.

In Chicago we changed trains and stations amid dozens of Red Caps and taxis. Finally, as we settled down in our seats on the Southern Pacific Railroad, we felt like we were taking off for the moon! We crossed Missouri, Kansas, Oklahoma, the Texas Panhandle — and the scenery was so immense! When the train stopped in Albuquerque, New Mexico, the Indians, dressed in their native costumes, came down to the station to sell their jewelry, rugs and baskets. We crossed Arizona, and, once in Çalifornia, on our way to Los Angeles, we stopped in Pasadena where we bought huge buckets of oranges for 25 cents. Finally we traveled up the breath-taking unspoiled coast to San Francisco, where we met Daddy. Then we all boarded the S.S. Sonoma and sailed for Australia on January 6, 1927.

We stayed in Australia for eight months. J.C. and I went to school but it didn't work because in the Australian school system boys and girls were separated. Worse yet, the kids didn't like Americans. So, because we were baffled, unhappy and homesick, Mother got us a tutor and we received the rest of our Australian schooling at home.

One night when we were living in Sydney, Olsen and Johnson had been invited to entertain the Duke and Duchess of York, George and Elizabeth (the future King and Queen of England) at a very elegant party.

One of their best jokes of the evening referred to Charles Lindbergh, who had just made his historic solo flight to Paris in a single-engine airplane. There was great excitement Down Under about this marvelous American nicknamed "The Lone Eagle" who had flown across the Atlantic ocean — alone! When Olsen and Johnson made their entrance at the party, Daddy asked, "And who are you?" Chic took off his top hat and, as a pigeon flew off the top of his head, he'd yell, "I'm the Lone Eagle!"

Normally for this bit, a small shelter would have been arranged in the wings off stage, and the bird's only meal of the day would be placed there so it would fly around for a moment and then head for its roost. But in all the excitement, the food for the pigeon had been forgotten. The confused pigeon flew around and around and finally committed a faux pas which barely missed the future king.

As part of the entertainment for this dignified crowd, Daddy, undaunted, organized a special dance which he remembered from his childhood in Indiana. He started the music with a flair and allowed those attending to choose partners and begin dancing. Then he stopped the music and said, "Now, gentlemen, take off your coats and trade them with the man standing next to you!" Stunned, then laughing good-naturedly, they traded coats. This was followed by more music, more dancing, and then the music stopped. Daddy then told the men, "Now, gentlemen, put your coat on the lady with whom you're dancing!" (It gets better.) Again there was more music and dancing. (Just remember, this was The Royal Party in Sydney, Australia, in 1927.) Daddy stopped the music again: "Now gentlemen, take the coat off the lady with whom you're dancing and put it on yourself." Well, there was genuine hilarity when the inevitable happened. A tall, distinguished British fellow found himself in a jacket three sizes too small for him, while a little five-foot-six, red-faced, laughing man was lost in a coat three sizes too large!

After they straightened out the huge mess in high good humor, Daddy started the music. They whirled around the floor before he stopped it yet again. "Now folks, make a circle!" (Obediently, laughingly, they made a circle.) "Now all the ladies take off your right shoe and throw it into the center of the circle!" Then he separated them — a circle of ladies going THIS WAY outside a circle of gentlemen going THAT WAY. "Now gentlemen, pick up a shoe and find the lady it belongs to and dance with her!!" It was a riot! They never had so much fun! Later, the Duke came up to Daddy and whispered in his ear: "What became of the pigeon?" (The stage manager had put him safely back in his cage.)

The party was an enormous success, and Daddy became very popular, and, of course, was often invited out. Mother grumbled about this, but never really wanted to go out and party with him anyway and she insisted he get home before midnight. Several evenings later, he was out after midnight with a distinguished member of the Royal Party. As Mother lit into him, he tried to defend himself by telling her who he'd been with. Listening to this heated argument in my room, I never will forget her answer: *"Nobody worthwhile is out after midnight!"*

I remember kneeling beside my bed many nights, sobbing and praying for them not to argue. Times of discord were bad for me, but I didn't pull into a shell to protect myself; instead, I jumped into the fray. I'd challenge Daddy, saying, "You did . . ." and "That wasn't fair," and I'd go to Mother saying, "Don't worry, it's OK," "Don't worry, because you know how good he is," and "He didn't mean to do that." Since I started that very early in my life, Mother called me her "Little Comfort" from the time I was four.

My parents often fought because they just saw things differently. For example, Mother would say to Daddy, "Don't lend that man any more money because you know he's never going to pay it back! You're a jellyfish! You don't have enough character to say NO!" And Daddy would lend the down-on-his-luck performer more money because the guy would cry on his shoulder, "Ole, we don't have any money and we need to pay the rent." Daddy would pay the rent. And who's to say that's wrong? Mother was right, but Daddy was right in another way.

□   □   □

After we came back home to Malverne from Australia, J.C. and I attended Central High School in Valley Stream on Long Island, and I don't think two kids ever had more fun in high school. I was elected student body president and re-elected until I graduated in 1932. I was also the chief cheerleader and led a squad of six. Daddy got us big white megaphones with "Central High School" painted in blue on them. J.C. edited and published the school paper. We had a lock on Central High School!

As I entered high school, our nation was in the depths of the worst depression in U.S. history. Millions were homeless, without jobs or enough to eat. Ironically, it was the "best of times" for us because Daddy was a star and theaters everywhere were a refuge for the masses who were suffering. Almost anybody could scrape up the 40 or 50 cents it took to escape into a world of music and laughter.

J.C. and I always had a car. Mother bought two Fords when we were in high school. Mine was a four-door convertible and J.C.'s was a spiffy little Model A roadster with a rumble seat. She paid $750 for both of them! And man, we had fun. We splashed fourteen directions at once. I used to love to pile as many of my friends as I could get into the car, drive up to Connecticut and try to get lost on the beautiful old country roads, but I always knew the way home. I also had a raccoon coat for the cold weather and a yellow "slicker" made of oil cloth for the rain. My friends signed their names on it with dumb little sayings like, "oh you kid!"

Bus Geiger, my steady boyfriend all through high school (whom I would've married as soon as he got a job making $25 a week), was the six-foot-four captain of the football team and, of course, center on the basketball team, the champions of Nassau County. After the games in the gym, which we always won, we'd pile in our cars and drive into Valley Stream tooting our horns happily, then crowd into the soda fountain for a Coke or a milk shake. In that gang, there was no drinking (that I knew about) — and drugs were unheard of. When we went to the school dances, since I was not quite five-foot-two, my chin hit Bus' belt buckle!

The first heartbreak in my life was when he began to pull away from me. It was painful for him, too, but although he loved me and my family, he was never comfortable in the world of the theater. And the gulf widened as I continued to be away more and more. We dated for almost seven years. When I went to Ohio State University, he sent me violets every Sunday to wear to church and he wrote to me every day. He was a strong, stabilizing part of my growing up, and wherever he is today, I salute him.

During those wonderful high school years, Olsen and Johnson were on the road down in Florida doing one-night stands. Mr. E. L. Cord, the great automobile designer and builder, was very fond of them and loaned them a fleet of Cords and Auburns — no charge! That's when we got the gorgeous Auburn Speedster and, in the course of the tour, wound up in Minneapolis.

How could I have been so lucky as to have a father who said, "Honey, how would you like to drive the Speedster down to Cincinnati?" (our next port of call).

Wow! I was in that car and on my way before Daddy got out of the dressing room. It was the first and only car I ever drove 105 mph! At seventeen, I liked to drive at night because there was no traffic on the road (forget an itinerant cow that might be strolling across the dark highway!). I've always loved to drive, and that night with the top down, with Minnesota flying past my ears, I sang at the top of my lungs — and looked up at the night sky and said, "Thank you, God."

The tour ended and we all spent the summer in Malverne. In those days, the early '30s, going to college wasn't top priority for the average girl — almost as if it were in the Bible — you got married, settled down, and had a family. So, while I waited for J.C. to graduate from high school, I went to Brown's Business School in Lynbrook near Malverne, to learn to type. Then, wonder of wonders, in 1934 we both enrolled at Ohio State University — and everyone wanted to know, "Why Ohio State?" Here's the story. A vintage Olsen Family story:

At the end of that summer in Malverne, Daddy had invited some friends of his — a theater manager and his family — out to the house for the weekend. The manager's daughter's name was Nikki Phelps and we enjoyed each other's company immensely. We went to the theater in New York, swimming out at Jones Beach and just generally bummed around. So, when it was time for them to go, J.C. and I said, "Why don't you stay? We're having such a good time!" Nikki answered:

"Because I gotta go back to school."

"Oh really? Where do you go to school?"

"Ohio State, where do you go?"

"Well, er, uh, we hadn't thought about it."

"So you'd better darn well think about it. It's September."

I looked at J.C. and J.C. looked at me and I said, "Why don't we go to Ohio State?" So we threw some bags in the car and away we went to Columbus, Ohio. We drove because we wanted a car at school (When we'd get low on gas, I'd get a date who'd always come up with five gallons!). Mother took the train. When we enrolled, our pictures were on the front page of the Columbus Dispatch with our father — we were the children of a star and we loved it.

I majored in journalism because I wanted to write, but I found out very soon that I wasn't interested in "Who — What — Where — When — Why" or in setting type. I wanted to write! Unfortunately, I didn't have a counselor to say, "Moya, you should be an English major." Darn it. But I did record the following in the school paper during that first year — not earth-shaking, but certainly prophetic: "My ambition is to marry the one I love and have a nice little home and children and write a book. Whether it will materialize or not is one of the deeper mysteries of my life and, characteristic of the Olsens, I'm not going to force any issues."

I didn't return to Ohio State for a second year. I wasn't accomplishing anything. I lived in Malverne and commuted to New York to attend Pace Institute down in the Wall Street district, where I continued my typing and shorthand proficiency because I wanted to get a job. I felt so grown up as I bought my copy of the New York Times, boarded the train, found a seat and, after I read the front page, flipped to Section B and read Will Rogers' column. J.C. finished two more years at Ohio State, and then transferred to the University of Southern California in Los Angeles, from where he later graduated.

Maybe the best thing to come out of that year at Ohio State occurred on May 5, 1935, when Mother and Daddy surprised us with a darling baby girl named Joy. Daddy called us at school in Columbus and said, "Your baby sister was just born." He called on Friday, and we were so proud, we took off after class and drove like two lunatics to Malverne (nearly 600 miles) — loved that baby and visited Saturday, drove back to school Sunday afternoon, and skidded into class Monday morning!

Once an interviewer asked Daddy about the surprise of such a late-life baby when he traveled so much and he answered, chuckling, "It's amazing what you can do these days with remote control!"

Chapter Four

In the mid-1930s, Franklin Roosevelt was in his first term in office, Hitler was Chancellor of Germany, Prohibition was repealed after fourteen years, Jesse Owens was sweeping the Olympics, gangsters were losing their grip and Edward VIII lost his crown over the woman he loved. And me? I was where I was happiest — backstage!

When I finished my studies at Pace Institute, Daddy offered me a job traveling with the company. I loved that. There were things I could do to make myself useful, and I felt a lot better working with the company than floundering around at home without work. I was a combination Girl Friday and advance press aide. Traveling with the advance man, I helped set up radio interviews. Sitting out front in rehearsals, I took notes on the show and made suggestions to punch up the dialogue, speed up the cues, and keep the show moving swiftly.

I remember we were playing the Main Street Theatre in Kansas City, August 16, 1935, when we heard that Will Rogers' airplane had gone down in Alaska, and that both Will Rogers and Wiley Post, the pilot, were killed. Daddy was always very fond of Will Rogers, and often reminisced about the time in Chicago when Rogers was appearing at the Chicago Theatre and Olsen and Johnson were conducting their madhouse right across the street at the State Lake Theatre.

During one of Daddy's shows, an usher came back to inform them that Will had slipped in to catch their show. Their spies had located Will — slouched down in his seat — about halfway down in the house. And just before Daddy and Chic got involved in their mystery scene where the gorilla followed the screaming girl up the aisle, they planted four stooges and three girl "screamers" around Will's location. When the cue came, the fusillade of shots that blazed out in the darkness around Will could have been heard in his own theater across the street. Then the screaming girls fell all over him. All he could do was sit there helpless with laughter.

He got so interested in what Olsen and Johnson were doing that he missed part of his own show. The manager of the Chicago learned that Will was in the State Lake, and Daddy had to page him over the loudspeaker. Will thought it was an Olsen and Johnson gag! That is, until the manager of his own theater came down the aisle and acidly inquired if it would inconvenience Will very much to step across the street and entertain a sold-out house, which the management would like to get out of the theater as soon as possible in order to seat the hundreds who were standing in line, anxious to pour money in the theater's coffers — which, in turn, would be used to pay Will Rogers one of the largest salaries ever paid a single performer! Then the manager stalked out.

Daddy also shared these memories and more with Goodman Ace (does anybody remember the "Easy Aces"?) at a radio station in Kansas City the day after the tragic loss of Will Rogers. It was in that interview that Daddy closed by reading a poem he had written about this heartbreaking event:

> Somewhere in frozen Alaska,
> A propeller is battered and bent.
> No longer it hums
> For fate beat her drums
> Then Death zoomed in tragic torment.

> Today the hearts of a nation
> Yea, the hearts of the world
> Are throbbing with grief
> For life is so brief
> When death's flags are too-soon unfurled.

> I spec' God was having His hands full
> And a laugh was what He needed most.
> So an Angel flew out for Will Rogers
> And he was piloted to Heaven by Post.

No one expected the deluge of response to the poem. And because many listeners wanted it, the girls at that radio station and I typed hundreds of copies. There was no such thing as Xerox or Kinko's, only a bunch of us making sure we got the carbon paper in right!

All in all, mine was a dream job with only one drawback. By this time, Daddy was a big star as well as being a genuinely warm, funny, handsome — and lonely man. I had not known before about the girls he saw on the side, and it was terribly disillusioning to see him in the front seat of a car flirting with one of the girls in the show while I was sitting in the back seat. I didn't want to see it. As I grew older, I came to understand that those other girls didn't change the love and respect he had for my mother. But my acceptance and understanding of this didn't come easily. I understood Daddy being the person he was, loving people and needing company all the time, and Mother being reserved — never comfortable with the crowd in his dressing room. Everybody visited Daddy in his dressing room — military officers, labor bosses, press, artists, spongers and all the friends Olsen and Johnson had made playing Omaha or Spokane or Denver or any little town in the country with a theater. I was just beginning to comprehend what a struggle it can sometimes be to keep love and a marriage alive, especially in show business.

□   □   □

Olsen and Johnson were enormously successful as comedians, and interviewers often asked how they did it. In one of his interviews, Daddy said:

> **"Humor is a commodity — ranks right up there with steel, transportation, communication and perjury! The next time you go to a show — preferably MY show — and have a good laugh, remember that somebody has gone through extensive training, has taken infinite pains, has made exhaustive tests to create and produce your laugh and to bring it to you. Also reflect that you have paid out good hard cash in return for something intangible — and just try to figure out who has the last laugh!"**

In another interview, he mused:

> **"You know, we're not really comedians in the true sense of the word — we're laugh manufacturers. We aren't funny in ourselves; we don't wear putty noses or baggy pants. We just create**

situations that get laughs — anybody could do it. Our only rule of thumb is to keep things moving — fast. Talent. Music. Comedy!"

"A young fellow asked me one time to what I attributed my success. I said, 'You have to jump at your opportunities.' 'But how do I know which opportunity to jump at?' the fellow asked. I explained, 'You DON'T know — you just keep on jumping'!"

By the late '30s, movies were pushing vaudeville into oblivion. Olsen and Johnson were still working because their act combined movies and their live show. They did four, five, six shows a day with a movie showing between performances. And the show at that time had a line of girls, orchestra, stage hands, a company manager, a stage manager and an advance publicity man.

Later, in 1938, Olsen and Johnson received the biggest boost in their career. While they were playing Philadelphia, a friend saw their show — "Hellzapoppin" — and suggested to Lee Shubert, the big-time Broadway producer, that he ought to see it. And Daddy said, "I don't think he expected to be too impressed with it. He sneaked into the theater one night reluctantly, totally unprepared for what he saw."

As it happened, Mr. Shubert saw the show the night the American Legion gave Olsen and Johnson a citation for their extensive work in veterans' hospitals. The theater was packed to the walls, and when The Drum and Bugle Corps came marching down the aisle, Shubert thought it was something they'd worked up for a smash finale. There was an excitement in that theater he'd never seen. He liked it!

The Shuberts invested $25,000 in "Hellzapoppin"— reluctant to invest more because they considered it a wild card. They used scenery from shows such as "Blossom Time" and "Student Prince," that had been gathering dust in warehouses, added a few musical numbers, and tried the show out in Boston. What happened next was nothing short of phenomenal in the history of show business.

Chapter Five

"Hellzapoppin" premiered Thursday, September 22, 1938, at the 46th Street Theatre. I think it was one of the only Broadway shows ever to open without an actual production script. It was my job to sit in the audience and take down the dialogue and action, lyrics and names so that a script could be submitted for copyright to the Library of Congress. This wasn't easy — matter of fact, it was almost impossible — because every show was different.

A film parade of famous faces opened the show — actual film clips of Franklin Roosevelt, Adolph Hitler, union leader John L. Lewis, New York mayor Fiorello La Guardia, not to mention Benito Mussolini. But the words and voices belonged entirely to the imagination of Olsen and Johnson:

> **Roosevelt: ". . . Our troubles are not over but we are on our way and we are headed for 'Hellzapoppin.' "**

> **Hitler: [In Yiddish dialect] ". . . Are you leffing? Am I leffing? I am tickled to teenchy veenchy pieces . . . Ah-hooray! Ah-hooray! Ah-whoopee!"**

> **Mussolini: ". . . As sure as big oaks from little acorns grow you can't go wrong with an Olsen and Johnson show!"**

"Hellzapoppin" was short on plot, long on audacity, and its energy ricocheted all over the theater. You had to be there! The audience

Baby Moya Olsen in the lap of her mother
Lillian; behind are Great Grandmother
Emick, left, and Mother Olsen. (Circa 1915.)

Lillian Olsen with, l. to r., J.C., Moya and Clem.

Moya dressed in a costume
belonging to Nan Halpern
who was on the bill with
Olsen & Johnson. (Circa 1923.)

Moya and J.C. with a dancer from the Olsen & Johnson show.

"Ole" Olsen, dressed as a Catholic priest to pick up his very good friend, Father Wagner, at Union Station in Los Angeles; note the saddle shoes! (Circa 1928–29.)

"Ole" and Lillian Olsen with Pierce-Arrow sales staff and new automobile. (Circa late '20s or early '30s.)

"Ole" Olsen, Moya, and cast of one of his shows, "on the road," in the late '30s.

Moya in the late '30s at "Ole" and Lillian's home in Brentwood, California.

"Ole" Olsen, "Chic" Johnson and Moya in the baby carriage, Santa Monica Beach, late '30s. Note in Moya's handwriting on back of photo reads: "Think this is a gag?? You should kno some of the things they made me do — and take dictation and type and stand on my head at the same time!! 'Course that was when I was good!!!"

The 1937 "wedding" of Lillian and John "Ole" Olsen; a renewal of vows on their 25th anniversary. Attending were Moya and her brother J.C.

"The House That Laughs Built" — "Ole" and Lillian Olsen's home from 1947 to 1954 was the second house built in Palm Desert, California.

Marquee for Olsen & Johnson's "Hellzapoppin" at the Winter
Garden Theater in New York, during its 1,404 performances
in the late 30s and 40s. Moya met Bill Lear backstage here on
Christmas Eve 1938. (Photo by J.C. Olsen.)

William P. Lear, as he appeared in the '30s when
he first met Moya backstage at "Hellzapoppin."
Photo was taken in 1932 in Chicago.

Bill Lear extolling the merits of his
new aircraft radio transmitter to
Amelia Earhart in 1935 at Roosevelt
Field, New York — two years before
she disappeared in the Pacific,
July 2, 1937. (Lear Avia Archives)

Bill Lear with the Lear-O-Scope direction finder antenna mounted atop his own
aircraft. He often tested new equipment while flying on business. Photo taken in the
mid-'30s. (Lear Avia Archives)

Moya Olsen and Bill Lear in 1939 when his Beechcraft crashed on a Christmas flight
from Santa Monica to New York. It was only the second fight Moya had taken.
(Lear Avia Archives)

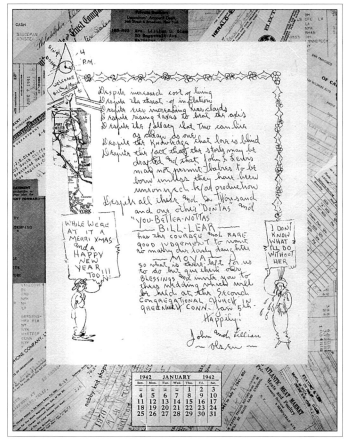

Invitation (matted in bills!) to Moya Olsen and Bill Lear's January 5, 1942 wedding.
Designed by John "Ole" Olsen.

Moya and Bill's honeymoon "getaway" car, suitably decorated á la Olsen and Johnson.

Four generations of Olsens: Moya, Mother Olsen holding Littlejohn, and Big John.

J.C. and "Ole" Olsen on stage in the '50s.

Civil Air Patrol member William P. Lear, Sr. and family in the '40s. L. to r., bottom row: William P. Lear, Jr., Moya Olsen Lear; standing: unknown, "Ole" Olsen, Lillian Olsen, William P. Lear, Sr., Harry J. Hutchins.

Moya and Bill at a traditional Japanese meal during their Hawaiian vacation, 1951.

THE *Collier Trophy*

Reprint of Bill with the Lear F5 Autopilot and Automatic Approach Coupler System for which he was awarded the Collier Trophy for 1949. (Lear Avia Archives)

President Harry S. Truman, Moya and Bill, December 15, 1950, receiving the Collier Trophy for 1949 for the Autopilot. (White House Photo)

Christmas Photo of Moya, with David (in her lap), Shanda and John. Taken at their home in Santa Monica about 1951.

Bill explaining something to Littlejohn who is trying to look interested.

Moya and Bill at Lear Inc. facility, Santa Monica, California. Mid-'50s. (Lear Avia Archives)

"The Flying Lears" as recorded on the January, 1953, cover of Flying Magazine. Pictured from l. to r., are Bill, John, Shanda, Moya and David. Photo was taken at the Santa Monica Airport, headquarters of Lear, Inc. (Lear Avia Archives)

The 1955 passport photo of the Lear children when first moving to Switzerland. Clockwise from top: David, Shanda, Tina, John.

The Villa Prevorzier, near Geneva, Switzerland. Bill, Moya (in dark coat) and family in the foreground. This was the Lear home during 1955–56.

Christmas in the mid-'50s taken at the Lear home in Pacific Palisades, California, before their return to Switzerland. L. to r., seated, Shanda, Moya, Tina, Bill, David, and John (standing).

Bill and friends in Santa Monica, California at the Lear, Inc. plant preparing for a weekend flight to Las Vegas (mid-'50s). L. to r., Bill, unknown, unknown (may be pilots), June Haver (Mrs. Fred MacMurray), Fred MacMurray, Bob Hope, Jerry Colonna, Moya. (Lear Avia Archives)

Bill greeting Moya upon her return from Europe in 1952.

Bill, King Michael of Romania, and Bill, Jr. (Circa 1956.)

"Le Ranch," the Cliff May-designed home the Lears built in Onex, Switzerland, near Geneva. This was home base from 1959–1962, during the early development of the Learjet.

Moya and Bill waving upon return from their controversial flight to Moscow, June 26, 1956. Lear was the first American private pilot allowed to land in the Soviet Union. (Lear Avia Archives)

Bill, Moya and Swiss aviation officials with son John after his aerobatics check ride — Geneva, Switzerland, 1960. (Lear Avia Archives)

had never seen anything like it, and they hardly knew which way to look next while Ole and Chic threw eggs and bananas from the stage, a man ran down the aisle selling tickets to "I Married An Angel" (a musical playing across town). There were gunshots, pratfalls, a gorilla chasing a screaming girl down the aisle (that was me!), a stooge hawking "BALLOONS! BALLOONS!" and a woman marching down the aisle hollering "Oscar!", and of course, lots of girls:

> **Ole (from center stage): "A show to be a hit today must possess novelty. Actors must possess ability. And a girl in order to be glamorous must possess . . ."**

> **The stooge (in the audience): "BALLOONS!"**

A woman would sing; a couple would dance (genuine performers with real talent). Then there would be more pandemonium — including rabbits and squirt-guns, bicycles and babies!

> **Detective: "Calling all cars! Calling all cars! Go to the corner of 49th and Broadway where you will find Mae West standing on a corner wearing a hat. That is all."**

> **Announcer: ". . . mothers make your babies happy with cellophane diapers and SEE what's goin' on!"**

Such gags were followed by more musical numbers, including a great quartet called The Charioteers, then another dance to keep 'em on their toes.

> **Ole: "And now we have a rare treat by little Sphinxy!" (opening sarcophagus and revealing mummy) "And after being buried for 25,000 years, I'm afraid she still does!" ("Sphinx," that is!)**

They had many running gags that kept the show moving in its own special way. At one point, Daddy would emerge center stage with a wild man in a straitjacket. Daddy would announce dramatically how this world-famous escape artist, Fiorello would now escape from this authentic Bellevue Hospital straitjacket in the "short space of five seconds!" (The name would change depending on who was in the audience — the night Jack Benny was in the audience, the escape-artist was "Jack Bennireno"!)

> **"ARE YOU READY, FIORELLO!"** (He'd nod, excitedly.) **Then Daddy would yell, "GO!" and the drum roll would start, and Daddy would count: "ONE! TWO!"** (Fiorello is struggling and squirming and kicking all over the stage.) **"THREE! FOUR! (pause) FOUR 'N' A QUARTER."** (Fiorello still struggling frantically.) **"FOUR NINETY-EIGHT!" Then a stooge in the audience would yell, "FIVE!" And Daddy would point excitedly to the guy in the audience and yell, "SOLD! TO THE GENTLEMAN FOR FIVE DOLLARS!"**

Fiorello (or whatever name he had in any given show) continued to struggle all during the show. Four or five times the spotlight would catch him still struggling on stage.

Other running gags included a man reading a newspaper on-stage and—let's not forget—the woman yelling for "Oscar" all through the show (it was really Catherine Johnson, Chic's wife). But the one everybody remembered with the most affection and delight was the "Plant For Mrs. Jones." The routine started when a clown came down the aisle early in the show, carrying a little green plant in a pot and calling:

> **"Mrs. Jones?"** (Timidly looking left and right.) **"I've got a plant for Mrs. Jones!"**

> A little later, he's back — but the plant has grown. **"Mrs. Jones! I've got this plant for Mrs. Jones!"**

> Later, here he comes again, only the plant is now 3- or 4-feet high. He still calls forlornly, **"Mrs. Jones!"** The audience howled with laughter every time he appeared.

At yet another point, the lights grew very dim and the musical theme of the radio show "The Shadow" suggested a very spooky scene:

> **Ole: "Ladies and gentlemen, now we want you to cuddle close together. Little children, run to the protecting arms of your**

mothers. Now we are opening our portals of death and into your midst come our spiders!" (At this point, stooges in the audience tossed beans in the air and dragged cellophane streamers on long poles over the heads of the audience.) "Feel them crawling down your neck. Feel them crawling up your spine! And now girls, pull up your feet — here come our snakes!" (Air hoses on the floor under the seats jumped and wiggled at their feet.)

During rehearsals for this particular bit, the stooges in the audience would not actually throw the beans — which had to be swept up — but acknowledged their cues by just saying, "Beans." Opening Night, the stooges themselves got so caught up in the fun they forgot themselves and yelled: "Beans!" as they tossed them over the audience.

The audience ached with laughter. Daddy and Chic gave away gag gifts at the end of the show — live chickens and blocks of ice! Then, as the audience stumbled up the aisle, still laughing, here was Fiorello, still wildly trying to get out of his straitjacket, only now he was in the lobby and he had a long white beard. And also in the lobby, still calling plaintively for "Mrs. Jones," was the clown — now sitting in the branches of a large tree.

After the first performance, producer Lee Shubert went backstage to tell Daddy and Chic that in the more than 500 shows he had presented, he had never heard such laughter on opening night before. Now, imagine this opening night scene after the show: the starring performers all congregate at two or three favorite spots to gulp down pastrami sandwiches, coffee or a coupla beers. They were noisy and happy, knowing that it was a great show because the theater was still rocking with the sound of laughter. They couldn't wait to see the reviews. Everyone checked his watch, waiting eagerly for the early editions that came out about four o'clock in the morning. Finally, they got the papers, all of them. Then suddenly, things got very quiet.

NEW YORK POST: ". . . it died young and in painful convulsions, the victim of its own energy . . ." (John Mason Brown)

BROOKLYN EAGLE: "To describe adequately the thing called Hellzapoppin that exploded at the Forty-Sixth Street Theatre last night, it would be necessary to be drunk." (Arthur Pollack)

NEW YORK TELEGRAM: "Some of the public may be able to survive an entire evening of din. A gentleman two seats away from me howled with delight through the whole show and, he was not, I am sure, being paid to howl. As for me, after half an hour of it, I longed for the peace and quiet of 'Our Town'. And as this review is written, my ears are still ringing." (Sidney Whipple)

NEW YORK DAILY NEWS: "There is good entertainment in this Hellzapoppin. Most of it happens early in the evening. But then it turns into a noisy and irresponsible riot!" (Burns Mantle)

NEW YORK TIMES: ". . . rowdy, confused, uneven—and no place to take jumpy nerves!" (Richard Lockridge)

NEW YORK JOURNAL AMERICAN: "Hellza, I would say, started to pop at the Forth-Sixth Street Theatre and then emitted a dull sickening thud!" (John Anderson)

We read these reviews, wiping our tears, but laughing at the way these critics tried to deal with "Hellzapoppin." With reviews like that in a country struggling through the depths of the Depression, how could a show survive? We survived because Walter Winchell, one of the great personalities of that era, wrote in his column for the *New York Daily Mirror* the following review (God bless him wherever he is):

> "The slapstickiest and slaphappiest troupe of maniacs ever assembled on any stage is to be hilariously enjoyed . . . Surely Olsen and Johnson's new show is Billy Rose's biggest threat in his career . . ."

> My confreres on the aisles can take "Candida," "Taming of the Shrew," "Our Town" and "I Married An Angel." Just so long as they leave "HellzaPoppin" to me and the rest of New York. It hasn't a dull moment, unless it's the Intermission."

Winchell's review, coupled with his comments on his Sunday night radio program, started a stampede at the box office. The 46th Street Theatre was sold out—every performance SRO.

Six months later, in Coronet, Sidney Carroll wrote:

> **"The critics jumped on Hellzapoppin because it was "rowdy," "slam-bang," "devoid of subtlety," and "offensively loud." The public took it to its heart — presumably for the same reasons . . . The Broadway trend has been toward ultra-smartness . . . Hellzapoppin is anything but sophisticated and its jokes make no bones about sex. The participants in Hellzapoppin shower beans upon the audience, a woman did her laundry in one of the boxes, a masher — one of the show's stooges — works on the ladies in the front rows between the acts. Olsen and Johnson, the stars of Hellzapoppin, throw bananas, eggs . . . The public is rediscovering the fact that nobody ever improved on the sock in the puss as a provoker of laughs."**

"Hellzapoppin," which cost approximately $30,000 to mount, ran on Broadway for 1,404 performances and racked up nearly $5 million. (Gee, if we'd only owned a piece of that!!) Many years later, I went backstage to see Dan Rowan of the famous '60s television show "Laugh-In," to tell him how much I enjoyed his show, and he said, "Well, you know where we got the material don't you, and gave me a hug.

□   □   □

Not all the entertainment at "Hellzapoppin"went on in front of the footlights. Daddy's dressing room was a combination Green Room, reception lounge, office, and souvenir gallery. Oh — and incidentally — a dressing room, with Daddy changing his pants right in front of anyone who happened to walk in!

From his years in vaudeville, Daddy knew people by the hundreds. A self-proclaimed mirth merchant, he said: "I'm selling corny comedy. So I shake hands, go to Lion's Club lunches, meet the Mayor and remember everybody's name. It's paying dividends now. I've got friends in every town that's got a theater, real friends. They come to New York and look me up or they tell their friends to, and I meet them, take them backstage, autograph programs, fix 'em up at night clubs, and they all go to the box office. See?"

And backstage they came — presidents and newsboys, grandmothers and generals, captains of industry and captains in the

military. Around Christmas in 1938, the Honorable Anthony Eden, a
future prime minister of England, was escorted to "Hellzapoppin" by
Mayor Fiorello La Guardia. The cast had been notified, the press had
been alerted, and Daddy was expecting them to drop by his dressing
room after the show.

About this same time, syndicated newspaper columnist Frank
("Bring 'Em Back Alive") Buck, chronicler of the odd and the strange,
sent Olsen and Johnson a three-legged jackass as a gag. They were
notified it was coming, but not exactly when. As it happened, the jackass and the dignitaries arrived at the same time — before the show!
Daddy's young assistant and right-hand man, Stan Seiden, saw the an-
imal being unloaded. He raced excitedly upstairs two steps at a time,
passed the dignitaries on the stairs and yelled, "The Three-Legged
Jackass just arrived." Daddy pushed him out of the way and stretched
out his hand to greet The Hon. Anthony Eden and Mayor La Guardia!

In addition to the typewriter and a couple of filing cabinets, one
more thing was squeezed into Daddy's dressing room — me. I tried to
keep things straight, answered the fan mail and the telephone, which
never stopped. (Daddy would have been in heaven if we'd had cellular
telephones in those days!)

Christmas Eve, 1938, "Hellzapoppin" was the big surprise smash
of the season. When it opened, tickets were $3.30. But when it be-
came apparent to the Shuberts that "Hellzapoppin" was going to be a
hit, they raised ticket prices to $4.40 and moved the show to the
Winter Garden. Daddy was upset: "Nobody's gonna pay four dollars
and forty cents to see Olsen and Johnson!" Nobody in the company
had any idea that in just a few months scalpers would be getting $100
a ticket!

□   □   □

December 24, 1938, I was in Daddy's dressing room having a fit.
I had people out front watching the show. I was getting theater
tickets, making hotel reservations, and travel arrangements (in
those days it was drawing rooms on a train or staterooms on a boat
if you were going to Europe), sending wires, wrapping Christmas
presents, acknowledging gifts, wishing I were anywhere but in this
dressing room!

I didn't have any social life. The theater was my life. I didn't drink,
because I just didn't care about drinking. I didn't go dancing because

there was nobody to dance with — and I was a good dancer. I didn't have any boyfriends. I didn't have anybody. Bus Geiger, my high school beau had dropped out of my life. I had a date once in a while, but with nobody special.

Every evening followed the same routine. We'd leave our house in Malverne at seven o'clock every night, listening to "Amos 'N' Andy" and then Fred Waring's "Pennsylvanians" on the car radio. We were at the theater walking through the stage door about a quarter to eight. Daddy would drive Chic crazy, skidding in just in time to shrug into his jacket and walk on stage. My work with the show sometimes wouldn't be done until two in the morning. And when I wasn't working, I was at home with Mother.

Now, I had already met Bill Lear, a young inventor. He had come backstage to see Daddy at the 46th Street Theatre shortly after opening night to thank him for a wonderful evening and a great show. I had been out front doing my job. I was trying to steal past Daddy's dressing room without him seeing me and get to my typewriter and copy my notes before they got cold. He caught me. "Hey honey! Come in here, I want you to meet somebody!"

He turned to Bill, one of his friends standing there: "This is my daughter Moya." And I said, "How do you do, Mr. Lear? (Daddy I'm awfully busy!)" That was it. No angels sang. No bells chimed. No fireworks went off. Just "how d'ya do, Mr. Lear" and I left, totally unimpressed. Bill Lear was just one of my father's thousands of friends. He came back a couple more times to take us out to supper after the show, still nothing happened even though I noticed Bill to be a well-dressed, handsome man. At about five-foot-eleven, he had an impressive bearing, clear blue eyes, neatly combed hair, and a very nice smile.

In Daddy's dressing room at the top of the stairs at the Winter Garden on Christmas Eve 1938 (I've often wondered how many great stars have used that dressing room since then.) I was stewing in front of the typewriter. When I looked up, there was Bill standing in the doorway, all dressed up in black-tie. I said: "Whatsamatter, are you lost?" Smiling, Bill answered: "No. I thought maybe you could come out and have a drink with me." At 23, I'd never had a drink in my life, but I said: "Duh . . . waitaminit. Don't go away!"

I called our company manager and said, "Denny, if Daddy's looking for me, tell him I've gone out for a little while with Bill Lear. I'll be back in time for curtain. Thanks, Denny." I put on my hat, smiled at Bill and said, "Lets go!"

He took me to the Stork Club! Now, when anybody ever took me out for a bite to eat, we'd go to the White Castle and get a Coke and a hamburger. Just think, you could buy a sack of ten hamburgers for a dollar in the late-'30s!

The Maitre d' of the Stork Club was standing behind that velvet rope with his table chart, looking out over the heads of the crowd leaning against the rope waiting to be seated. He spotted us coming through the door and smiled as he said: "Good evening, Mr. Lear. We have your table for you." Well, let me tell you, I was very impressed!

After we were seated and settled, Bill said, "What would you like to drink?" and I said, "Uh, well, see I don't drink. How about a Coke?" Bill looked up at the waiter and said, "Scotch 'n' soda and a Coke." We blah-blah'd for a few minutes, and then he asked me to dance. I thought if he's a good dancer, I'm sunk — because I wasn't going with anyone and I was lonesome and he was fun to talk to.

Not only was he a good dancer but he took my breath away! When we reluctantly sat down, I asked, "What're you all dressed up for? Y'sure didn't put that black tie on for me!" And Bill, smiling, said, "I would've, but I didn't." (He was charming my socks off.) "No, it's just that my third wife served me divorce papers this afternoon, so I thought I'd celebrate."

I hoped the shock didn't show on my face. He'd said it so casually. Then, too, there was something in his face. Something in his eyes I'm sure he didn't realize that I could see — his vulnerability. I didn't stop to figure what those divorces were all about. I just suddenly felt so terrible for him — that this woman would wait until Christmas Eve afternoon to serve divorce papers.

It was the first time I jumped to his defense (and it certainly wasn't going to be the last). Going back to the theater in a taxi, Bill reached for my hand. He didn't make a pass. He didn't grope. He just reached for my hand, and I didn't realize at that moment, as I slipped my hand in his (with my heart pounding), that it was going to stay there for the rest of his life — and mine, too!

BOOK TWO

Mrs. William P. Lear

(1942–1978)

Chapter Six

When I fell in love with Bill a lot of changes took place in me. For openers, my hair grew thicker and longer. The rain — instead of being wet — was clean and cool — and the streets were black and shiny, reflecting the millions of lights in New York City in December 1938. The wind, instead of being just cold, was zippy and bracing. And the stars, I never saw so many stars — nor had they ever been so bright! Colors were more vivid and beautiful. I smiled at the world because I was drop-dead in love.

While I hadn't had a lot of experience, I knew I would get married someday and have children, but it was never a big concern of mine. I was unsophisticated and I didn't date much, but because I was Ole Olsen's daughter, nobody monkeyed with me. With Bill I was always comfortable. I was where I wanted to be. I loved his stories, the sound of his voice. I felt very close to him. For the first time in my life, I didn't want to go home. I had found my place, which I would never lose, and that place was with Bill.

From our first date, he told me all about his childhood, his mother, his ex-wives, his girlfriends and all the trouble he got into. I heard it all. It was very confidential stuff that normally a guy would try to sweep under the rug. But Bill was very up front and open with me. He always found that kind of peace with me. And being a good listener is inherent in my character. I'd say, "And then what happened? Where is she now?" And those times drew me closer to him.

Bill endeared himself to me by sharing with me his most personal thoughts. He didn't edit what he told me — it just poured out of him.

He'd tell me about his mother, Gertrude, who never understood him, she was like a hen who hatched a duck egg. (His words.) He was so full of imagination and creativity, but she'd beaten him down. She belittled him. And when he started to build an airplane in the basement of their house when he was an adolescent, she berated him mercilessly because he didn't have enough money to buy supplies to finish it.

"Why'd you start it when you couldn't finish it!" she yelled at him. "You'll never amount to anything."

All that stuff had gotten tamped down inside him, but when he talked to me by the hour a lot surfaced. And I was just hypnotized by him.

He told me about running away when he was fifteen years old. He packed some socks and a sweater, and left. But he wanted "home," he needed an anchor. He kept going back to his mother, still hoping, still yearning, blaming himself for her anger. He needed a sense of security which she never gave him. He never had any self-respect or self-esteem with her because she never let up. When Bill first got married, she said, "You'll never be a good father because you're going to bring babies into the world and they never do anything but pee and smell bad."

His mother even apologized to her family because Bill made so much money (inventing radio transmitters and receivers) and she didn't understand it. She was suspicious. "But Mother, I'm in the radio business," he'd say. And she'd say, "Well, Elmer Smith has a whole store of radios and he doesn't make that kind of money." They were living in Chicago then and she'd say to her family, "Well, he's got this gorgeous apartment and his own airplane! And you can't tell me that he's not involved in bootlegging, he can't be making that much money honestly."

Bill told me about his former wives, too.

His first wife was Ethel, a very pretty girl. They had a little girl named Mary Louise. But they were both too young, and Bill had that irrepressible spirit. It was too soon to try to tie him down.

The second marriage was to Madeline, the mother of Patti and Bill Jr. But Madeline tried to control him: "I want you home at six o'clock for dinner," and, "You said" and "You promised" and "You didn't do what you said you would do." And so she drove him away.

The third marriage should never have happened. Bill knew it was wrong from the start. Along with all those marriages ran the threat of

Natalie (not her real name), his secretary and later, his mistress for many years. She was always there.

I loved Bill's deep and harmonious voice. They talk about special voices of leaders such as Churchill, Roosevelt or even Hitler. Bill had a distinctive voice too — a very warm one. And that warm voice on the telephone — no matter how mad I was, no matter how "through" I was, no matter what had happened before — could say, "Hello, baby" and whatever I was angry about was gone. Bill's voice moved down through my whole body. I heard him with everything in me, not just my ears.

By 1939, when our romance was flowering, Bill was already recognized as a successful young inventor.

In the early '30s, Bill had brought his newly invented car radio to the attention of Paul Galvin, who later became president of Motorola, and Paul had said, "Aw, come on Bill, don't come to me with your harebrained ideas, they will legislate against it in Congress because it will be distracting to the driver."

One of his "harebrained ideas," the electromagnetic interrupter, converted, for the first time, the direct current of the car battery to AC (alternating current) through the use of a small, simple, inexpensive device. (My thanks to Sam Auld, a top engineer and lifelong friend of Bill's, for providing the explanation!) Commonly referred to as the "vibrator," it became the basis for the automobile radio, which Bill named the "Motorola." Providing miniaturization and simplicity to the design, he made it possible to put a radio under the hood of an automobile. Before that, early attempts at car radios had used large, separate batteries or a motor-generator to provide the high voltage DC (direct current) needed by the vacuum tubes. Bill's miniaturized RF (radio frequency) coils, for example, were thumb-sized instead of fist-sized.

Bill, with his powers of salesmanship, ultimately persuaded Paul Galvin to build 100 units. The multi-billion dollar automobile radio business began in Chicago with that little 100 unit order, which was sold in 10 minutes on the street in front of the plant! With that single event, Bill fueled an entire industry and shortly thereafter sold his one-third interest in the company (which became Motorola) and moved to New York. Every car radio made anywhere in the world for the next 25 years used Bill's invention until in the 1950s when his invention was replaced by the transistor, which could operate directly from the low-voltage DC of the car battery.

But my new-found love hadn't begun life with a silver spoon in his mouth. Bill was born William Powell Lear in Hannibal, Missouri, on June 26, 1902. He was the only child of Reuben Lear, a gangly carpenter with big dreams. His mother — Gertrude — was a big redhead who'd rebelled against her father. She'd married at seventeen, had Bill at eighteen. Not long after, she walked out on Reuben. She lived with a succession of men and fought with all of them. But when Bill was six years-old, Gertrude settled down with an easygoing Dubuque man named Otto Kirmse. She finally married him after five years.

Bill's mother had found religion and become a fanatic. She railed against sin and once beat Bill with a broomstick for giving a girl in his eighth grade class a ride on the new bicycle he'd gotten for his birthday. She then took his bicycle away from him and didn't give it back until the following Christmas. Otto, a kindly man, many times stepped between Bill and his mother to ward off the blows she meted out to her son with whatever was handy. I can't help but think that in this day and age (the '90s), she would have been put in jail for her physical and mental abuse of Bill.

But nothing, not even his mother's abuse could curb Bill's immense curiosity and relentless tinkering. By the age of twelve he had built a radio set, learned Morse Code, assembled an elementary telegraph set and read every book he could find on electricity — as well as every Horatio Alger book he could get his hands on. He also spent hours and hours in the basement of a friend whose father worked for a utility company, experimenting with the many electronic parts he found there.

School bored Bill. He'd often skip class and ride his bike along country roads, where he frequently found stalled cars. Bill could fix almost any engine problem and often did, his fixed price for starting stalled cars, 25 cents. He finally quit school early in the ninth grade to become a mechanic. When he was eighteen, he left home to join the Navy, and that's where he deepened his knowledge about and fascination with radios.

By the time he was twenty, Bill had his own company: Quincy Radio Laboratories. By 35, he'd been in and out of business a number of times, had been very rich and flat broke, but held seven patents. Along with his electronic wizardry, he was totally fascinated with airplanes.

At seventeen, he had even worked for free as an airport mechanic in Chicago. But the first time he flew — in a DH-4 "flaming Coffin" with an airmail service pilot — the plane ended up landing hard, flipping over and tossing Bill out the window onto his head on the grass. Bill later bought his own airplane and took his first flying lesson. The next day his instructor came to the hangar and asked, "Where is Bill Lear?" He was told, "He's out flying." "He can't be," said the instructor, "he hasn't got a license." Bill Lear was out flying anyway.

Because of Bill's early passion for flying, he was building an impressive bank of knowledge in communications and navigation for pilots. He told me that passion started when he discovered that he was lost only once as a pilot, and that was from the time he took off until he landed!

He was extraordinarily gifted, with the ability to design and machine new parts himself and refine them until they worked perfectly. For example, Bill had started the first major work on the Automatic Direction finder in the early '30s. When we met in 1938, he was already planting the seeds for the ultimate development of his automatic pilot. Just imagine, he had only an eighth-grade education! But then, Bill was also a former Eagle Scout, further proof of his fierce desire to be the best.

We talked for hours and hours in those early months when we weren't fighting or making love! — he was my first real lover, and I was enthralled. In him I'd found someone I could finally talk to. Someone who would listen to me. But I was much more curious about his life than he was about mine.

I told him about Daddy and the fun we had, about growing up, and the funny things that happened in our family. I told him about what I loved to do, which was to direct and to write. I particularly enjoyed working to improve the dialogue for Daddy's show so that it was smoother, to suggest ways for making the action move faster, to say, "That's a good bit and we should make a running gag out of it." (For example, the midget in the big sombrero, who ran across the stage during some of our shows, was very funny. So I said, "Don't waste it, it makes a great running gag." As a result of my suggestion, four or five times during the show, the midget would go tearing across the stage in his enormous sombrero.).

The more I knew Bill, the more I loved him — I watched him move with an incredible intelligence and I listened to the sound of his voice, his deep, throaty laugh. He had so much zest for life. He passionately enjoyed whatever he was doing, and, if you captured his interest, my God, jump out of the way because the effect of his full attention would awe you. His warm, blue eyes, which would crinkle when he smiled (which was a lot), were full of mischief, but sometikmes they would look right through you with such an intensity that you'd better have something fantastic to say.

Bubbling over with stories, he'd clap his hand over his mouth when he had to wait his turn to tell them. He listened with attention and an appreciative ear to storytellers who were usually in a bar, somebody's kitchen, or dinner partners at some fund-raiser; but, such stories would also be told in the cockpit, in the board room, or on the telephone. His was an irrepressible sense of humor, lusty and delicious.

Bill was also a salesman with a very high-frequency antenna tuned to signals most of us never hear. His implicit faith in himself transferred to others. That's how he kept his gang together. His engineers loved him; they'd have followed him to the moon because he helped them believe in themselves. Once, in Reno, he told a young lady, "You know what you should be doing? You should be drafting." He sent her to drafting school, and she became one of his best draftspersons.

But the flip side of all this was a problem for him and those around him who tried to keep him out of trouble. Bill was an easy mark when his enthusiasm was aroused, and he could be sold wild ideas because his imagination was capable of visualizing glowing wonders in anything the other guy was pitching. Fortunately, he was exposed to the world at an early age, or he might have been a chronic investor in the Brooklyn Bridge!

Anyway, as time went on, our relationship increased in intensity, My life had sure been turned upside-down. I was still working at "Hellzapoppin," but I didn't want to be there. For the first time in my life, I didn't want to go home; I wanted only to be with Bill. For me, time was no longer measured in minutes and hours, but was a matter of how long I had to wait until I could be with him again, or at least, to hear his voice on the telephone. I could have my eyes closed and know that Bill had walked into the room, for I could feel the sparks of his magnetic, boyish nature. I was in love. I was walking into walls! I crawled inside myself to better deal with what was happening to me. My mother was very disturbed and upset, and said, "You're not the same little girl." But after all, I was twenty-three, and I thought, Oh, Mom, you're right about that. I will never be the same, but I'll be better, smarter, prettier!

We danced at various popular New York clubs like El Morocco, the Stork Club, the Copacabana and the Rainbow Room, where we listened to the Big Bands playing the music of Cole Porter, Irving Berlin and Rogers & Hammerstein. We both loved music and also loved to dance.

Bill also took me flying. I wasn't all that comfortable in a little airplane when it was bumpy. My first flight had been in a Ford Tri-motor when my father sent my girlfriends and me to Washington, D.C. to celebrate our high school graduation. That ride was so turbulent — I got so sick — that I decided I was never, ever going to get into another airplane.

Then I met Bill and changed my mind. For openers, of course, I was persuaded to get into an airplane, a single-engine Beechcraft. Not only did I get into it, but he convinced me to fly from Santa Monica, California, to New York for the Christmas of 1939.

At the Santa Monica Airport, we stowed the baggage in the airplane, climbed in, buckled up and took off. Bee Edlund (the future Bee Burtis) was with us, on her way to New York to start a new career as Daddy's secretary. (I had finally resigned.) We dipped our wings over Douglas Aircraft Company to say goodbye to our friends, and as we headed east we settled down for the long trip ahead — which suddenly became a very short trip. As we flew over Los Angeles City Hall, the engine suddenly quit, just like that. Everything was dead quiet.

"Get in the back seat," Bill commanded us. "But I wanna see!" I said. "GET IN THE BACK SEAT AND FASTEN YOUR SAFETY BELT!" he repeated firmly.

Then, in the ominously silent Beechcraft, we soared in big circles while Bill looked anxiously for a place to land. "Do you want a golf course or an empty lot?" he said. I made a quick decision, "The empty lot!" We both were thinking of friends who had recently landed on a golf course, with tragic consequences.

Bill landed perfectly on a piece of land which would be the site of a brand-new May Company shortly thereafter! Because the ground was a soft silt, the gear plowed through it deeper and deeper until the plane flipped over on its back stopping next to a school. The kids ran out sure that someone would have to call an ambulance, but we were simply hanging there, upside down, secure in our safety belts.

Bill yelled firmly, "DON'T UNFASTEN YOUR SEATBELTS!" This was very good advice because people have broken their necks or suffered concussions by doing that very thing. Just think of the things I was learning, and I wasn't even married yet, things like — "Don't unfasten your seatbelt when you're upside down in an airplane — on the ground!"

A *Los Angeles Times* reporter took our picture. We were smiling and unruffled in front of our over-turned Beechcraft. Bill then called his plant in Santa Monica and the insurance company; I telephoned Daddy in New York to make sure he knew I was all right. After we'd fluffed up a bit, Bill and I went to Beachcomber's for dinner, and the next day, we commercial'd to New York. As long as I was with Bill, I simply didn't care what else happened, and through the years a lot happened!

One postscript to the crash: I had been crocheting an afghan during the flight, and my work was in a basket that survived the crash intact. Prior to the accident, Bill was so funny about the basket. He'd grumble that we looked like a bunch of peasants, "Dumb basket. Don't ever bring a basket. What's in it, anyway?" "It's an afghan, honey." "Well, leave it home." " 'Kay." (What's wrong with a basket?) Well, I finally finished the afghan and won first prize at the Los Angeles County Fair in Pomona in 1941. The truth was that Bill loved that afghan. Every time we settled in a home (including our home in Reno), there was the afghan, the coffee perking and the bread in the oven. Then we unpacked.

□   □   □

Among the unusual friends we had was an exporter/importer in the Orient. Many years before we knew him, he had been walking down a narrow street in Shanghai, stumbling through noisy crowds, when he became aware that a fight was taking place right in front of him, blocking his way. It was a mother beating up on a little girl about eight years old. Our friend stepped between them and tried to reason with the mother. He was fluent in Chinese and got her immediate, stunned attention because for an American to be fluent in her native language was a surprise to her.

His intervention led the angry mother to say, "Well, if you think she's so great, why don't you take her?!"

Our friend said soothingly, "Now you don't want to give your little girl away. There must be a solution to this."

"There is," said the Chinese lady. "You take her. I have seven more children and I can't feed them."

Our friend wound up with the little girl, signed adoption papers and brought her to the States. He educated her; she spent most of her growing up years in excellent boarding schools. Extraordinarily bright, she graduated from Vassar, and he later married her! I met this darling girl while going with Bill in New York. Matter of fact, we double-dated.

During a very tense evening at the Stork Club, I was sobbing in the ladies room, heartbroken. I had just found out why Bill had, sometime earlier, broken our date for the Fourth of July. For that occasion I had planned a great picnic, and did so look forward to it. During a pause in the dancing we stopped and chatted with the orchestra leader whom we both knew. He said, "Nina (the singer at the Stork Club) will never forget her ride with you on the Fourth of July!" Of course, Bill could have strangled him.

My Chinese friend found me sobbing in the ladies' room. Trying to wipe my tears, I told her what happened, and she said, "Moya, don't ever cry tears over any man. None of them is worth it, except mine!"

I had to smile, despite blowing my nose, and I said, "That's the way I feel, too!"

Bill and I didn't fight a lot. He had to really work at it to make me mad because I don't ruffle easily, but I didn't want to discuss the other girls — it was a sort of tacit agreement. Don't embarrass me. Don't flaunt them. There was no way I could insist on fidelity and get it. But that Fourth of July date bothered me because he'd gone out with another girl on my time.

I left the ladies' room, got my coat without Bill seeing me and left, the doorman whistled for a cab, and as I climbed in Bill tore out of the club and tried to apologize and get me to stay. I looked at him through tear-filled eyes and said, "Go to hell!" I then went to Penn Station and took the next train to Malverne. It was early in our love affair and I had a lot to learn, but so did he, and I was mad and stayed mad for, I guess, a couple of days. I stayed home in Malverne and went to the beach with Evvie, an old girlfriend who belonged to a beach club. Bill knew about it and found me there on the telephone.

MOYA: Hello.
BILL: Hello, Baby, will you come in town and have dinner
        with me?
MOYA: (frostily) No.
BILL: Aw c'mon, honey—promise me you'll have dinner
        with me.
MOYA: No!
BILL: (laughing) Then promise me you won't!
MOYA: I'll be there on the next train, you bastard!

I found out it was painful to love the way I loved. There were other times during our turbulent courtship when I got mad at him about something, and I was through; I wanted no more part of Bill Lear, ever. He could have all of his girls and to hell with him and them.

I called my friend Evvie and said, "Throw a bag in the car. We're going to take a trip." She was a wonderful friend I'd had throughout high school and was ready to go anywhere with me, anytime. We got in the car and took off. I drove up through Connecticut and Massachusetts and wound up in Rye, New Hampshire, where I remembered a play I'd been typing and working on with an old friend, Grant Garrett. It was called "Bedtime Story" and was going to be tried out in a barn up there.

When I got to Rye there was nothing there but a Coast Guard station and a big, old resort hotel. We registered in the hotel and asked the clerk if there was a theater group in a barn nearby. Pointing down the road, he gave us directions: "Turn left, continue to a tree in the middle of the road, turn right, then there'll be a barn on your left."

We finally found our way and there was a fellow sweeping up in the little theater. "Is there anyone here who's rehearsing a play called 'Bedtime Story'?" I asked.

"I don't know. I just sweep up the place, lady, but there's somebody upstairs," he replied.

I went up the stairs two at a time. All the doors were closed on the second floor, but I heard a phone ring and heard a girl behind a door say, "Moya? Moya Olsen? No, there's no one here by that name." My heart started to pound. I banged on the door and said, "I'm Moya Olsen." A lady in a robe opened the door and said, "It's for you."

I picked up the phone in total shock and heard Bill say, "Hello baby, you thought you could get away from me, didn't you?"

I was miles from civilization. How he ever found me there I will never understand. That's just one of the magic things that happened in my love life with Bill. There was something that pulled us together just when I thought everything was going to pieces. I knew that he loved me, but I also knew that his love wasn't "all out" like mine was.

He had a terrible reputation about girls and everybody tried to persuade me not to marry him. Daddy had a fit because he, like everybody else, knew Bill was a ladies' man. It was part of his blood, his bones, just the way he was. He had a strong, strong sex drive. And the business of fidelity? Uh-uh, you better learn how to deal with his infidelity — or leave now!

By the fall of 1940, my parents were wondering just what Bill Lear's intentions were regarding their daughter. Bill and I had discussed getting married, but he always avoided any commitment. We finally agreed to announce our engagement at a party around Thanksgiving.

I was with friends decorating for the party, eagerly awaiting the phone call telling me what time to pick him up at the airport. When the phone did ring, it wasn't Bill, but his west coast representative calling to tell me Bill couldn't make it. I was devastated — just devastated—that he didn't have enough courage to call me himself. That's when we broke up. It would have helped if I could have been angry, but I wasn't angry. I was just heartbroken.

That Christmas, Mother, my sister Joy and I went by train from Los Angeles, where we were living at that time, to New York to spend the holiday with Daddy. I was totally out of it, really suffering, and my parents were furious. Daddy even told the doorman at the Winter Garden, "Don't ever let Bill Lear walk into this theater."

I didn't want to get away from him as badly as I wanted to get away from those who were trying to "straighten me out about Bill Lear." I loved him so desperately and I knew it would never stop no matter how many years I worked at it. Try as I might to suppress my feelings for him, I could never stop loving him.

That's when Daddy decided to send me to Rio de Janeiro for Carnival because he could see how unhappy I was. He had a friend who lived in Rio, so Daddy got the tickets and I went shopping up and down Fifth Avenue for cruisewear. I was in the B&G coffee shop for a bite to eat when I opened the paper and saw on the front page of the

New York Times: "W. P. Lear Crashes Into River in Florida."

Heart pounding, I raced to the nearest phone booth and called the hospital in St. Mary's, Florida, where Bill had been transported, and got the nurse who was attending him. He couldn't talk because his jaw was broken and his chin was wired shut, leaving a scar that would stay with him the rest of his life. The nurse read to me — in her best, conscientious, R.N. style — Bill's scrawled lines: "I love you, darling — have a good trip!"

I mumbled "Thank you" to her and hung up. I leaned against the phone booth and sobbed into a handkerchief — loving him so terribly, no longer wanting to go on this cruise and wishing I could be down there with him. Matter of fact, this was one of the things that kept us in touch with each other — because I wanted to know if he was all right.

The night the ship sailed in January, he sent a huge bouquet of roses to my stateroom, and when my mother saw who they were from, she was furious. She steamed, "Why doesn't he let you alone!" The whole gang from "Hellzapoppin" came down to see me off. They had rushed off stage after the finale and they were all there on the dock.

No one saw my heart aching. I have always been pretty good at keeping my deep personal feelings concealed. But then that incredible "Boom" of the ship's horn sounded and I felt the motion of the ship in the harbor — leaving New York — on my way . . . where? To Rio de Janeiro, in South America! What craziness had made me agree to this dumbbell caper? Panic seized me — I wanted to get off. But before I could, I got very busy just trying to hang on to my bunk in the tossing ship.

Appropriately, the ship left New York Harbor during a tremendous storm. The ship heaved and shuddered. My belongings were all over the floor. Mirrors were broken. The freight in the hold was knocked loose. Everyone was sick. About this time, there was a knock on the door and I groped (no lights) and stumbled and crawled to the door to find a guy with a telegram. It read:

HAVE FUN HONEY SIGNED MOTHER AND DADDY!

I had fun in Caracas and Rio, then went down to Montevideo and Buenos Aires. Back in Rio I stayed a couple of months with a girlfriend. We had an apartment with a great big picture window that opened on the Bay of Rio de Janeiro with Sugar Loaf right in front of us. We also had a Brazilian cook who not only fixed our dinner, but told our fortunes every evening at 6 o'clock while they played the "Ave Maria" on all the radios in Rio.

I ran around with a little gang and enjoyed the company of one of the guys. I wasn't comfortable with an affair, but I was so mad at Bill, I tried. When my pal said goodbye to me in Rio, he said, "I will bet you fifty bucks that your Bill is going to be waiting for you at the dock." When I got back to New York and Bill wasn't there, I sent my pal a telegram that said:

YOU LOST YOUR BET.

South America was fun, but it didn't help because I still loved Bill, and I knew that he loved and needed me.

I returned in the spring of 1941, and after a few days in New York with my father and the gang in "Hellzapoppin," I went back to Los Angeles. Bill and I had restored communication during my trip. When I was mad at him, I'd send my cables collect. And when I was making up with him, I'd pay for my cables. But back in the States, Bill and I had to devise a way of communicating because my mother would tear up the mail; so, he contacted me through close friends. For awhile, we went around and around, and then, in the fall of 1941 after many letters and cables, I met him in New York. I went out to meet his plane at La Guardia Airport.

As I waited for him to get off the airplane, I thought I would never have the strength to be near him without crumbling under the force of the power he had over me. When I saw him get off of that plane, my heart turned over. Just the bulk of him, and his energetic enthusiasm, he almost ran to see me with a big smile on his face. And those blue eyes. He was genuinely glad to see me. He sure had a hold on me. And he does, even now.

I was limp with excitement just having him in the taxi after all the months of not seeing each other, of trying to believe that our relationship couldn't work, that he didn't want to get married, that it was all finished. But after we got together, he confessed that he couldn't live without me. We wanted each other so much, we could hardly wait to get out of the taxi and into the Lexington Hotel.

We started the most dad-blasted affair — just couldn't wait — couldn't wait — and my family would have blown sky-high if they'd have known. J.C. knew I was having an affair because I was just on fire with it! Mother must've known too; she worried about Bill because he was older and I was innocent. (I wasn't a virgin but I was naive.) I knew our love was a great love, but I didn't know back then how special it was for the two of us to love as much as we did.

On Thanksgiving 1941, he called and said, "OK Honey, let's tell the world." And we both cried on the telephone, both of us. The same day Daddy had taken Mother to the Army-Navy game in Philadelphia. Now, the train is a terrible place to be after a football game — everybody is rowdy and drunk, and Mother hated the trip home. But as soon as she arrived, I opened the door and said, "Mom, Bill called and we're going to get married!"

She answered, "Come in the bathroom and tell me about it." There was no way she would have gone near the bathroom on that train!

So I sat on the tub and she sat on the pot while I told her, "We're going to be married, Mom."

"Honey are you sure?"

"Yep, positive."

"Well, let's go into town and tell Daddy after the show."

So Mother and I joined Daddy at Lindy's to have "night" lunch and after Daddy recovered from the shock, he wrote the wedding invitation on the back of Lindy's menu:

Despite increased cost of living
Despite the threat of inflation
Despite ever increasing war clouds
Despite rising taxes to beat the axis
Despite the fallacy that two can live as cheap as one
Despite the knowledge that love is blind
Despite the fact that the stork may be drafted
and that John L. Lewis may not permit babies to be born unless
they have been unionized before production.
Despite all these and a thousand and one other "Don'tas" and
"You Better Not-tas"
BILL LEAR
has the courage and rare good judgment to want
to marry our lovely daughter

MOYA
So what is there left for us to do
but give them our blessings and invite you
to their wedding which will be held
at the Second Congregational Church
in Greenwich, Conn. Jan 5th, 4 p.m.

Happily!
John and Lillian Olsen

And while we're at it, a Merry Xmas and a Happy New Year,
Too!

We were married in Greenwich, Connecticut at the Second Congregational Church because you couldn't be married in New York if you had been divorced, and remember, Bill had been divorced three times! No happier bride ever walked down the aisle. When it came time for the minister to ask, "From whose love and care cometh this young woman to be married?", Daddy was supposed to smile and say, "From ours." But no one could hear him because his emotion made him choke on the words. He found his way back to his seat beside Mother, who was also mopping up. Then we tried to hear Bill repeat his vows (I took out "forsaking all others"; I was going to take care of that one myself!), but no one could hear him, either. At our wedding, I was the only one who wasn't emotional, for my heart was singing, as was my voice — loud and clear:

I, MOYA, TAKE THEE BILL, TO BE MY LAWFUL WEDDED HUSBAND — AND BEFORE GOD AND THESE WITNESSES, I GIVE THEE MY HEART AND HAND, TO GO WITH THEE THROUGH LIFE, TO SHARE WITH THEE ALL BLESSINGS — TO COMFORT THEE IN ALL SORROWS — TO LOVE THEE WITH MY WHOLE HEART — TO BUILD WITH THEE A CHRISTIAN HOME. AND THERETO, I PLIGHT THEE MY TROTH.

After we left the church, we had one reception at the Kent House in Greenwich (dry—because my mother said so!) followed by a caravan of cars into New York for another reception at the Park Sheraton (not so dry!) We stayed in New York overnight, had lunch the next day at the "21," and then left for our new life in Piqua, Ohio.

Chapter Seven

Piqua, Ohio? Yeah, well I never would have heard of it either, except that Bill had moved his operations to Ohio in 1939 to be closer to military operations at Wright field in Dayton.

It was wartime and the Piqua plant was prosperous. Military contracts were pouring in. During the war Bill filed successfully for 43 new patents, most bearing his name, and his reputation was growing in stature. He was profiled in magazines and newspapers, and the fame delighted him. Meanwhile, Lear Avia's workforce expanded a hundred fold — from 41 to 4,000. Sales increased eighteen-fold, to almost $37 million a year! The company switched from making direction finders, transmitters and receivers to gearboxes, actuators, screw jacks, and all the other things needed to maneuver the mechanical functions on warplanes from wing flaps to bomb bay doors to gun turrets to landing gear. I was totally unaware of the magnitude of the man I had just married. We pulled into the driveway of Bill's tiny white house at dawn, January 7, 1942, exactly one month after Pearl Harbor. I looked at my new home with my heart soaring. With a little stream that meandered right past it, my new home was right on the fourth fairway of the Piqua Country Club, and had an apple tree in the front yard. Everything was frozen, so I couldn't have anticipated that the following summer, caddies would be dropping their clubs and finding shade under that apple tree in front of our house, and I would be slicing watermelon and taking it out to them while the players would yell, "Hey, how about us?"

Our nation was at war and I, just like all housewives, saved red stamps for meat and butter, blue stamps for canned goods, worried about not having enough sugar stamps, and read the headlines of the newspaper with dismay. But even though the world was in chaos and there was war news everywhere, I found absolute peace as a bride moving into my own little home in Piqua.

I loved that little house from the first time I laid eyes on it. Even on that freezing January dawn, it looked like heaven to me. On our trip from New York, when we stopped to eat, Bill had called his maintenance man at the plant in Piqua to turn on the heat and start the Capehart (a fabulous new record-changer that ate records by the dozens). When we walked in, the house was warm and cozy and the famous torch singer, Hildegarde, was singing "I Can't Get Started With You!"

When we woke up the next morning, Bill went to the plant. His parting shot was a quick hug and "call me if you need anything." I stood bewildered at the back door where he left me. Having been raised in hotels and restaurants, I didn't know from up in the kitchen. My darling mother never liked to cook more than was absolutely necessary, so I never learned. Fortunately, Bill taught me to cook (he was good); he taught me how to thread my sewing machine; he even taught me how to iron a shirt on a mangle! (He'd learned a lot in his marriages!) He literally taught me to keep house and I loved it.

I adored my little home; cooking, washing and ironing. It was all new to me, and I brought peace and order and warmth to Bill. And for the first time in his life he was ready for it. The first thing I cooked all by myself in my own little kitchen was chicken curry because he said he liked it. I didn't know anything about curry, but I was going to learn. I got the recipe out of a Boston Cooking School cookbook, and he had a fit because it was so good. He told me that he'd "never tasted anything so delicious." It was so sweet and encouraging for me to have him rave about my cooking.

One Sunday morning soon after we arrived in Piqua, we built a fire in the tiny fireplace and unwrapped a lot of wedding presents. Bill kept throwing the boxes, paper and ribbon in the fireplace. (Sometimes he wasn't as bright as he was smart!) Pretty soon the fire got out of hand as flames began to lick the wooden mantel. Bill was running back and forth with pans of water and wet towels and more pans of water, and I was stretched out on the couch, roaring with laughter.

As he got the fire under control, he asked me (a little testily) what was so funny. I said all I could think of was the bit in Daddy's show where the guy runs down the aisle with a paper cup, runs up the steps onto the stage, across the stage to the water cooler, fills the cup, runs back across the stage, down the steps and up the aisle. After this happens two or three times — interrupting Daddy trying to make an announcement on stage — he demands: "Now wait a minute! Wait a minute! What's going on here?" And running past him with another cup of water, the man yells over his shoulder, "Don't stop me, man, the men's room is on fire!" That was all I could think of, watching Bill running back and forth from the kitchen. Did I help him? Nope, I let him take care of it.

After we'd been married about a month, I was standing at attention one morning waiting for him to finish dressing and hurry out with his associate, Dick Mock, who had been tapping his foot and looking at his watch for about a half hour. I had Bill's fresh-squeezed orange juice in my hand waiting for him to grab it, drink it, and leave — but oh, no! He sat down at the kitchen table.

BILL: How about coffee, Dick?
DICK: Sure, Bill, but we're late.
BILL: (comfortably) Don't worry, they won't start without us.
DICK: (grumbling) Y'got that right, but . . .
BILL: Toast!

He wanted a piece of toast! Now, I hadn't set the table, because I knew these two fellas were going to fly out the back door headed for the plant, so I started to steam.

MOYA: Here, ferhevensakes, take mine.
BILL: I want jam and I need a knife and goddamit — when I sit down at the table I want a knife 'n' fork 'n' spoon!
MOYA: (losing it) Is that right? Well, I'll throw the whole box at you!

I picked up the big box of silver we had received for a wedding present, and I would've thrown it at him — and hopefully hit him — but they both had already made a hasty exit out the kitchen door!

After lunch, I was in town with a marketing list thinking, what a dumb thing to have a fight about. So I stopped at Western Union and sent him a telegram:

QUOTE   NOW   UNQUOTE

I signed it: **ITTWBAY.**

All during our courtship he had told me that if I ever needed him I just had to send a wire that said: "Now!" and he would come immediately. The letters in the signature were the first letters of "I'll Throw The Whole Box At You."

Now, Bill had gone to Chicago the weekend before all this happened and among other things, he'd gone to a cocktail party. The hostess had cornered him and grumbled about her husband never being home, whereupon Bill threw out his line to her, grinning, "Well, if you ever need me, just send me a telegram that says 'Now' and I'll be right over." He laughed mischievously when he told me this story, safe in the knowledge that it would never happen.

I had returned home from town and was putting the groceries on the kitchen table when the phone rang

BILL: (in his sweet voice) Hello, baby.
MOYA: (melting) Who is dis speakin'?
BILL: This is your lover. Should I come home?
MOYA: (certain he had received my telegram) Yes!
BILL: Right now?
MOYA: (smiling at the game) Yes, right now!

We had a wonderful afternoon, and a happy ending to our first married quarrel. Now, fast-forward to the following Sunday morning, when eating Bill's heavenly scrambled eggs and onions, drinking sherry and loving the wintry, snowy morning, he mentioned the telegram.

BILL: Honey, remember the story I told you about the gal in Chicago last weekend?
MOYA: Yeah. (remembering very well)
BILL: . . . and how I said "If you ever need me, send a wire that says . . ."

MOYA: Yeah, I know. (I've been there!)
BILL: (laughing) Well, guess what?
MOYA: (innocently) What?
BILL: She sent me a wire (I can't believe my ears!) that said
quote now unquote. Isn't that cute! I would never do
anything about it so I could tell you.
MOYA: You dumbbell! I sent you that wire!
BILL: (You should've seen his face) You sent it?

He was completely dumbfounded. Then we started to laugh. Hysterically.

BILL: (gasping) Just think if I'd gone up there and she'd opened
the door and I'd said "Here I am!"
MOYA: Well, the funny part is you made all the right moves. You
came home right now! What did you think ITTWBAY
stood for?
BILL: Oh, I just thought it was some kind of Western Union
code!

We never forgot that story and laughed every time we told it. A few days later, Bill had just gotten out of the shower, and I was standing at the bathroom door chatting with him. While he was shaving, he said: "All my other wives used to lay my stuff out for me."

I let that sit there a minute while I sorted it out — then I thought: What's the big deal? I can do that! So I said: "Is that a fact?"

"Yep. That's a fact."

So, for 36 years, folks, I laid out his stuff every morning. Underwear, socks, shirts (put the stays in the collars like we used to have to do) and picked out his ties. It was part of my morning — like putting the coffee on, squeezing the orange juice and making the toast. And now, let's fast-forward to the '70s, and I'm laying out his stuff.

MOYA: Honey . . .
BILL: Hmmm?
MOYA: Did your other wives really do this for you?
BILL: (shaving — he looked sideways at me and twinkled when
he replied) No.

I picked up one of his shoes and chased him with it. Would it have changed anything if I'd known? (If I had him here right now, I'd look sideways at him and twinkle as I said: "Nope!")

Right from the beginning, the patterns of our marriage were established. Throughout his career he traveled extensively, and I kept home nailed down for us. I was always there, and whatever happened "out there," he came home to me. As time went by and the months melted into each other, I realized (as he did) that he really did need me. My being there was vitally important to him, and I bloomed and flowered with that need.

Prematurely on December 4, 1942, we were blessed with a beautiful, blue-eyed baby boy we named John Olsen. My father said, "Not one of your children better ever come up to this dressing room and call me 'Grandpa.'" From now on I'll be 'Big John' and this little rascal will be 'Littlejohn.' "

When John was a baby, in the cold winter of 1943, I would pull the diapers out of the washing machine, take them outside in a clothes basket and hang 'em on the line. It was about fifteen degrees, and after I pegged those diapers on the line, I'd run back in the house to get warm. When I went out 30 minutes later, they were stiff as tortilla chips and I stacked them up in the basket and set it down in the kitchen. In fifteen minutes the stack went limp and they were all damp again! I didn't understand where I'd gone wrong. Nobody had explained to me that the damn diapers would freeze on the line.

Somewhere along in here, Bill "scheduled a trip to Seattle," so I went to New York to spend time with Daddy and show off my baby, Littlejohn. While I was gone, Bill added a great big living room (doubling the size of the house), with a huge brick fireplace. He also enlarged the kitchen, paved the driveway, and installed green and white awnings — all in about five days!

To keep up the pretense that he was out West, he got the operator to say, "Mr. Lear's calling from Seattle." I was totally unaware of what he was doing, so that when he picked me up at the train station and drove me home, I nearly dropped Littlejohn when I saw the beautiful transformation. Everyone had helped. His boys at the plant, his children who lived in Dayton (Bill Jr. and Patti, who had become like my own), even the delivery people!

But, even after building our home, even being busy at the plant, Bill didn't like Piqua. He thought it "small" in every dimension. One evening we went to an open house, and when it was time to leave, I went upstairs to get my coat. The host made a pass at me. He tried to throw me down on the bed. I said, "Whoa!" (You'd be surprised how strong a girl my size can get if you try to make her do something she doesn't want to do!) I was so offended. On our way home, I told Bill about the unpleasant incident. He said, "OK, that's it. We're out of here." (I'm cleaning up his comments a little.) "We have to grow and we can't grow in Piqua."

Another time, he received a call at the plant alerting him that "Mrs. Lear was seen marketing in downtown Piqua—in slacks!" What he said then was totally unprintable. Then we laughed and started to pack. But I cried when we moved from that little house in 1943. Bill, trying to comfort me, said, "C'mon, honey, we'll be coming back." I looked at that house for the last time as we backed out of the driveway and I said, "No, I know we'll never come back." And we didn't.

Another big problem was keeping top-notch engineers and their families happy in a tiny hamlet like Piqua, Ohio, in 1942. So Bill expanded his operations to include New York, Los Angeles, and moved his production to Grand Rapids. While I didn't have any involvement with his business decisions, I always served on the board of directors because Bill said, "Honey, I want you to know what is going on." But my main task was always to establish a home wherever Bill decided to locate, a challenge I was to meet thirteen times.

When we chose to live in Los Angeles, we bought a beautiful home in North Hollywood, at 10063 Toluca Lake Avenue. We paid $35,000 for that house in June 1943. It was a big, sumptuous home with everything, including nine bathrooms, a swimming pool, badminton court and an elegant pool house. But, of course, our whole lifestyle changed with that house. And my secret heart yearned for my first little home in Piqua, which would've fit into our new pool house.

That's not all that changed. A couple of years later Lear Avia was renamed "Lear, Incorporated." We were building peacetime products such as wire recorders. And this was the beginning of Bill's interest in high fidelity music recording. We also built a low-priced automatic direction finder for private pilots, the Lear Orienter, as well as VHF transmitters and receivers. The Air Force was still buying actuators, screw jacks and automatic controls, but sales had dropped 80 percent from the $30 million annual gross of the last year of the war.

Chapter Eight

Not long after our major move to Los Angeles, we discovered another baby was on the way. While we were waiting, we made a trip to New York. Sitting with Daddy in the dressing room at the Winter Garden after his show, we were discussing what we were going to name this little soul. Daddy, with his incorrigible sense of humor, started putting names with "Lear," and he made the following pronouncement: "Now, if it's a girl, her name has to be 'Shanda,' if it's a boy it's 'Gonda,' and if you aren't sure, it's 'Cava'!"

The baby turned out to be a dark-eyed darling baby girl, and we did name her Shanda Lear. Shanda was as dark as Littlejohn was blue-eyed and fair.

While I was learning about making a home and being a wife, Bill was learning something from me — that he could be a good husband and a good father. All his mother had told him about having children had convinced him he was going to be a bad father, but he learned nothing from her about the love, the joy, and the delight a child brings into your life.

Bill loved his children when they were little. But when they got older and started to argue, he wasn't tolerant. In spite of my faith in him, he didn't understand how to be a father. I wished he had been home more often even though he did phone all the time to talk to us. But I was always the one who tucked them in, read them stories, got them that drink of water.

□   □   □

I've been amazed to find so many letters I wrote to him — mainly, I'm sure, because of the efforts of loyal and capable secretaries who scooped them out of his desk drawer among secreted candy bars and put them in a file folder. Some of the letters were written because Bill spent so much time away from home. Some I put in his bag to be read when he had time and some were mailed. I wrote him hundreds of letters about the children, our home, loving him and missing him. I wanted him to know that he was safe at home, that nothing could hurt him. I wanted to help him believe that he could be a better father, a better husband, and that I would kill anybody who hurt him! I tried to understand his frequent absences, but occasionally my loneliness would creep into my letters:

> I'm at Mother's — and we've been showing off Shanda 'n Littlejohn!
>
> I'm very lonely for you. We've been apart too much, my darling. It's no good for me. What fun is there in being married — or having a home? Gee, you can only spend so much money a month! Can't you be successful and happy in achievement without beating your brains out week in and week out — missing MONTHS of our precious babies —
>
> Darling we love each other — we should be together — I have so much stored up for you.
>
> YOU'RE important to me, not whether the hell Lear Avia lives or dies — only insofar as it affects you. I think you'd be infinitely happier with a successful company half its size and with twice the time to love 'n laugh 'n watch our treasures learn about life.
>
> It's just a plea for more time together — and less material wealth. Less of you having to slug the days out in a world apart from me 'n the babies. It's no fun without you.

A lot of what was so lovable about his little ones he learned long-distance from my letters:

> While I'm giving Littlejohn a quick "Bye beebee" in the settle, Shanda plays peekaboo with me in her bed with her blanket. She pulls her blanket up over her head and then with great glee — drops it suddenly — for me to say "peekaboo!" This inter-

feres a little with Littlejohn's mood, because he wants peace — and he wants me to sing to him quietly — and Shanda just gets in his hair! Did I ever tell you about his little music box? It has a lot of pictures of fairy story characters that move in a little frame to the music that plays. Well, when the old Witch with the tall pointed hat and the old gnarled stick appears, Littlejohn gets very excited and says "DA DA." And I always hafta recognize you and say 'yes, darling I see Daddy' and he's satisfied. When he tries to tell me something and I guess what it is, he looks at me with the sweetest proudest little smile and the expression in his eyes is a treasure I will keep in my heart always.

He will have to wear braces because his little thumb is very important to him now and the little baby pearly teeth are making way for it. If you want him broken, YOU'LL hafta stay home and do it — because I WON'T!

Shanda climbs up on the furniture — gets into the ashtrays — knocks over lamps. I'm just proud that she can climb up on the furniture (the little bit of a thing!). She makes faces at me and giggles when I mimic her. Talks a streak — and goes like lightning whether on foot or on her knees.

We had high drama one day in Mother's house in Brentwood. It started as a scolding and ended in a big-time problem in child psychology. Shanda was 2-1/2 and Littlejohn was 3-1/2. They were spectacularly beautiful babies. Shanda was a cut-up from birth, loved to laugh and make jokes, and Littlejohn worried about her. Well, Shanda started to peel wallpaper every time she woke up from her nap in her crib. When I first discovered it, I scolded her and said, "Shanda, this is Nano's house. You must not peel Nano's wall paper!"

"OK, Mommy."

Next day, another little ribbon of peeled wallpaper. "Now listen, you little squirt! Mommy's gonna have to find you another home if you peel Nano's wallpaper again!"

"I won't do it again, Mommy."

Next day, I couldn't believe my eyes. "OK," I said to this little baby doll (in retelling this story, I can't believe I did this!), "get your sweater." I put a quarter in her pocket, "You might need some lunch money." "I won't do it again, Mommy!" "I know you won't, not in

Nano's house, we're gonna find you another house."

Well, for her, this was all getting to be pretty interesting, but not for Littlejohn who had a fit: "You can't take my baby sister away!" he raged. As I put her in the front seat of the car, I told him, "We have to find a family who will take a little girl who peels wallpaper!" I had signaled my sister to go down to the corner and wait. I drove Shanda around several blocks and then dropped her off on the corner of our block a couple of houses down from our house.

She said, "Is this the house?"

"I don't know," I said. "You have to knock on the door and ask them if they want a little girl who peels wallpaper." And as she got out of the car, ready for anything, I was sorry I had started it and wished I hadn't been so impulsive.

As I drove away, three things happened. Shanda started to cry, Joy ran across the street to scoop her up, and an alarmed neighbor stepped out of his front door to see a car drive away leaving a little girl in red corduroys on the sidewalk in front of his house! Joy knew the neighbor. He had given her a kitten named Marmalade. After she explained to him what had happened, he laughed. "I'll take her," he said. "She can peel all the wallpaper she wants in my house!"

Afterwards, when we were reunited in the driveway of Mother's house, I held Shanda tight in my arms and said, "Oh my darling, you know Mommy would never give you away, don't you?"

I wiped our tears and she said, "Yes, Mommy, can we go swimming?"

We all learned important lessons from that episode:

A. She never peeled wallpaper again.

B. I strongly urge you never to threaten to give your child away no matter what they do. There are many less catastrophic ways to deal with discipline. I learned the hard way.

C. Sometimes we make mistakes in our mothering. This had to be one of my more creative blunders!

□   □   □

Another letter to Bill dealt with playground management:

I actually JUMPED out of bed this morning feeling wonderful! Bright sunshine — happy babies playing in the yard!
I made earrings for Shanda out of two fuchsia blossoms —

and tied a couple to one small beautiful ankle over a precious little bare foot — and away she went — feeling truly like the Queen of the Fairies!!

John is cross and irritable — and hard to get along with — one minute I accuse him of disturbing the peace — and send him to his room — 'n pretty soon he reappears like nothing happened!

We've used strategy twice in the last day or two. The eating goes on all day — "I'm hungry — I'm hungry — I wanna cracker — I wanna banana — I wanna sandwich."

I had an inspiration. We had a meeting. I said 'This is not really a meeting, children. Because we're not DISCUSSING anything. I'm TELLING you! From now on there will only be three meals served a day—where you'll sit down and eat what's served. In the morning, after breakfast, you will each be given a snack box with your name on it and you will make the contents (John: What's 'contents'? Mommy: What's in it.) last all day. When you get a little yen (John: What's 'yen'? Mommy: Desire—y'want it. John: Oh.) for something, you dip into your box and eat a few raisins or a graham cracker or a marshmallow or whatever Mommy put in your box. You eat sparingly because you want it to last all day, do you understand?' 'Yes, Mommy.' 'We will also put a pitcher of fruit juice out in the playhouse in the morning and in the afternoon and you can pour your own drink when you are thirsty. Okay, now go. The meeting's adjourned.' (John: What's adjourned? Mommy: Ended. Over. All washed up!)

Okay, now get lost, the three of you! (Cousin Ronnie was spending the weekend when all this took place.)

Five minutes later an outraged Littlejohn and Ronnie came in and reported at the top of their voices that Shanda had drunk every last bit of the fruit juice and she was a dirty rat.

Shanda was sitting placidly out in the playhouse. I said, 'Did you, Shanda?' And she said, 'Yep, I did.' I was tempted to say 'Oh' and walk away, but I was afraid of the two furious little boys at my heels. So I said weakly, 'Well, don't do it again.' And she said (after she had raised her hand to her mouth to cover a rumbling burp. 'Okay, Mom — I won't.' I was laughing to myself, SURE that she wouldn't!! At least, not today — again!!

I turned around and walked past two deflated little boys with their mouths open, frankly disappointed that there hadn't been any torture or murder . . . or that I hadn't at least put her in jail!!

It was during these wonderful years in the '40s while we were living at 222 14th St. in Santa Monica when Bill decided to teach his 8-year-old son Littlejohn a lesson in economics. He'd heard they were selling lemonade in front of the house.

The scene is dinnertime and Littlejohn is jubilant. Dad asks, "Why?"

JOHN: (proudly) We made $9.72 today selling lemonade.
DAD: Wonderful, John. How much were the lemons?
JOHN: We got the lemons out of the 'frigerator.
DAD: (persisting) How much was the sugar?
JOHN: Mommy gave us our sugar.
DAD: (going in for the kill) All right, John, how much did you get for a glass?
JOHN: (practically) We didn't sell the glasses!

□   □   □

In my letters I tried to tell Bill everything the children did:

I was up in the bedroom working and I heard this struggle and grunting and puffing — came downstairs to see what was going on and there was Littlejohn — triumphant and radiant — standing in the middle of the living room floor with an old dead Christmas tree evidently dragged clear down the alley from someone's trash. He was so proud. He presented me with it, complete with mess all over the living room!

I knelt down and put my arms around him and tears spilled out of my eyes. His precious little heart was pounding with excitement. I believe it was his first 'loot'.

I said, 'Oh my darling — Mommy loves you for bringing her a present — but I have no use for it, sweetheart,' (so far so good) 'and besides, Christmas is over — we don't need a tree now. (Wrong thing to say entirely!)

'We'll save it for next Christmas, Mom.'

I got the tree out of the house only because I went to college and have read a couple of books. We battled very quietly and legally for about a half an hour.

Oh, what a wonderful little guy! What an amazing, satisfying, precious little person! His struggle to be independent is almost savage sometimes. His disposition, when it's bad, is the worst I've ever seen exhibited anywhere. When he's good — I lose my breath I'm so proud of him. One night I was dressing to go out and he went into absolute ecstasy over my black lace panties. I told him I was his party girl that night. So a coupla nights ago I arranged for a sitter and he overheard me and he said, 'MOMMY! are you going to be a party girl tonight and wear those bruutiful pants!!!'

I giggle at Shanda two or three times a day — she'll get a paper bag over her head — or tell a wild story rolling her eyes and laughing and say 'dija ever hear of such a funny sing Mudder!!' Some darn way she'll wrangle a laugh out of all of us during the day. Her little foot taps with the music and she sings, 'Twinkle twinkle little star how me wonder whats you are' until you think the only thing to do is walk her over an open manhole!!!

When we come home, we roar in the side door and say, 'Hello House . . . hello you old stinker bogey man house!' When I come in alone — I stand still by the door and whisper, 'Hello house' . . . and I shut my eyes and yearn for you — my heart says, 'Oh come HOME, my darling . . . come home so we can love you!'

If you go broke — I hope with all my heart it won't be necessary — but if you do — we still have each other. We have the most wonderful babies in the world. We have our home.

We'll always have enough to eat and a place to come in out of the rain.

I'm Always your Mom.

Chapter Nine

In the midst of all this intense living, I happily found myself pregnant again. When Littlejohn was born he was not only premature, he was a difficult breech delivery. A week later, I started to hemorrhage, and that sent me right back to the hospital, where they quickly began transfusions. In the urgency of the situation they mis-typed my blood, and consequently, I nearly died. Even though it was touch and go for a couple of weeks, I finally got to go home. Shanda's birth was a blessing.

But, in a letter to Bill I confided my worries about the possibility of facing another difficult delivery:

> As badly as I want this baby — as anxious as I am to have it all over with — I'm petrified. I awaken sometimes at night in a cold sweat — praying that Dr. Krahulik can do for me what he's done for so many other women.
>
> I love babies so! Why can't I have mine like Junie Johnson had hers! (Junie, Chic Johnson's daughter, told me she'd thought she'd at least have a HEADACHE during delivery! She just popped her baby out!)
>
> And I argue with myself so often — about wanting you to hold onto — and yet I couldn't subject you to just watching me suffer though another labor.
>
> I love you. I love you much more than anything in this world. I will never have to choose between you and Littlejohn — because he is you — he's my love for you — our love. He fills

**your place when you can't be here — close to me. Still I want to
lean on you these days.**

When we moved to Grand Rapids in January 1946, it was a chaotic
move for me, and I was uneasy and uncomfortable from the start. I
had carried Littlejohn and Shanda easily and outside of the first
month or so, had no discomfort during pregnancy (deliveries were another matter). But my current pregnancy, now in its sixth month, had
been trouble from the beginning.

Littlejohn was four and Shanda not quite three and the sight of
the moving van backing up to our home in Toluca Lake was something they remembered for a long time. " 'Member the big truck?"
they asked over and over again. I remembered the "big truck" with
my heart sinking.

Bill, the children and I spent that Christmas in Chicago with
Mother and Daddy, J.C. and Joy, on our way to Grand Rapids. (Daddy
was playing the Shubert Theatre.) Bill wouldn't move us from the
Blackstone and Daddy had to stay at the Hilton, so we were in different hotels across the street from each other. It was a noisy, hectic
Christmas and I was miserable, desperate for quiet, sick at my stom-
ach, and unhappy.

When the children and I arrived in Chicago, Bill got very upset
after discovering I had allowed the people who bought our house in
North Hollywood to move in "before escrow had closed." I couldn't
believe the tantrum he threw. We had been packed and ready to leave
on December 20, and the people who had bought our house had
asked me if they could move in for Christmas. I said, "Of course!" We
were out after all. The house was empty and we were spending
Christmas in Chicago before settling in Grand Rapids. What was the
big problem? The problem was "before escrow closed"!

And guess who defended him? My mother, that's who! I was
taking a hot bath in our suite in the hotel, sobbing, when she tapped
on the door. She cracked the door, took one look at my face, slipped
in and closed the door behind her. "Honey, he'll be all right. He's
just more aware of the problems in business than you are. Be patient
with him!"

I couldn't believe my ears. Be patient with him! I was sick of being
patient with him. I was tired of coping with him. I wanted peace.

(Little did I know that I had more than 30 years to go. I think if I'd known that then, I'd have drowned myself in that tub!)

The misery of going through a bad pregnancy, of being uprooted, moving again, with all the furniture, of being the general in charge of the move, I felt overwhelmed. I struggled through the holidays — usually a happy time for me. But not that winter of 1945-46 in Chicago en route to Grand Rapids.

After taking the train to Grand Rapids with the children, we discovered the movers had unloaded "the big truck," on December 31, 1945, and stacked and stuffed our entire Toluca Lake household — furniture, kitchen, dishes, lamps, linens, nursery, rugs, books — into two rooms, clear to the ceiling, and left! If I'd had the strength, I'd have hunted those men down and killed them.

Bill was remarkably patient. He got a team from the plant. I sat in the mess and told them where to put everything. It was a total nightmare. Fortunately, there was a wonderful big basement where we put everything we didn't know what to do with.

All this activity didn't help my pregnancy a bit. I was hurting, and worried. I told Bill something was wrong. It wasn't the same as my other pregnancies. Unfortunately, he was susceptible to all the cuckoo cures that anyone suggested. So, when some local doctor produced this cockamamie electronic buzzer that he claimed would cure any pain if you just put it on the place that hurt, Bill probably said, "Oh, that's just what my wife needs!" (Right, Bill, and I have this Joy Juice that cures bunions, cancer, depression — especially depression! — and it comes in this bottle. Ladies and gentlemen, only 25 cents for this incredible cure!)

Well, I humored this doctor (and Bill), and went for the "treatments," but my problem persisted until finally I made an appointment for a checkup at University Hospital on the campus of the University of Michigan, in Ann Arbor. I drove over with a friend who was visiting from California. We stayed with some friends who lived about 20 miles out of town.

I was more than seven months pregnant, big and uncomfortable. The nurse took me to an examining room, helped me up on the table, and said the doctor would be in to see me soon. And of course, what couldn't happen did. They forgot me! Then everybody went home! I was on my back and hurting. I called. I yelled. And finally, when I became aware that everyone had gone, I struggled to turn over and got off the table. I got dressed and got out of there. My friend was waiting and couldn't believe the story. I was going back the next morning, and, don't worry, somebody was going to hear about it.

But the next morning, out at our friend's house, 20 miles from town, I started to hemorrhage appallingly. I made it to the bathroom and filled the john with blood and clots. My friend was frantically trying to get an ambulance.

After a maddening length of time, came the ambulance. Now if an ambulance could stroll, this one strolled up the driveway without even a siren. My life was pumping out of me with every heartbeat. There wasn't even a stretcher. They put me on a chair and lifted me out of the house and into the ambulance, then drove 35 mph all the way into town. The stolid old boy driving would not exceed the speed limit, and, when my friend hammered on the glass divider for him to hurry, he pulled over, got out, came back and asked what was the matter!

Needless to say, I was an emergency case, in shock, when I finally arrived at University Hospital. But the Lord was with me because Dr. Norman Miller, Dean of Obstetrics, just happened to be in his office (it was a Saturday afternoon), chatting with a couple of his students. It was a Code Blue and everyone went into instant action. They were superb.

When I regained consciousness, I discovered I couldn't move because they were pumping blood into both arms and both legs and had an oxygen tube up my nose. I had lost our baby girl (it was a placenta previa — she suffocated). Bill was standing by my bed and I had never seen such anguish in his face. It was the first time I knew that he really did treasure me. And when I could talk, I said, "Honey, this doesn't mean we can't have any more children, does it?"

Wiping the tears from his eyes, he said, "Oh my God, maybe you can, baby, but not me. I couldn't live through another nightmare like this!"

At the moment this conversation took place, Daddy had been asked to be guest host on Don McNeil's "Breakfast Club" radio show in Chicago while Don went on vacation. Daddy was on the air when Bill reached him on the telephone, sobbing as he told him that I had lost the baby and my condition was critical. Bill's anguish had been intensified when a nurse gave him my rings, which he interpreted to mean the end was near. Daddy, shaken, said, "I'll be right there."

He finished the program, but not before he started the "Sunshine Shower for Shut-Ins" segment, a shower of gifts and cards. That morning, he dedicated the first shower to "his little girl" who was in University Hospital in Ann Arbor, fighting for her life. "Please send her a card," Daddy said.

Well, barrels of not only cards, but teddy bears, other toys, and hair ribbons deluged the hospital mail system.

Physically, I recovered quickly, but I suffered with the loss of that baby. I lost my faith for a time. I wrote to Mother:

> "Where is MY God who is usually so close to me and says 'C'mon Moya dear, I'll help you.' "WHERE IS HE?"
>
> Mother, I feel I have to work this all out so that I can have something to give to Littlejohn and Shanda. And that's been my biggest worry. How to teach THEM what I believe.
>
> At least that was my biggest worry until I looked at that big light over the operating table and realized I don't have a leg to stand on.
>
> Bill sat with me for hours and hours and talked quietly to me and so lovingly. And as he spoke in his low comforting voice, I finally went to sleep, holding on to his words, "faith is the substance of things hoped for — the evidence of things not seen."
>
> I just wanted you to know, my precious Mother, that I'm not going on blissfully ignorant of the importance of religious training. I'm only sorry I can't find the comfort you do from Christian Science. All I want to preserve is my faith. Bill said we'd go to different churches together to find one we both felt comfortable with, but I doubt very much if I'll ever be a member of any church again.
>
> Mom, when we were down at the desert for Easter, I was out in the children's room, sitting on the edge of the bed, trying to tell them what Easter was REALLY all about — that it's not the Easter Bunny, and chocolate eggs and jelly beans. And my tears started. I tried to tell the story of Jesus so that they would understand. I wiped my tears. I blew my nose. I started over. I was terribly upset with the urgency of telling this story, when Shanda, on her back on the floor with her arms folded under her head, said comfortingly, "Aw, Mom that's okay, all's I want to know is where's my bathing suit!?"

After we moved from Grand Rapids to Santa Monica, California, to the little house on 14th Street in December 1946, I regained my faith.

Bill was happy to be back in California. He loved the weather. And he loved the action. Los Angeles was where all the major aircraft plants were based: Douglas, Lockheed, Northrop, and many others. Our plant was on Santa Monica Boulevard in West Los Angeles.

I joined the first Church of Christ, Scientist in Santa Monica, put the children in Sunday school and sent them to Berkeley Hall, a Christian Science school in Beverly Hills. It was a fine school and I was at peace with the world and myself.

Bill never challenged my religion. He said if he could give me anything better, he would. I wasn't as devout a student of Christian Science as Mother was; for example, J.C. and I had never been to a doctor. We had measles, mumps, whooping cough, were even quarantined for scarlet fever, but there was never a doctor — and we were always the first to recover in the school. (Just think: Mother was sick the whole nine months she carried me and lived on soda crackers. So much for vitamins!) She respected the law, but she always demanded her religious freedom. We were never vaccinated. Bill, however, insisted on polio vaccinations. And in that, as in everything else, we made room for each other.

I began to embrace my religion with a fervor I had never known. It was like water out on the desert. I couldn't get enough. I had class instruction and managed to answer most of my own questions. We all find our own way and maybe it doesn't always seem logical, but a profound faith transcends logic. For a while, I straightened out the uninformed folk who said, "Oh yeah, that's the one where it's mind over matter, yeah, I know that one. Except you don't believe in Jesus."

No, my friend, it's not mind over matter, it's the power of prayer. It's knowing who God is, and Man's relationship to Him. It's knowing that we were created in the image and likeness of God and we were given "power over every creeping thing that creepeth upon the earth," and that the teachings of Jesus are the basis of our religion. When we have children, we'd better be ready. I love the T-Shirt that says, "Because I said so, that's why!" But it doesn't work when you have inquisitive, intelligent children who want answers. We won't always have the answers, but we can teach them right from wrong. We can teach them to walk away from trouble, to tell the truth, to try to be unselfish, and the rest they have to learn themselves.

Chapter Ten

In December 1946, Bill wrote me a sweet letter that touches my heart to this day when I read it:

> Darling, you're so precious to me and I hardly realized how necessary was your presence and love until you were nearly snatched from me last Spring. Then I knew for sure how much I loved you—how necessary you were to me, to my happiness and my success. Who else in this world could I share my achievements, accomplishments and moments of elation with but you? Who else would have the depth of understanding to at once know the thrill and appreciate the cost — I'm sure you're THE ONE.
>
> Darling, I write you so seldom and mostly when I do it isn't nice writing but this is my bouquet to you, my living loved one. I'm terribly glad you're alive. So glad you were born and so happy that you loved me, love me and always will love me. It's TERRIBLY IMPORTANT to me!
>
> I never want to leave you, ever — you've become so important to me, Darling. I call you each day to hear your voice tell me you love me. I hunger for it during the day and I feel so helplessly inadequate to express my appreciation when I do get to hear it at night.

Reading his words, it's hard to imagine that during our marriage there were other women, but there were.

I always felt secure that he loved me. And though I always knew that there were other girls around, they didn't threaten me. No one threatened me, because we had a special bond.

We were always very close in bed at the end of the day, the best time for a couple to be close. Because the rest of the day is consumed with associates, work and children, arguments, and going to market and getting food on the table. The end of the day should be a time for summarizing the day together — problems, aspirations and dreams. A lot of couples lose being close. Love-making becomes a mindless physical exercise and they get disenchanted and stop caring. But we cared. And Bill was very sweet with me. He was a wonderful lover, he knew exactly what he was doing. He was very warm and he wasn't selfish. The whole business of making love was part of him and part of me. He was rare for his time, a truly considerate lover.

Early in our marriage we had a big fight. We had moved to Santa Monica, but were back in Piqua visiting friends. During the afternoon, I was with our host and hostess, waiting for Bill. Everybody in the house knew Bill was with this girl — he was out with her all afternoon, knowing that I was waiting for him. And I was furious!

The girl was Carla (not her real name), the pretty wife of a Piqua man, who Bill had met while setting up the plant in Piqua. When we'd first moved to Piqua, Bill had brought her to the house with her two little girls in bonnets. He introduced her as a nice little friend for me. He liked her, and I did too. She helped me cook, showed me how to iron.

This was the first time in our marriage I knew Bill was being unfaithful. I was disgusted with him, ashamed of him, and embarrassed by him. I packed and was going back to Los Angeles, but there was no way to get out right away. The train station was in the next town and the drive was too far. So we managed some degree of making up. Bill was genuinely remorseful. He was good at winning me back. But in bed, after such an incident, I wouldn't let him touch me. I was revolted. I had to get through that. In the end, my love for him was so powerful that it made situations like that seem insignificant. I never felt inadequate or insecure, and that was the blessing. It wasn't because I learned how to do that, it's just the way I was. And he was lucky, I never was vindictive.

I can't help but wonder where my balance came from — the ability to step back, look at, and deal with Bill's infidelities in such an objective way. I guess I could see what was happening with Bill. He was traveling — he wasn't going to be alone in his hotel room when he'd been busy all day. He'd go out to dinner, have some drinks with friends, and nine times out of ten there'd be a cute girl. Things could very easily escalate into a quick little affair. I couldn't control that. I couldn't be in two places at once and he just was the way he was.

Bill had a great personality. It was his voice, the way he could play, dance, laugh, coax. He was a very positive, happy person, seldom morose. He was complimentary to the girls. "You look so pretty. I love the dress you're wearing." He really talked to them. "What did you do today?"

His saving grace with me was that he never wanted to hurt me. He always held me close and made me understand how much home meant to him, how much my happiness meant to him. There were things that I thought I'd never get over — but you do get over them. For instance, I thought I'd never get over "Barbie."

One day I was straightening up the bedroom and decided to tackle a chest of messy drawers. I separated the socks, handkerchiefs and underwear, and a Thanksgiving card surfaced. I opened it innocently and read: "Dear Bill, I'm sending Thanksgiving greetings to the fathers of all my children, so of course you had to be included." A picture of a little girl about two years old — just Shanda's age — fluttered out of the card. She looked just like Bill. The Lear stamp went on all his children: the strong nose, that Lear face. Suddenly I had to sit down — there was no chair handy so, I sat on the floor. Shock and disbelief surged through my body. I could not believe it. I knew the mother was Carla. And while I was fond of her, I was not THIS fond. The picture was of Carla's little girl, who I would later discover was named Barbie.

Years later, when Ed Bradley interviewed me for "60 Minutes" he said "Gee, Mrs. Lear, you show a remarkable tolerance for this sort of thing. Did you just yawn and turn the other way?" NO! I didn't. When Bill came home, I was ready for him. I wanted to kill him. I'd never been that angry in my life, before or since. I screamed and hollered, bit and scratched, and slammed doors and chased him with scissors (and don't worry, if I'd have caught him, there never would've been a Learjet!).

He ran up the stairs, and I ran after him. He got into our bedroom, slammed the door and locked it. I was banging on the door so hard I made marks on that door with my wedding and engagement rings. I was too furious even to cry.

The whole house knew there was a major fight going on. Nils Eklund and his wife and little boy, Peter, who was about two, were staying with us. Peter was pushing cookies into the crack under the door. And I said, "Don't feed him!" Anyway, Bill stayed barricaded in the bedroom long enough for me to leave.

I put on my coat and drove for a couple of hours, thinking: OK, do I want this to be the end? Do I file for divorce tomorrow? Finally, I went back to the house. After all, I had to pack some clothes if I meant to go through with it. Also, I would have to leave the next morning to get a ticket and go to California. But even though I was out of control with rage, the love I had for him was still strong. It always was. And I would never have left him. I went up to the bedroom. Bill was standing in his bare feet and pajamas with a stricken look on his face.

"Oh, Mom, I'm so glad you came home."

I put my suitcase down, shrugged off my coat, walked across the room, put my arms around him and said, "You're such a dumb bastard."

"I know, Mom."

"You can't do things like that," I said. "How come you didn't insist that she have an abortion?"

"Because she wanted that baby and said she would never come to me with problems about it. And it wasn't my call."

Both of us wept. It was an intense time in our marriage. We worked our way through it. Mostly because I understood. I played out the scenario. They'd had an affair. And when you monkey around like that, you're playing with fire — somebody's gonna get pregnant and it won't be him!

His latest betrayal of me made it hard for me to go to bed with him, but the love we had soon brought us through, even this time. He was never one to send flowers, but he always called and was there for me when I needed him. Strangely, some of the worst major fights do have a way of pulling you closer to your spouse. Because you go through that stuff with each other, you experience a very strong force that keeps you together instead of polarizing you. That force bonds you again, only stronger than before because you've been through it. You've seen it. You know what's happened. And you're hurt but you're not bleeding. And you put your arms around one another and cry together, kissing the tears away.

Girls were always available to him, and he had a lot of them. But he only had one of me. That's where home was, and he didn't need a direction finder to get there! I really did nearly kill him that time. I've been assured that it would've been Justifiable Homicide! Actually, I had three options: divorce, murder or suicide, but with any one of these I would have to face life without him, and I wasn't ready for that.

Subconsciously, I was resigned that every once in a while Bill would have an affair. From my point of view, men and women are not only built differently, they have different drives. I never contemplated an affair to get even. I think it's wrong for girls to even think about getting even. It's vindictive and it doesn't pull a marriage together. You can kiss your marriage good-bye when you start playing games like that.

I'm reminded of a story Bill told me about one of his girls in New York, who said one day:

"You're NEVER going to divorce Moya and marry me!"

"Well, why would I do a thing like that?"

"Why wouldn't you?"

"Okay, first I'd hafta move Moya out of town."

"Yeah — so?"

"Then I'd hafta move you in."

"And what's wrong with that?"

(helpfully) **"Well, the problem with that is — where would I find another girl like you in New York?"**

(indignantly) **"Well if you think I'LL put up with what Moya puts up with, you're nuts!"**

(laughing) **"You just figured it out all by yourself!"**

When he told me these stories, he laughed — and so did I! He never intentionally did anything to hurt me. And he never let me doubt that he needed me and loved me.

The last part of the Barbie story went something like this: I was in

New York visiting my family and Bill was in St. Louis. We were going to meet in the next day or two in Grand Rapids. The phone rang in my room. It was Bill calling to give me his itinerary, so we blabbed on the phone for a little bit.

"Bye, honey!"

"Bye, Barbie!" (And he hung up.)

I sat there and looked into the telephone — dumbfounded. Barbie? Where was she in the roll call? I had never heard him mention a Barbie. (I didn't know that was Carla's daughter's name at the time.) But I'll bet there's more to this than he intends to admit. I sent him a wire:

> **YOU'D BETTER HAVE SOMETHING VERY FUNNY TO SAY ABOUT BARBIE. STOP. SEE YOU IN GRAND RAPIDS. STOP. LOVE ANYWAY. MOYA**

Both of us finally wound up at home in Grand Rapids. After the baggage had been taken upstairs, we sat down in the living room. I smoothed my skirt and planted my two feet on the floor and hauled off with:

"Okay, I'm ready. Who's Barbie?"

(Honest to God, this is what he said:)

"Oh Mom, c'mon! I was saying 'baby' when I meant to say 'darling' and it came out 'Barbie'!"

Well, of course I had to laugh — and if you laugh, all the fire goes out. I told this story to our son, John, he roared with laughter, gasping: "Oh Mom, ask Dad if he can think up one like that for 'Nancy'!" I let it drop. I let him win. It wasn't important enough to break up a marriage — not our marriage anyway.

But there was one real heartache, and that was Natalie, the one girl who had a strong, strong hold on him. Still, even with her, he could only stay for a day or two. All she did was love him. She wasn't vindictive, or spiteful, or ever a problem. Bill felt guilt, but he never married her. And even when he established an enormous trust fund for her, I was still OK because I knew a lot had gone on before I appeared on the landscape, and I couldn't change any of it. But it still took me a long time to work this one out so that I could wind up with some peace of mind.

One hot summer night as we lay in bed holding hands and looking at the ceiling, Bill turned to me and said — "Honey how about the one where you divorce me, and let me go marry her — and I give her a baby — and then I divorce her and come back to you. How about that one?" (I couldn't believe my ears!)

I got up on my knees to look at his face to see if he was kidding. No, he wasn't kidding. He was dead serious. I said, slowly and carefully, "Honey, you know that wouldn't work. You know that in your heart! I couldn't be happy. She wouldn't be happy when you left her with the baby. And you couldn't end up happy either 'cause you've got some bad scenes in store for you if you ever try to pull a caper like that."

But I talked to him about it. I didn't scream, "Are you out of your mind?", or make a scene. He could talk to me about anything, and he did. He told me stories about all his girls. As a matter of fact, he even told me about making love to one of them years and years ago and reading the funny papers over her shoulder. I laughed about that because it was so outrageous!

I didn't discuss my situation with anyone, not Mother, my sister, or my friends. It was my problem, and nobody got to drag it over the coals. I didn't need to talk. I have no idea where my strength came from. Oddly enough, I was much more hurt by Daddy's affairs than I ever was by Bill's, maybe it was because I was younger and it involved Mother and Daddy whom I idolized.

Still, it was important not to let resentment build up. I never harbored anything. I put letters on his pillow, and letters in his bag when he went on trips. I avoided one-on-one conflict because I never knew what problems he would be coming home with. He might be running out of money, or having trouble with the design of a product, stuff that I had no idea how to fix. All I could do was make home comfortable. I didn't want to confront him with another problem, so I wrote a letter.

Letter-writing is a way of communicating without conflict or hollering or without saying things that you're sorry you said. In my letters to him I'd put down all the things in my heart for him to read when he was ready. I think timing's very important. I let certain letters "ripen" for a day or so. I raised hell with him in some letters. But I always had a sense of humor, which evidenced itself in the following letter:

A scene flashes through my mind: the Lexington Hotel in New York around New Year's Eve. You called Clarissa to come over. To myself I said "Come on over and I'll fix you GOOD You nasty little no-good hoofer, you!"

Y'know, everything was all right until I knew she tried to get you away from me. If I had known the whole story, I NEVER would have been so nice. NEVER!! I'd have killed her first and gone to jail.

I hate 'em all . . . but I can't help but understand how wonderful it must've been for them! (and I don't blame THEM, either). The dancing, the dinners, the fun in bed, even the tears. You made women out of 'em, sweetheart! I'm sure of that. I'd spit right in Clarissa's eye if I had the bad luck to run into her again.

The scene described above took place in the '40s, and there was a great song that was popular then which I loved called "Speak Low." But I found out she loved it too:

> Speak low, darling, speak low
> Our summer day withers away
> Too soon. Too soon . . .
>
> . . . our moment is swift
> Like ships adrift
> We're swept apart.
> Too soon.

Too soon, my foot!

As I wrote to Bill:

I can SEE that. I could even rationalize on your behalf . . . Playing games — little love games. But suddenly I'm alerted (and what's very funny about the whole thing) LONG after it's over! I found that it wasn't 'ships adrift' at all! She tried to STEAL MY BOAT!

Darling, we're a pact and a union and a song . . . I'm the melody that haunts and remembers, and you are the bass and

the highs and the harmony. The pianissimo and the crescendo. You take my melody and 'rend it to bits.' You weave it and mold it. You sing it. Chant it. You beat a drum. Tear at it and cling to it. It will always be there. And our music is like nothing anyone has ever heard. It is strange and sweet. It has strength and power. It never ends. And we never tire of it.

I never lit into him or gave him an ultimatum, but I gave him plenty to think about! For example, in 1944, I wrote and illustrated a little book for him entitled, "On this Business of Being an Understanding Wife" (a reprint of which can be found in the back of this book).

I always let Bill know how I felt, not only in letters but in hand-lettered books, personally illustrated and some even bound by me. And, of course, many square miles of needlepoint. One piece has been part of our home for nearly 50 years. Mounted under glass on a flip stand in the form of an antique face screen, one side greeted him with, "Welcome Home, Darling!" After he'd been home long enough, I'd flip to the other side that read: "Get Out Of Town!"

For his 50th birthday, I worked a piece with "Ah L'amour" in the center. Then I filled it with the names of his ex-wives, ex-mistresses and "ships that passed in the night"; then, I stitched it with a border reading: "Some I've Forgotten and Some I Didn't Know About." I matted my work with bitch pink velvet. I then stitched a smaller sign in an identical frame that said, "No Vacancy!"

What he was doing was not OK with me, but not all that earth-shaking either, certainly not grounds for divorce. When I give talks around the country, girls tell me, "If I ever catch my husband monkeying around with another woman, that's it!" Well that shouldn't be it if you love him — because then you lose your whole marriage, the father of your children, your home, everything, just because you get hard-nosed about him stumbling.

Now if it's flagrant, if he says, "Up yours! You married me, and that's it!" then you leave him. That isn't what I dealt with, ever. He loved me. He didn't want to hurt me, and although he sometimes wrote letters saying, "I can't be as good as you think I am, and I'm a bastard and that's the way it is," I knew he wanted to be a better person. I appreciated his honesty; it was my choice to accept the ground rules.

When I started digging into letters and archives to prepare material for this book, a close friend, an author in his own right, said a little scornfully, in a teasing way, "Oh, Moya, I know — you're going to try to clean it up!" No. I'm not trying to clean it up. I'm trying to tell you what happened and how I dealt with it. And in going over letters I wrote to him, I found it truly wasn't easy. But three things were crucial to our staying together:

1. **I loved him with a true, knock-down, drag-out, unconditional love.**
2. **We respected each other.**
3. **We both had a healthy sense of humor.**

Start with that and you can conquer just about anything. The key is unconditional love. Love him the way he is. And God help you if you think you're going to change him. They do change because they mature, and if they love you at all — which he did—they try to be better. And he did become a better person.

If we had fought over every one of those girls we never would have made it through our marriage. I understood why he got into this kind of trouble. As I said before, he was built that way — the sexiest guy I ever saw in my life! But with such brilliance and so much character — in every other area — it wasn't important enough for me to disturb the peace of my home or my heart. He was happy when he was home with me, and for me there was nothing to equal that. He needed a home and that's what I gave him. I truly was his mother, his wife, his mistress and best friend.

We had something remarkable. We really did.

Chapter Eleven

After World War II, a bunch of pilots came to Bill and said, "Hey Bill, you know what we need worse than anything in the world of general aviation? An automatic pilot that's small, practical and works for us!" That conversation sent Bill on one of the most challenging and rewarding projects of his career. When the pilot's approached him, Bill's reputation was already solid. He no longer was the brash young inventor, but a very respected force in aviation.

What made Bill's autopilot such an exciting success was the fact that it was small, practical, and still did the job. It helped pilots fly in heavy weather even at zero zero visibility. At that time the only existing automatic pilot was a big, cumbersome affair, a prohibitive payload and, worse, not licensed for operation in turbulent weather. In addition, it was horrendously expensive and absolutely useless to the little guy. That added up to a very desperate and urgent need which Bill addressed when he designed a practical automatic pilot.

Private pilots in the late '40s were flying Italian Trecker Amphibians, built by Piaggio, and American-built Bonanzas, Navions, converted B-26s, DC3s and Lodestars — anything they could patch up and make fly higher, farther, faster. Right? (Jet? Whatsa jet?) But it was impossible for them to find their way in fog or touch down under "minimums" — the minimum altitude needed for enough visibility to land an airplane. Bill emerged as an aviation innovator and flourished in this age of utility. This was right up his alley. He turned our home in Grand Rapids into an informal boarding house for engineers, so they'd be handy during the design and development of the autopilot.

Bill's work on the Automatic Direction finder (ADF) prepared him for the challenge of the autopilot. The idea was to give our fighter pilots more than just a ten-minute respite while flying on a mission. But the complete device had to weigh less than 40 pounds. To design this, Bill had to gather together a team of engineers who were brilliant enough to contribute real ideas and dedicated enough to submit to Bill's exacting management style and his demanding hours. Fortunately, Bill had hired in Nils Eklund in 1943 — a Swedish engineer with an original mind who was well-versed academically and was as skeptical of "book" knowledge as was Bill.

As usual, Bill had to move against the wind. Even with his most-famous invention, the car radio, he'd been told: "They'll legislate against it in Congress because it will distract the driver." Now he was being told: "Bill, none of these private pilots are going to spend that much money for an automatic pilot."

And what about the airlines? In 1935, Eddie Rickenbacker, founder of Eastern Airlines, had called Bill's Direction finder, which was the first practical automatic direction finder, "the most important air navigation aid developed to date." But now, when Bill came to him with his autopilot, Eddie said: "No automatic pilots in the cockpits of Eastern Airlines — my pilots are going to fly my airplanes!"

Then Bill, persisting, said, "But Eddie, with an automatic pilot, they would never get lost."

To which Eddie roared, "Eastern Airline Pilots are never lost!"

Not long after that conversation the entire eastern seaboard was tied up while Air Traffic Control tried to locate an Eastern Airlines flight bound for Charleston, South Carolina. The pilot had veered off course and gotten lost in very nasty fog. Finally, after nearly an hour of agony in the cockpit, he announced triumphantly that he had landed at Charleston. The fellows in the tower at Charleston said, bewildered, "Eastern 731 is not on the ground at Charleston."

The exasperated pilot said, "The hell I'm not — I'm parked right under your tower!" To the embarrassment of the Eastern pilot, the professional voice of Air Traffic Control in Charlotte, North Carolina, announced to the air waves, "You're parked under our tower, sir!"

So Bill, with his powerful, uncluttered reasoning and creative, spontaneous bursts of inspiration, addressed himself to the problem — and with a skilled group of dedicated "can-do" engineers, designed and built the first small high-precision autopilot for jet fighters in the

Korean conflict. And they tested it, and tested it, and tested it.

Bill's search for excellence was a character trait that often drove his production people crazy. The engineers on the production line would say in frustration, "The boss changed it again!" Bill explained, patiently sometimes, (and sometimes not) that if they didn't make the change he asked for, the equipment would make the full circle from the factory to the salesmen to the owner back to the factory for repairs.

Someone wrote a book about a search for excellence many years later. The author didn't know Bill and Bill didn't know the author. But they spoke the same language.

Money was not the reason Bill loved to work; it was the problem-solving that excited him. He not only loved to create, but to produce what he had created in the best possible way, so it truly was excellent. He got so mad when they said in the aviation periodicals that Lear made "Mickey Mouse" equipment, because he wanted to make the best. The problem was that after he made the best, he neglected to develop the necessary support systems to repair and service the equipment.

He was the happiest when he was engulfed in a project. When the project was over he became very depressed. He didn't feel a sense of accomplishment. What he did feel was a void, an emptiness because the challenge wasn't there anymore. The need to accomplish wasn't there anymore. He'd done it.

From my side of the bed, I thought I was going to die of old age before I ever saw the end of the autopilot project. It was an intense, fascinating, all-consuming challenge for Bill. He ate, drank and lived the autopilot. The project tapped all of his energies (which were immense) and his thought processes which were brilliant, especially considering the level of his education. After watching him solve complicated mathematical problems intuitively, Bill's engineers said, "Boss you tell us what you want it to do and we'll develop an equation for it!"

His intuitive powers — which came from what he called his "Infinite Source of Supply" — came into full flower with the auto-pilot. He truly believed it when he told me never to worry: "There's an Infinite Source of Supply of Ideas — I just dip in!" There was absolutely no doubt in my mind that he could do whatever he set out to do.

Every day, every night was filled with test flights. He'd change the design and test fly, then return with Nils to the hangar and leave a note on the engineer's bench about the change in design.

Climbing in the Twin-Beech with the children, stepping over all the wires in the aisle, and settling them in their seats (I think they were born knowing how to fasten their seatbelts) was standard procedure. I'd build my nest in the seat opposite to and behind Bill so I could watch him fly blissfully armed with only the autopilot in his lap, a screwdriver, and happiness. The autopilot was an eight-inch-square black box which was mounted in the nose of the airplane. As Bill worked on the instrument, he kept it on his lap, watching an indicator on the control panel, calibrating roll, pitch and yaw with a screwdriver.

Early on, we logged thousands of hours (I can't be more precise, because he never in his life kept a log book!). He told me to watch for birds — they could be sucked into and stop the engines. And I learned how to navigate — even nudged him awake when we went over Air Traffic Control check points, radio signals from the ground set up at positions corresponding to flight maps. I memorized Emergency Landing Procedures. I knew how to click 121.5 — the emergency radio frequency — knew where the throttle was, how to adjust it and how to maintain speed and altitude, but prayed fervently that I would never have to do it!

Bill, with Nils Eklund, a wonderful scientist, physicist and friend, spent hours, months, years on the autopilot project (as did, of course, the whole team at Lear, Inc.) One winter night in Grand Rapids, it was snowing and I was waiting with a casserole in the oven, the children were in bed. Finally, about 11:30 p.m., Bill and Nils came in the back door — white with exhaustion from such work. I took their coats and sat them down at the kitchen table. I got a bottle and two glasses, lit a candle, and found a copy of "The Rubiyat" (which they both loved to read aloud to each other). I spoon-fed them from the casserole and finally got them both to bed.

But Bill's autopilot team found time to relax. I also found time to relax with them. For example, we had a lot of fun playing poker. And on summer evenings we sat out on the front steps of the house and sang songs, harmonizing. Bill and I also played thousands of games of gin rummy during this time.

Sometime later, I was down in the basement of the house doing laundry. It was a big, cool area and I loved being down there with the children — doing nice dumb stuff like taking the sheets off the line out in the backyard, then going down to iron and stack folded work in a basket.

Between the music on the little Learadio and the babies chattering (we used to say John talked "monkey talk" and Shanda talked "bird talk"), I was totally content. Then the phone rang.

"Honey, Jack (the co-pilot) and I are going to fly down to St. Louis this afternoon. We'll be calibrating the Autopilot. Come on and go with us — you can visit with Louise" (my cousin).

"Oh, honey, I'm right in the middle of something (nothing really) and besides I don't like to be in the airplane when you're calibrating the autopilot!"

"Come on, Mom, I really want you to go!"

"OK," I grumbled, resigned. I looked around at the unfinished laundry. I'll need the baby sitter, I thought. Quickly assessing what I would have to do, I said, "I'll be out there in an hour."

"Great! I'm glad, honey."

Darn it, I didn't ask him if we were going to stay overnight. Well, just in case, I'll pack a nightie and a toothbrush. And I'll bet a clean shirt is the last thing on his mind, so I'll tuck one in. And I musn't forget my needlepoint or my book.

By the time I reached the airport, they were standing around the airplane waiting for me. I thought: he really is the limit. Why in the world does he want me in the airplane for a dumb flight to St. Louis to calibrate the Autopilot? Shoot! I grumbled as I climbed into the airplane. They stowed my suitcase, but I kept my book and needlepoint, as I sat down, fastened my safety belt and we were off. I read for a little bit, did some needlepoint and then, as I thought about all the things I should be doing at home, I tipped my head back and fell sound asleep.

When I woke up, the light had changed. It was getting dark. I couldn't believe I'd slept that long. I looked out the window and it sure didn't look like Missouri to me. I unbuckled my safety belt and went up to the cockpit. And there, to my wondering eyes did appear: the skyline of Manhattan framed in our Beech 18's windshield — right out in front of us — brilliant, dramatic, breathtaking. My surprise was complete. I was speechless.

He'd flown me to New York to see "South Pacific"! (Y'build up a lot of Brownie points with stunts like that, you know!) But I suffered a momentary twinge of guilt and a very deep tenderness for him — remembering how hard he'd had to argue to get me on that airplane —

"We'll be calibrating the Autoplot" — HAH! He hadn't even brought a screwdriver!

Finally, the autopilot was finished. The prototype was completed early in 1949 — less than two years after development had begun. What's more, the Air Force demanded an autopilot for the F-86, and Lear, Inc. developed one after four intense months of work. The device led to a production contract that would bring our company almost $1 billion over the next dozen years or so.

The night the Federal Aviation Administration was to announce the autopilot's certification, Bill and I sat up in our home in Santa Monica drinking tea (honest), eating chocolate chip cookies, and waiting for the phone to ring. When the ship landed, the pilots and FAA inspectors and engineers who were in the airplane lined up outside a phone booth at the airport at 10'clock in the morning to tell Bill the good news.

The Lear autopilot was an incredible achievement and was soon installed in jet fighters during the Korean War. Its principles are still used throughout the industry today. For it, Bill was awarded the Collier Trophy for 1949 — the highest award in aviation. It is presented by the President of the United States:

"To William P. Lear, Director of Research and Development of Lear Incorporated, for his outstanding achievement in the development, perfection, application and production of the Lear F-5 Automatic Pilot and Automatic Approach Control Coupler System which makes possible the safe landing of Jet Aircraft regardless of extreme weather or visibility conditions."

Of course, everyone in Lear, Inc. celebrated — and Bill acknowledged them all. He really owed debts of gratitude to many, but the list was headed by our great friend, Nils Eklund.

The high point in all the celebrating was our trip to the White House. While we were waiting with the news media before being admitted into the Oval Office to see President Truman, I was so excited I could hardly stand up. Everything thrilled me about being there. When I reached for Bill's hand to squeeze it (knowing he had to be twice as excited as I was) he leaned down to me and whispered, "Don't worry, honey, I'll put him right at his ease!" Can you believe him? When we finally all swarmed in, they took pictures of Bill and me and President Truman, as well as pictures of Bill and the Collier Trophy. Finally, President Truman said, "Mrs. Lear, do you ever help your husband in the business? Do you ever tell him what to do?"

I looked up at him smiling and said, "No, Mr. President, I never tell him what to do. I sometimes tell him where to GO, but . . ."

Bill said, "Yeah and y'know what — I don't hafta go there!"

Winning the Collier Trophy meant a lot to Bill. The recognition was a confirmation of his genius, but nothing changed at home. Life went on exactly the same as before.

On another late afternoon in Grand Rapids, Bill called and said, "C'mon out to the field — we're going to Chicago for dinner!"

"Whoopee!" I hung up the phone and lunged for the closet to jump into a cocktail dress, and to check my makeup. (Big deal — I never was very careful about makeup. Matter of fact, one of my granddaughters said, "Ma, we know you put on your lipstick while you're walking — but, talking?")

I picked up my keys and tore out to the field. When I skidded into a parking place, he was still on the phone! He looked at me blankly and said, "Where'd you come from?" I pointed and smiled, "Right down the road a piece. Were you expecting somebody else — did I beat her?" He put his arms around me and held me close. Then he pushed me at arm's length and looked deep into my face saying, "You know there's no one else, don't you!" And I said, "I know there's no one else like me!" "Y'got that right, honey!" he smiled.

Then we walked out to the airplane, arm-in-arm. He climbed up on the wing to the pilot's seat, and I followed him in my high heels and cocktail dress (never a tight skirt, so I could always maneuver that step up on the wing of an airplane in the '50s, gracefully!).

We buckled up and Bill called the tower, telling them we were taking off (as opposed to asking for instructions!). The tower called back and said, "You're cleared for takeoff, Bill."

After we took off and achieved our altitude, Bill pushed the yoke over to my side, pulled his hat down over his eyes (against the setting sun) and said, "You take it, honey — wake me up when we get to Chicago!"

He was out of his mind! "No," I yelled "Don't you dare do this to me. Absolutely not. I won't do it! I can't fly this damn airplane and you know very well I can't!"

Bill spoke patiently — as to a hysterical child: "I know very well that you can. Y'see that instrument? That's the artificial horizon. Just keep it level, like it is now, and follow the lake around to Chicago. I'm going to sleep." And in about two minutes he was snoring.

"He's serious — he really means it," I thought, "I have to fly this damn airplane to Chicago!" From the little cockpit of our Bonanza, I searched the sky so I'd be sure to see that airliner I was certain would be bearing down on me. "Birds!" I thought frantically. He had always said to watch for birds. He was kidding, right? If I saw a bird I should turn left to avoid it. I did keep the airplane straight and level in a turn — all around the lake — and when I saw Chicago I tapped Bill on the shoulder. "Mr. Lear, this is your wake up call!" He smiled when he looked out and saw Chicago. He was proud of me. Matter of fact, I was pretty proud of myself!

I loved him for his patience, being able to explain it all in Brownie language. It was never: "You dumbbell, you'll never get it, will you?" He never talked down to me. He respected me and I respected him. That's part of what kept it together when the going got tough. And we went through some pretty heavy weather together!

Chapter Twelve

The year 1949 brought us an even greater joy than the Collier Trophy: our third child, David, born September 22. By this time, we were living in Santa Monica, with Bill commuting to Grand Rapids. My life was a constant parade of schools, music lessons, ballet, carpools, Cub Scouts, Brownies, March of Dimes fund-raisers, picnics, pals, pets, and peace-making! I don't believe in letting children beat up on each other, so we held family meetings to settle disputes. By the time David was a toddler, he was the usual suspect if a toy was broken or missing:

"David broke my truck!"

"David's been messing with my electric trains again!"

We always had some little dog pooping on the carpet because somebody missed a turn taking it out:

"It's your dog!"

"Well, it's your turn!"

Bill finally had enough of the daily bickering and called a family meeting:

"Everybody in this corner! I'm tired of all the quarreling about whose turn it is to feed "Mother Dear" (the cat). We're going to give "Mother Dear" away."

"You can't give "Mother Dear" away, she's my cat!"

"OK, she's your cat — you feed her!"

He threatened to dispose of two or three other pets that were quickly claimed the same way. Then John voiced his concern:

"Now Dad, about David — "

"No matter what you say, David stays!"

Sometime in 1953, when David was not quite 4 years old, we were flying with my mother and the children to Grand Rapids in our Learstar when Bill accidentally strayed into the Aircraft Defense Identification Zone (ADIZ) where only military aircraft are allowed. The Pentagon's decision about the location of the zone didn't make sense, and it frustrated most pilots trying to get from Petosky, Michigan, to anywhere. Pretty soon, Bill saw two F-86s from Selfridge Air Force Base gaining on him fast. He said:

"Quick! Everybody! Away from the windows—down on the floor!"

He buckled David into the pilot's seat, told the delighted little boy to fly Daddy's "airpane," put it on autopilot and got down on the floor with us at about the count of one, two, three! We all stretched out flat on the floor, laughing — can you imagine my mother laying on the floor of that airplane laughing with the rest of us? Those F-86 pilots looked into our airplane, totally empty except for a four-year-old boy in the cockpit doing what his daddy told him to do. I'd have loved to have been a fly on the wall when those pilots told their story back at the base.

Bill had a way of getting people to follow his lead. At Lear, Inc., when lunch time rolled around, he'd round up his boys and go to their favorite Chinese restaurant, The Scotchman's, near Santa Monica Boulevard. The first time he went, the music was blaring. After Bill had asked the proprietor a couple of times (unsuccessfully) to lower the volume, he asked his boys, "Anybody got a pair of wire cutters?"

Someone replied, "Yeah, here's mine." Then Bill walked casually over to the juke box and with a snip, there was silence. He returned to the table, and they went on with their conversation.

Next day at the same restaurant where they ate frequently because the food was excellent, Bill and his gang walked in and the beaming proprietor welcomed them. The music was raucous and Bill headed for the box, wire cutters at the ready and the Chinese gentleman said, very proud of himself, "Misser Lear, I fix switch. See!" He flipped the switch — silence. Bill roared. They were very good friends for years, the restaurant owner and my husband.

Bill also had a friend, Jack, who was a great sports fan. He knew the players, the odds, the backgrounds, the history, everything. When he placed a bet, it was calculated and he knew what he was talking about. In contrast, Bill would throw a dart and wherever it landed, that was the team, horse, airplane or car he'd bet on. And he usually won, which annoyed Jack. One day, they were having lunch together, and Bill ordered a hamburger rare (and then said to the waitress):

"And may I have my hamburger exactly the way I want it?"

The waitress said, "Of course, sir."

So Bill spelled it out for her. "I would like it with no pickles, tomatoes or cucumbers on it, around, above it, under it, or was on it!" (The waitress probably wrote: "no garnish.")

This provoked Jack, who said, "You don't have to draw pictures, Bill. Geesus, this is a first-class restaurant. All you have to say is, 'hamburger rare, no pickles or tomatoes.' Is that so difficult for you?"

BILL: OK, smart ass. Y'wanna bet it comes with pickle 'n' tomato?
JACK: I'll betcha fifty bucks it comes without pickle 'n' tomato.
BILL: You're on.

A few minutes later, the girl came through the swinging door with her tray. She saw them, spun right around and went back. Jack grinned and said, "I'll take a check." When she came back with the tray, she put Bill's hamburger in front of him and said, "I nearly forgot your pickle 'n tomato."

JACK: I'll be a sonuvabitch!
BILL: (handing the hamburger back to the waitress and smiling) I'll take cash.

□   □   □

Like the rest of the world, aviation was growing ever more complex, not at all the way it was in the '40s, when Bill took me flying in the Beech 18. Once back then, about 30 minutes out of Dayton, Bill started to contact Dayton Tower:

"Dayton Tower — this is NC15405 — come in please."

Minutes droned by. He repeated patiently:

"Dayton Tower. 1-5-4-0-5 — Dayton Tower. Come in please."

Still nothing. His voice became short and abrupt:

"Dayton Tower Dayton Tower. 15405"

Silence. Then, singing like a child on a playground, Bill mocked:

"DAY — TON — TOW — ER!"

Clearly and immediately the tower responded:

"Whaddaya want, Bill?"

Listen, I just laughed. That was then. It wouldn't happen anymore. But oh what fun it was to fly then — early, when the airways weren't so crowded, when most of the tower operators across the country knew Bill, when there were some laughs.

Bill and a friend were swapping stories one night in San Antonio. His friend told him about a tower operator asking, "Who dat dude talkin' V2 speed wid' a wooden tail skid?" He must have been talking about Bill, because our lives were about to assume V2 rocket speed! — but without a wooden tail skid!

□   □   □

We had a spirited discussion on New Year's Eve, 1953, with a couple of Bill's older children about family planning; for example, we discussed how many days after our period can we be sure to get pregnant, and how many days we can be sure not to get pregnant; afterwards, Bill said impatiently, "Oh, you can't work it like that. You never can be sure. And you can't say, 'Now we'll go to bed because I want a baby,' because all the love-making goes out the window."

Well, maybe, but I knew that if the experts were right, that night was my night!

The next morning as Bill was dressing for a trip to Europe and I was packing his bag, I smiled. As he checked for his passport and ticket, he looked up at me with such a sweet expression, came over and put his arms around me; holding me to him, he said, "I love you, Mom."

"Oh my darling, I love you to death!"

A horn tooted — his ride to the airport. As he went out the door, he called, "Don't forget, honey, no matter what you hear, I love YOU the best!"

A red flag went up and I thought "Waitaminit — what is he saying?"

Later, I inadvertently discovered that he'd rendezvoused with an old girlfriend in Europe. I wanted to jump off the world, to just disappear, to be gone forever when he called. My heart broke — again! How much more of this could I take?

I sat alone in our wonderful 222 14th St. house in Santa Monica. So much love had gone into that house. I couldn't cry. The pain was too cold and hard. I felt, "OK I've had it!" I told Connie (the wonderful woman who lived with us and helped me keep things together) that I wanted to drive to San Francisco to be with Daddy, who was playing the Geary Theatre.

She said, "Go!"

While I was driving up the coast, the dam broke and I wept for hours. How could he continue to tell me he loved me and do stuff like this? Tell me — I could understand that. He can tell me anything (and often did). But love me — how could he love me and put me through this again!

I arrived in San Francisco, checked into the St. Francis Hotel, then walked over to the theater where there was more discord (a fight over paying a singer). Daddy wasn't his usual booming, happy self, but seemed rattled and harassed. His eyes didn't twinkle. I helped where I could, stayed backstage during the show and talked to everybody — had supper with Daddy later and left the next morning.

On my way back down the Pacific Coast Highway, I healed. I felt at peace. I knew it would be all right. The gal was no threat to me. And besides that, I had a secret that made me incredibly happy. I was so happy to see my children when I got home. I gathered them all in the car and we went to the Hot Dog Show in the Palisades for a quick supper and saw a movie. John was eleven, Shanda, ten, and David, six — and oh, how much I loved them. I put them all to bed and smiled with my secret.

Bill came home. We had quarreled over the phone, but it was over. Peace was declared. When God put me together, he gave me generous portions of objectivity and flexibility, and an incredible power to set priorities. So here I was, strangely happy, completely at peace, and smiling quietly to myself with my lovely secret.

Valentine's Day was upon us and we had invited a couple of close friends over for dinner. It was going to be a warm family evening and I told everyone (including Bill) that I had a surprise for them.

"What's the surprise? What's the surprise?"

"You'll know at dinnertime," I said, closing the louvered doors to the tiny dining room, while telling them not to dare open them until I said so. Finally I called:

"Okay, everybody, dinner's ready. SURPRISE!"

They all gathered around the table, looking unsuccessfully for the surprise. I had a lovely centerpiece of flowers with a tiny toy train moving around it.

JOHN :   C'mon, Mom. What's the surprise?
SHANDA: Yeah, Mom, what?
MOYA: C'mon you dummies! LOOK!
JOHN: We're looking. Pretty flowers. Cute train.

Bill and our friends were looking at the table, bemused.

JOHN: (persisting) What's that in the caboose? It's a little
              doll. It's a baby! (light dawning) It's a baby! Mom's
              gonna have a baby!

Everyone rejoiced. My friends embraced me "What a delicious surprise, Moya!" The children were beside themselves. Bill, however, was stupefied to the point that the children said, "Look at Dad!" (who was speechless!) "Look at Dad!" indeed! Our eyes met across the table and mine smiled, Gotcha!

When Bill later told this story, he'd always add the World War II story about a couple of G.I.'s in North Africa at Mail Call: Joe starts jumping up and down with delight.

MIKE: What're you so excited about?
JOE: My wife's gonna have a baby — that's what!
MIKE: Hey, man. We've been over here for two years!
JOE: What's that got to do with it? There were three years
         between my brother 'n' me!

Now, let's fast-forward to September. I'm driving the children to school.

MOYA: Isn't it just incredible that we're going to have a new
         baby in this family in one more month?

CHILDREN: (long pause) Yeah.

JOHN: Mom, c'mon. How do y'know that in one more month
we're gonna have this baby?

MOYA (carefully): Well, it's like I told you, honey. It's nine
months from the time the Daddy plants the seed.
(Whew!)

JOHN (triumphant): Ha, ha, Mom. Y'can't give us that, anymore.
Dad was just as surprised as we were!

Valentina (forever after became Tina) was our last baby. And Bill,
for the first time in his life, climbed in the nest with me, so delighted
was he about this baby.

Chapter Thirteen

Somehow, in the course of the first ten or fifteen years of our marriage, I earned the dubious reputation of being some kind of an airhead about money, of not balancing my checkbook. I'll admit there might have been something to some of the complaining when we were first married, but not everything!

Although my brother and I were given an allowance, I never had a bank account until after I was married. In my growing-up years, my parents took care of the money.

When I was going with Bill, one of our good friends was Jerry Orbach of Orbach's department stores. Jerry had said, "Come by the store, we just got some new stuff in." I tried on some things and thought they were nice, but I didn't have any money with me — I never had any money with me. So he said, "You can write a check can't you?"

"Sure, I can write a check." (I knew how to write a check because I'd been taught at Pace Institute how to write a check. You put in the date and the amount and who it's to and you sign it. That's how you write a check. Can you write a check? Sure!)

But it was Daddy's account and I didn't have a checkbook. Jerry said, "We have a counter check, you can sign that." I said, "Sure." So I wrote a check to Orbach's for the amount and signed it "Moya Olsen." I never thought a thing about it; I'd paid for things hadn't I?

The bank president in Malverne called Daddy: "Ole, Moya wrote out a check on your account, did you know that?"

"No, I didn't know that."

Daddy called me into the dressing room and said, "Honey, don't you know you can't do that? You have to have an account of your own to write a check." In all my life, I'd never known that. If Daddy had an account at the Bank of Malverne, certainly I could write a check there! It's hard to believe that I could be that naive, but I was.

Even though I had never had any experience in keeping track of money, I learned to be more careful. Bill was a wonderful provider and I wanted him to have a home that was worthy of him. A few years into our marriage, after we'd moved to 10063 Toluca Lake Avenue, North Hollywood, he said we needed to cut back.

The end of World War II meant the cancellation of contracts. The bottom fell right out of the war economy. At that time, our household staff was comprised of a married couple and a nurse named Thelma. I wrote him in part:

> **Our static monthly expenses including $170 mortgage average about $325. The couple and Thelma are $300. I've allowed $100 a month for me and the babies. And between $150 and $175 for the house. This varies greatly according to whether you are home or not. Takes care of meat, groceries, baker, paper boy, waxer, household goods of all kinds. All this only brings it to $1,000.**
>
> **You said $1,100 should be ample. And it's more than enough.**

In Grand Rapids after the war, Bill's company controller said, "Well, Bill, you might as well lock up the place, you're broke."

I thought, "Wow! What does that mean? What happens when you're bankrupt?" I thought, "Do they back up a truck, load up your furniture and drive away? What happens?"

He came home that night, put his arms around me and said, "Mom, don't ever worry about bankruptcy; they can't bankrupt my mind. His was such a positive philosophy — he passionately believed that there is such a thing as an INFINITE SOURCE OF SUPPLY OF IDEAS, and he proved that in his career, over and over again.

In our years together, I never worried about money. How much we had didn't matter to me; I could always get along. I didn't care if I lived in a mobile home, so long as he was there and I had my babies. But I also had absolute faith in his incredible philosophy, that he could tap into the creative force of the universe, and it did seem true for him. My faith in God sustained me through many crises, but Bill's faith was also very strong. He believed that the Lord had given him more than he ever deserved.

Because Bill always looked for the next challenge, he went through a lot of downers. One time in the '30s when he owed alimony and payroll and the bank, he reached that scary bottom of the heap and decided he would leave this world. He bought a bottle of Scotch, got a room on the 30th floor of a hotel, and was going to jump out of the window. He entered the room, closed the door firmly behind him, put the bottle of Scotch on the coffee table and, for the first time in his life, discovered he had acrophobia! There was no way he could get near that window, let alone jump out of it.

"Now wait a minute, I not only can't do that, but it would be too permanent." So he went back to his office, sat down and tried to figure it all out. His positive nature kicked in and he thought, there must be something this world needs that I can provide. He started sketching an idea, which he subsequently sold to RCA. His idea, the concept for a very small and very efficient turret tuner that contained his miniaturized coils and special wire, could be used with every chassis RCA manufactured. They would install the same small tuner into the various chassis they built for different radios. The turret tuner contained all the coils necessary to tune the various bands, together with a much more simplified switching arrangement. Many years later, the concept would find wide usage in the tuners of television sets.

After Bill had built a model, he made an appointment to see the vice president of RCA. On the way up in the elevator, he decided that he wanted $25,000 for his idea. Then he ticked off his options: "If I can't get $25,000, I'll take $20,000; however, $15,000 will take care of my debt at the bank, but $10,000 is my rock bottom. With his model under his arm and high hopes in his heart, he gave his name to Mr. Cunningham's secretary and was admitted immediately.

In the course of negotiations, Mr. Cunningham, the vice president of RCA, said, "Mr. Lear, how much do you want for this idea?"

"You're in a better position to judge its worth." Bill said.

Mr. Cunningham went to talk to his associates, came back, and said to Bill, "Mr. Lear, we will give you $50,000." Bill blanched at the amount and Mr. Cunningham, thinking it wasn't enough, said, "But that's not all, we will also give you a consulting contract for $25,000 a year for five years." Bill continued to sit there, unable to speak, and the vice president said, "We will also give you $15,000 worth of work a year for five years" — making it $40,000 a year, or a total of $250,000 for the entire deal!

At the conclusion of this meeting, Bill was so stunned and exhilarated that, with a check for $50,000 in his pocket, he walked all the way back to Greenwich Village where his shop was because no earthly transportation system could get him there as fast as he wanted to go.

Chapter Fourteen

Around the first week of August 1955, we were driving from our home in Pacific Palisades over to friends' for dinner. We'd moved to Pacific Palisades in 1954 when Tina was coming and we didn't have any more room in that old 14th Street house.

Bill said, "Well, y'better fasten your seatbelt." I buckled up and smiled at him. "OK, I'm ready" (thinking: Oh, oh! Now what?).

BILL: We're gonna move to Switzerland!

MOYA: Right. (pause) When?

BILL: As soon as you can pack.

MOYA: But — but pack what — a trunk, the house, the children?

BILL: Don't argue. Just do it.

MOYA: (soothingly) Honey, be reasonable. First, Switzerland is a country. Where in Switzerland?

BILL: I haven't made up my mind yet. We'll call Sylvan when we get home.

Sylvan Ginsbury was an old friend who had been an usher at our wedding and lived in Geneva. Several factors influenced Bill's decision to set up operations in Switzerland. A pool of trained engineers remained from the war years. Lear products had always sold well internationally and might do even better with a European subsidiary. Most important, this division could be devoted exclusively to Bill's consuming interest — aircraft engineering. So — lock, stock and barrel — to Switzerland — now!

MOYA: But . . . honey! School, dentist, passports!
BILL: Don't argue!
MOYA: (grumbling) Yeah, right — just do it.

Y'wanna know what I did, folks? In three weeks, I packed eleven trunks, 35 pieces of baggage, got passports and vaccinations for everybody, leased our Pacific Palisades home to Grace Kelly, moved into a furnished house on the lake in Geneva, and enrolled the children in the International School! We left Los Angeles en masse on TWA in September 1955.

Once in Switzerland, our friend Sylvan introduced us to one of the great human beings of the world, a Swiss businesswoman named Germaine Stoll, who was the greatest blessing of our entire stay in Switzerland. She was about five years older than I, unmarried, spoke several languages and had excellent contacts all over the country. She was warm and intelligent, with a lovely sense of humor. She gathered the entire Lear family in her arms and we were hers! She was an unbelievably wonderful friend helping us all — Bill, the children, but especially me. God, she was great.

She mopped up so many tears, jumped in and settled so many conflicts, helped with the homework, carefully monitored the music lessons, the ballet. She told us what was acceptable and what was not. She'd say things like, "C'est pas comme ca," which, roughly translated into English, meant "That ain't it, honey!" She hired and fired. She taught me how to market and where: on Tuesdays, here; on Fridays, there. She taught us about centigrade and kilos and centimeters. She made airline reservations, sent us on trips with our tickets and currency of the country to which we were going — France, Germany, Italy, Holland, Spain, England, Greece — secured reservations at the hotel of our destination, then met us at the airport when we returned. She interpreted the customs of each country in a way that made them seem reasonable — even if they weren't. She even had a facility for making us be reasonable — when we hadn't been (in her opinion).

We got so that if Germaine wasn't there, we stood around and looked at each other and said, "Duh, now what?" She helped us with our French and we all learned to say the alphabet so that if we had trouble with the international telephone operators (If!?), we could at least spell it.

I eventually learned to make my way in "taxicab" French. The children were fantastic. Shanda soon spoke excellent French and even the boys did great, considering that David was only six and John, twelve. Tina, of course, was bilingual almost from her first burble.

Bill, however, was terrible, and although he memorized more vocabulary than any of us, he just couldn't rattle off French the way his children could. He could say "vooz-ett tray johntee!" (with a terrible accent). He could say, "Bon Soir, M'sieu — Madame," and "Merci, beaucoup." And he was absolutely delighted when Germaine taught him to say, "Chateau La Pompe" which was slang for "water"! (Fortunately, Scotch and soda is the same in French.) He also learned to say, very graciously, "l'addition, s'il vous plait." But it really bothered him not to be fluent.

We had leased a Charles Addams-type chateau, a huge old estate on the lake in the Canton de Vaud, with the imposing name of Prevorzier. The rooms on the first floor had extremely high ceilings. It drove Bill bananas that there were no base-board sockets; instead, an electric cord with a socket on the end hung from that high ceiling! All I saw, however, were the gorgeous floor-to-ceiling windows opening out on a broad expanse of lawn that stretched to the lake. It was a very elegant Old World house and all very fascinating to me, but I wasn't married to an Old World guy. So Bill Lear declared war on the real estate broker for the entire year we were there, and, in his absence, guess who had to keep the peace? Me, with my broken-down taxicab French.

Anyway, we held our Lear, Inc. Board of Directors meeting in Geneva that year and gave a dinner, which was very elegant and formal, at the house the night before the meeting. The table was set for about ten directors and their wives; Bill was seated at one end and me at the other — with a pair of two-branch silver candelabra in between (I had just bought them on a trip to Rome so I could see him at the other end of the table).

We had just started the dessert course when six year-old David wandered in. He walked up to the table and said, "Hey Dad, guess what?"

Bill, thinking David discovered there were fish in the lake, took another spoonful of chocolate mousse, smiled and asked, "What, Dave?"

And David said conversationally, "'Crap' means pancakes in French!"

The distinguished Board of Directors of Lear, Inc. fell off their chairs and there was no more formality that evening. If one were to give our exploits abroad a title, it could easily be, "The Raw Life and Times of the Lear Family in Geneva!"

Chapter Fifteen

On June 18, 1956, Bill suddenly asked me during breakfast at home in Geneva, "Wanna go to Hamburg with me tomorrow?"

"Sure!" (I'd learned never to turn down an invitation like that!) And I would discover that what seemed like just another trip with Bill would turn out to be one of our greatest adventures.

"I have to address the FAA gang in Hamburg in the morning and we'll come back tomorrow night," he said. (Just a nightgown and toothbrush to pack, I thought.)

He called back from his office later in the afternoon and said, "We'll leave this afternoon for Heidelberg. We're invited to a party there and I've invited Jim Chown." Jim was Bill's aviation consultant for Europe. (Cocktail dress, I thought. Now I've gotta take a bag. If it's hot, I'll need this; if it's cold, I'd better bring a sweater; in case I spill something, bring a spare; or we might get hung up in Hamburg and get a chance to go to the theater, so better bring my lace sheath . . . and while I'm at it, don't forget an umbrella.)

Off we went, Jim Chown — who only brought a shaving kit (silly man), Bill and myself. We went to a wonderful party in Heidelberg, saw a fantastic palace and famous opera house. The next morning, we flew to Hamburg, where Bill addressed the FAA group on instrument requirements for private pilots in Germany. He had very strong views about this, encouraging pilots everywhere to get their instrument ratings. He told them that an artificial horizon isn't going to help you in bad weather, when, for example, the fog closes in and you don't know which way is up.

From the air, Hamburg had looked like a great city with a large, well-lighted airport. After waiting for Bill there almost all day, however, I wanted to SEE the city! Finally Bill finished his speech, he called me at flight ops and said, "Grab a cab and come on into town." There we ran into an old friend of Bill's, Paul Penrose, who had a car and showed us around.

We decided to stay in Hamburg overnight and called every hotel in town for accommodations, but everything was booked solid. So we logged some time in a bar, and the boys "remembered when." We made so much noise laughing at the stories the guys were telling that we were asked to leave the bar.

Well, feeling great and having a ball, Bill had Paul drive us to the Atlantic Hotel. Paul said, "C'mon Bill, can'tcha read signs? Don'tcha listen? They don't have any rooms!"

Bill said, "Waitaminit!" He got out of the car and walked forthrightly into the hotel. In a minute, sure enough, he came out for our bags. The only catch was, we had to move out the next morning for the Shah of Iran! Even so, we had a great time. After some quick sightseeing, we danced our feet off, and finally went back to our gorgeous suite at the hotel.

When I think back to the next morning in that great city, and how close we came to going back to Geneva, I can't help but think— as I often do — that there was a FORCE guiding Bill to do the things he did. We got a cab to the airport the next morning, ready to return to Geneva (or so I thought, totally unsuspecting). Poor Jim Chown only expected to go to a party in Heidelberg. He didn't know anything about Hamburg — at least I knew that much. By this time, he was thinking about the things he should've done before he left Geneva.

On our way to the airport, Bill asked, "Hey! How would you like to go to Berlin?"

"Berlin?" I said, "Absolutely. Great! I'd love to go!" But Jim gulped and wondered how to ask for a 16 1/2–33 white shirt in German.

We got out to the airport, paid the driver, unloaded the baggage, and Bill went into flight Operations to file his flight plan to Berlin. The guy looked at Bill's flight plan and then up at Bill and said, "It'll take a minute."

Bill said, "What'll take a minute?"

"Well, you need an OK to fly the corridor." The Four Powers

who'd divided Germany after the war had left a narrow air corridor over Communist East Germany to the divided city of Berlin.

Twenty minutes later, as we waited in the plane, with Bill ready to say, "the hell with it," a fella ran out and said permission had been turned down. Bill, kind of surprised, said, "OK, back to Geneva."

I was in the back seat, reading — hungry — and not paying a whole lot of attention. "Please, let's get something to eat! And if we can't go to Berlin, let's go home!"

So Bill went back to flight Ops to file for Geneva. While he was standing there, the Telex started to stutter. The operator tore off the message and smiled as he handed it to Bill (I found these messages in the archives):

> **THIS AMERICAN PRIVATE flYER WILL GO TO
> SCHOENEFELD AND WANTS TOWER FREQUENCY
> DO YOU WANT A flIGHT PLAN FROM
> BERLIN/TEMPLHOF TO BERLIN/SCHOENEFELD
> PLS ADVISE**

This reply came back:

> **WE KNOW OF THE FLIGHT GOING TO
> SCHOENEFELD AND THE FREQS ARE BEING
> PHONED TO HIM AT THE PRESENT TIME**

Bill came back from flight ops, climbed in the airplane and said, "OK, off to Geneva." (Not a word about Berlin.)

By this time, I was starving! "That's too bad, but gee, it's at least a three-hour flight to Geneva!" I said. "Oh we'll be there in no time," he said comfortingly.

"No time." — I grumbled as I scrounged around in the back seat for a piece of candy or gum or a cracker! But I remembered what the minister had said about for richer or poorer, for better or worse, and I went back to my book, resigned to my hunger, glancing down at the beautiful country now and then.

Pretty soon, I could see the edge of a city under us and Bill was losing altitude. I thought, Oh, he's gonna be a good boy and feed us! This must be Frankfurt. But in about two seconds I could see this fantastic city spread out all over the map and I knew it was Berlin. I closed my book and hit Bill on the back of the head with it. "It's Berlin, you dirty rat, and you let me sit here reading a book when I could've watched every inch of the way!"

We landed with no trouble at all, but the Director of International Traffic called Bill up to his office. "I'm supposed to dress you down for flying into Berlin."

Bill grinned at Dick Pears — an old friend. "Why?" he asked.

Pears said, "Because you didn't observe correct procedure!"

"What is correct procedure?"

"That's just it! Nobody knows!" He laughed and said that the Four Powers Safety Council had just directed him to write up the correct procedure for a private pilot to fly into Berlin, so Bill offered some good-natured suggestions.

We chatted and laughed for a while, and then went into town — into town? I write that like we drove into Pittsburgh! This was Berlin! What a great city — still scarred, bleeding and torn to pieces (four ways), but a beautiful, busy, well-lit, well-dressed city. West Berlin, that is.

We finally had lunch, and during lunch Bill dropped his next salvo! "We're this far, what do you say we try for Moscow?"

I gulped. "Do you think they'll let us?" "We'll ask." (I kept putting food in my mouth and forgetting to swallow it.) Jim's eyes got glassy and Bill laughed.

"Not you, Jim, you can go home."

"Whew!" said Jim (I'm outta here!).

It took a special kind of nut to want to fly a twin Cessna into Moscow in 1956. I think Bill was the only "nut" around at the time. (What does that say for his wife, who went along for the ride and thought it was great?)

We had asked Dick Pears about problems going into East Berlin, the zone occupied by the Soviets. "No trouble, just get in a cab and go. You might get a driver who won't take you across the border (no Berlin Wall in 1956) but the embassy is only a block away from the border, so you could walk." When we told him what we were thinking of doing, he said he didn't think it was possible but — he grinned at Bill — "If anybody is crazy enough to try, you're the best candidate I know."

It was a year marked by Cold War tension, heightened by the Hungarian Rebellion. Feeling like characters in a TV series, we went to the Soviet Embassy in a cab but couldn't find anyone who spoke English. On our way out, an English girl told us to try the East German Consulate a block away. Inside the consulate (my heart pounding because it was very dark and gloomy and untidy) we were finally directed to the second floor.

We met a youngish man named Krevoshei who was likable and courteous. We found out later that all the boys in the press knew him. Bob Tucman, an Associated Press writer who would soon be transferred to Cyprus, told us that Krevoshei was very proud of his American haircut. Bill explained to Krevoshei that he would like to be the first private pilot to fly to Moscow, and asked, "Is it possible?"

Krevoshei said yes, but that it would take time, and asked about how long we could wait. When Bill said, "Oh, I can wait till tomorrow afternoon," Krevoshei laughed. He had a nice face when he laughed. He shrugged and said we could only try, telling us to "Come back tomorrow at 2."

We went back to West Berlin, to wait. The stark difference between East and West was unbelievable. The people in East Berlin were poorly dressed with little expression on their faces. We saw no lights, flags or gaiety, and no traffic. There was no evidence of a better world for the working masses.

We went directly to the hotel. While we were putting ourselves together, Tucman called us and said he was taking a movie star out to dinner, would we like to go?

Bill said, "Sure. Who is it?"

Tucman said, "Bob Cummings and his wife Mary."

Well, we nearly fell through the floor because they were very good friends. Cummings was a leading man in the movies and television. But he and his wife were the last people we expected to run into at the dinner table in Berlin.

Having discovered trouble with our brakes in the Cessna, we had called Krevoshei the next day to tell him to postpone our trip until June 26. As it happened, for the next several days, we stuck close to Bob and Mary, so we flew over to Stockholm to be with them for Sweden's annual Midsummer Festival. While we were there, the people who represented Lear, Inc. in Stockholm fixed our brakes before our planned "Invasion of Moscow."

Back in West Berlin, we had our passports stamped at the

American Embassy, giving us the OK to travel in Russia. Because the United States had diplomatic relations with Russia — confusing as they were — we could travel there. People at the consulate were interested, surprised, and amused that we'd gotten our Soviet visa so quickly — due solely to Bill's famous habit of "rushing in where angels fear to tiptoe." We jumped through all the hoops, and everything was finally in order. We were ready for the count-down!

In the days that followed, Bill had to shrug off many false and nasty criticisms. He was accused of making this trip without permission — just heedlessly taking off without the required visas. On the contrary — the Russian sector at Schoenefeld wrote up our visas to include not only ourselves, but our airplane, a Cessna 310 with the N numbers 77L. The State Department in West Berlin had stamped our passports appropriately, and because we both had carried the old wartime passport, forbidding travel into any Communist country, both passports were updated.

The night before our flight we checked in at a little hotel at the airport to facilitate our takeoff the next morning. When I looked at our key and saw "411," I had to smile at the incredible coincidence of how the numbers we considered lucky — 4, 7, 11, and 13 — followed us around.

The next morning, brushing my teeth in that bleak hotel room, I looked in the mirror and thought: "Here we go girl. This isn't L.A./ Palm Springs, or Grand Rapids/New York! This is a trip for posterity — for the children to write papers about at school — for the next National Business Aircraft Association convention — this is Berlin/ Moscow! And I'm taking this flight with this darling man of mine, a straightforward, fearless, up-front fella who loves to wade through bureaucracy and come out the other end whole!"

But we were totally unprepared for what happened.

The press was out en masse at West Berlin/Templehof when we took off, but not hostile at all. We had absolutely no indication of the blast about to occur. When we landed at East Berlin/Schoenefeld, we met the Russian navigator assigned to go with us. He spoke no English, which made communication very interesting, as they made mathematics their sign language! An interpreter sat in the cockpit helping Bill and Nicolai (wouldn't you know he'd have a name like that) coordinate their signals — it wouldn't do for them to tangle high over Moscow with Nicolai zigging in Russian and Bill zagging in English!

So, while I sat in the flight ps building waiting for Bill to yell, "Let's go!" I mentioned to the interpreter that it was Bill's birthday. Smiling, he started to sing the "Happy Birthday" song in heavily accented English. I, delighted, said, "You know it! Let's sing it to Bill." Then I shoved him out the door and to the parked Cessna, where we sang: "Happy burssday to you! Happy burssday to you!" I finished with, "Happy birthday, dear Billski, happy birthday to you!" Everyone laughed and shook hands. We climbed into the Cessna, buckled up, called for clearance from the tower, and we were off!

We flew the first leg to Vilna, capital of Lithuania. With a good tail wind, it took us 2-1/2 hours to fly the 460 nautical miles. But I was surprised to see how underdeveloped the countryside was. For example, there were houses that looked like huts, and the roads were muddy — where there WERE roads. The main cities were linked by highways, but everything else was extremely primitive. While what we saw was beautiful agricultural country, there was no evidence of any real planning in its cultivation; instead it looked very haphazard — as if a farmer had gotten a new plow or cultivator and gone nuts with it — as if everybody in town had taken a turn. I wondered how they kept the spirit of the people jacked up in this backward country, since they were in their sixth "Five Year Plan" since 1925. Somehow, the farmers were doing a terrific job. They also gave us a cheerful welcome, smiling broadly and waving their caps delightedly, when we cranked around to land at Vilna, June 26, 1956.

At Vilna, they invited Bill up into the control tower, and he was stunned by the antiquated radio communications equipment. After refueling, we tried to pay, but they said it was impossible. There was no gauge on the truck. Why should they have a gauge, they said, the trucks belonged to the state. The fuel belonged to the state. The airplanes belonged to the state. So who cared how much fuel went into what?

We flew the leg from Vilna to Moscow with my heart pounding. I had climbed into the back seat to make sure Bill and Nicolai did their jobs. Diving from one side of the back seat to the other so I didn't miss anything, I watched Bill and Nicolai "navigate" — smiling and pointing and shaking hands.

The entire press corps met us at the airport in Moscow. I was overwhelmed. But Bill was in his element! He was used to meeting the press head-on. Gad, there must've been 25 of them, many with cameras. We answered their questions. "Why did you fly to Moscow?"

Bill said, "Because I wanted to be the first private pilot to penetrate the Iron Curtain."

Simple? It was to Bill. We still had no suspicion of trouble. We were delighted to be in Moscow. And, yes (in answer to their questions), we were going to see the sights. We wanted to see L'Hermitage Gallery in Leningrad. Would we like to go to the opera and see *Aida*? YES!

Unfortunately, there was a little secret Bill hadn't shared with me. Bill had been asked by a friend who worked with the CIA to look into something for him. He'd asked for Bill's help in identifying a little railing along the outside of the fuselage of the Tupolev 104.

Hah, no problem for Bill! That sneak was on a mission! After we'd been there a couple of days, Bill asked our guide, Vladimiroff, if he could arrange for Bill to see the Tupolev 104. We both got to see it — and so did a Life photographer they weren't expecting. She pushed in and no one said "No." She took pictures of all their radar equipment, radio communications (antique), the entire interior — lace curtains, red brocade upholstery, everything! In the cockpit, Bill was asking questions of the engineers and getting answers. Outside on the ramp, he pointed to the little railing and asked, "What's that?" The engineers said it was an antenna. "Transmitting or receiving?" Bill asked. "Both," they said.

Then they had a small conference and came back to Bill and asked, "Why do you want to know?"

Bill answered: "I'm a specialist in that field and I'm interested in the design." (By this time, he was!) There were about nine people crowded in and around our Cessna, and it was a fascinating exchange of ideas. They knew of Bill's work on the autopilot. The conversation was totally open and extremely friendly. They answered Bill's questions in detail and respectfully. Then Bill asked if they'd like to go for a ride, which they certainly would. Bill said he'd like to make about a half-hour local trip around the airport carrying four passengers, but one of them had to be Vladimiroff, the only one who could speak English. Vladimiroff's first assignment was to find an English-speaking tower operator. Once everyone was on board and Bill was ready to go, he asked for clearance from the tower. The tower operator replied, "Two minutes please. Two minutes." About 30 seconds later, he came back on the wire: "OK, Lear. You're cleared to runway 6-2." In Bill's own words, this is how it went:

> The tower operator said, "All right, you're cleared to runway six-two for a local flight. Remain at three hundred meters altitude and watch for other traffic." So with no more than that, with no flight plan, we taxied up and took off and flew around for half an hour. My passengers were very surprised that the automatic pilot actually worked! They asked me if it was possible to make a turn and to climb or dive at the same time. I didn't realize then why this was a matter of any importance to them. So I made a turn, climbed and dove, and they made motions to me by giving me a 'thumbs up' signal to show that they thought this was really a wonderful capability.
>
> On this flight around Moscow, one of the things that impressed me was that at one time when I got to twelve hundred feet altitude, which was about three hundred feet above my prescribed altitude, I was immediately detected. The tower came on and said "Moscow tower to Lear. What is your present altitude?" I said, "Three hundred meters." They said, "Three hundred meters?" Then I looked at the altimeter and saw I was at twelve hundred feet which was about four hundred meters, so I went back down to three hundred meters right away. I suspect that they had a pretty good radar system and that they were able to determine my altitude without any trouble.

Bill landed, shook hands, said, "You're welcome," locked up the airplane and came back to town with Vladimiroff to meet me. We thought we had been invited to a cocktail party for U.S. Air Force General Nate Twining — representing the Air Force on a mission — and some American friends. But it wasn't a cocktail party at all. It was a hornet's nest. We arrived as Gen. Twining was giving his briefing.

The press was already simmering and unhappy because, not having been included in the junkets with Gen. Twining, they had been stuck in their hotel rooms with no story. They'd had to wait until the end of the day for his briefing and they weren't happy! A reporter for the Baltimore Sun was the most aggressive. He went after Twining with guns blazing: "What about this guy Lear who just flew in with all this classified equipment?"

Gen. Twining: I don't know anything about it.
Reporter (hostile): Well, don't you think it's your business to know about it?
Gen. Twining: (over his shoulder to his aide) "Find out what Bill's doing up here."

That request translated into headlines all over the country:

"TWINING ORDERS INVESTIGATION OF LEAR, INC."

We weren't prepared for the blast, and I know Nate Twining had no idea what he started. We were just walking down the corridor looking for the cocktail party! We had started to hear American voices when Twining said to his persistent interrogator, "There's Bill now. Why don't you ask him?"

The entire press corps stampeded down that corridor and pasted us against a wall, everybody firing questions.

"Why did you really fly to Moscow?"

"What about the classified equipment in your airplane?"

"Are you selling anything while you're here?"

"We heard you took 'em up for a flight. Why?"

"Who's paying for the fuel?"

Et cetera. Et cetera. Et cetera.

I was getting p.o.'d at the tone of the inquisition, but Bill was patiently fielding their questions. (It was usually the other way around!)

Bill: My wife and I got in our Cessna and flew to Moscow because we wanted to be the first representatives of general aviation to penetrate the Iron Curtain. I thought it was time! There is No, repeat No, classified equipment in my airplane. Everything in it you can buy off the shelf from any distributor in the United States. I'm not selling anything, gentlemen. Don't you people know that nothing on the airplane is on the NATO embargo list?

Yes, I took interested spectators — three of 'em and an interpreter — for a half-hour local flight over Moscow. They had heard about my autopilot and were genuinely impressed with its performance. I couldn't sell it to them but I was proud to show it to them. I tried to pay for the fuel in Vilna and discovered that they don't have any meters on their trucks. They wouldn't let me pay for it!

We felt comfortable with the interview. General Twining asked us to have dinner with him and Mrs. Twining, but we told him we had been invited to the opera. It was all very cordial. But in view of what happened next, we should have forgotten the opera and had dinner with the general! Bill had a very colorful way of saying, "C'est la f——g vie!"

We didn't know we were an "incident" until the next night, our last night in Moscow (we arrived late Tuesday afternoon and left Friday about noon). We had left our hotel room with Alex Vladimiroff, the man from the Board of Trade who took care of things for us, when I realized I had forgotten my purse. I sent them down in the elevator and went back to the room. As I picked up my purse, the phone rang. It was Bill Jr., calling from our office in Geneva. I sat on the bed stunned and sick at heart while he read me some of the teletypes from our plant in Santa Monica, the sort of stuff which had hit the newspapers worldwide:

> **Some employees have threatened to quit because they didn't want to work for a firm selling equipment to the Communists.**

> **General Twining has snubbed us.**

> **We moved to Geneva so that it would be easier to do business with the Communists!**

I told Bill Jr. briefly what had actually happened and that his dad would contact him the next day when we reached Berlin. I went down to the dining room in a state of shock! Up until this minute, everything had been intensely interesting and exciting. I sat down with Bill and Vladimiroff and said, "We're in trouble." Vladimiroff's expression changed from amusement at the story Bill had told him to one of genuine concern. While I was telling them what Bill Jr. had said, Clay Blair (writer for *Time* magazine) and Jim Haggerty (aviation editor for *Collier's*) walked in.

We invited Clay and Jim to have dinner with us, and when we got to the restaurant, an amusing thing happened. When we asked the waitress if we could be seated at a larger table, she promptly picked up our table set for four and moved it across the dining room! She then got another woman to help her lift a table set for six over to where we were sitting! Then Clay and Jim told us what had been happening in the press camp.

According to them, all the aviation writers understood the situation, but the guy who started the trouble, kept it stirred up and actually printed out-and-out lies was the Baltimore *Sun* reporter. He filed the inaccurate story that our Cessna was full of classified equipment; that Lear, Inc. was doing business with the Communists; that we had moved to Geneva to facilitate these sinister transactions. It was one horror story after another. I remembered the McCarthy trials — the witch hunts and Congressional hearings for prominent Americans who were allegedly Communist — and felt enormous sympathy for those unfortunate victims of that mindless persecution.

Later, when we visited the American Consulate, they asked Bill why he came to Moscow. Bill said, "For publicity." They grinned and said, "You got it!" We were the first to penetrate the Iron Curtain with a private airplane all right, and in light of all the wretched publicity, probably the last. The fellow in the State Department at the consulate was a real dumbbell. Among other inane remarks, he asked Bill, "How do you know they aren't out there at the airport right now copying your equipment?" (It was an all-time low for me to hear such a stupid remark in such a high place!) Our airplane was parked and locked under guard, right underneath the wing of General Twining's DC6. Bill didn't say, "You dumb bastard!" like I thought he might (God help us!); instead, he said, "Well if they take it apart, I hope they get it back together right because we're leaving tomorrow!" When we were ready to leave, the State Department man opened the door just a crack to let us out for fear someone would take his picture with these two American lunatics who'd just paid him a courtesy call.

On the plus side of the trip, we saw "Aida," and I've never seen such a production in my life. I'm sure the scenery too ranked with the greatest in the world. The beautiful opera house had six golden tiers of balconies, every one of them jammed! People were hanging out of that sixth balcony. The whole trip, on balance, was totally fascinating. And Bill wound up calling our Cessna the "Moscow Mule" — because it kicked up such a fuss! When we returned to Geneva we were again attacked by the press who refused to believe the innocence of our story.

Unfortunately, John, who was then attending Le Rosey, a very prestigious boarding school outside Geneva, was more adversely affected by what had happened in Moscow than our other children. Fellow students gave him a hard time because of the press reports that Bill was selling classified equipment to the Communists.

David was there at the door with his hugs to greet us. We could have been in Zurich for all he knew. Us being home was a whole lot more important to that little boy than where we'd been. Shanda wanted to hear all about the trip, and Tina stood in her crib and smiled her beautiful smile with her arms up to be held.

So even though we took a lot of flak because of that trip, I wouldn't change five minutes of it — and I'll never forget it.

□   □   □

In September 1956, our lease on Prevorzier expired and we moved into the Hotel Richemond while we engaged prominent California architect, Cliff May, to start building our home. At the hotel, we took up almost an entire floor for nearly two months. During that time, students sympathetic to the Hungarian Rebellion were demonstrating all over Europe, protesting Soviet aggression.

One evening, an anti-Soviet demonstration involving students from the University of Geneva erupted violently outside our hotel. Police immediately barricaded a two-block area around the Richemond, which was adjacent to the hotel where Soviet diplomats were holding their meeting.

Just before the demonstration, a bunch of our American friends in Geneva had come in for drinks and dinner. When they couldn't leave because of the angry crowd on the other side of the police barricade, they established a "beachhead" in the Gentilhomme (the bar at the Richemond) happily (if uneasily) caught in the middle of an uprising. It was a very exciting evening, but it shook us all up.

That incident, along with the closing of the Suez Canal by the Egyptians, plus gas and food rationing because of fears about an oil cut-off was making me uneasy about staying in Geneva any longer. And I was determined to leave after talking to a pal in London (Brigadier General Dick Lassiter, Strategic Air Command). I invited him to Geneva for a visit, but when he said, "I wish I could, Moya — but we're on 24-hour alert," my heart sank. I said, "OK, that's it, everybody home!"

We discussed the wisdom of leaving John at Le Rosey and decided (wrongly, as it turned out) to keep the family together and bring him home with us. I packed up everybody, including my mother, and TWA'd to Los Angeles. Bill followed soon after.

We were happy to be back home in Pacific Palisades, but we had to stay in our guest house until Grace Kelly left for Monaco to marry Prince Rainier! I was so impatient to get back into my own home. When Miss Kelly was finally ready to leave, we walked up the drive-way, through a crush of media with cameras, to say "Au revoir," and Bill told her if she ever needed transportation to call him! And I promised myself to work a piece of needlepoint to hang over our bed:

"BILL LEAR AND GRACE KELLY SLEPT HERE."

□   □   □

In 1959, Cliff May kept coming to me asking, "What kind of hard-ware do you want in the Geneva house? What kind of wallpaper? What floor covering?"

"I don't care," I'd tell him, "we're never going to live in that house. Just finish it. It's only an investment." That's what I thought.

That year, Shanda and I accompanied Bill to Tokyo and, when he returned to Santa Monica, we continued to Hong Kong, Bangkok, New Delhi and on around the world. Bill had asked us to stop in Geneva and see if there really was a house there. If so, he'd pay the bills. He also said he couldn't wait to see us at the Paris Air Show.

When Shanda and I arrived in Geneva from Cairo, we took a taxi out to the house: Le Ranch, a fabulous home with sprinklers watering the lawn, huge fireplaces, and spacious rooms, including an enormous kitchen. I called Bill in Paris and said, "Listen, we've never built our own home. We've got to move into this house and at least turn on the showers and put fires in the fireplaces because it's too pretty not to live in it for a little while."

That move from Pacific Palisades to Geneva was a major one, and the whole family was involved, including my sister's two little boys who were about three and four-years-old. I had gone through the en-tire house with red, green and blue strips of tape, designating what was going where. Blue to Geneva, red to Bekins and green to Palm Desert. It had taken me all day to figure where each piece of furniture would go, mark it with the appropriate tape and record an inventory. At the end of the day, when I was sitting with my feet up sipping a glass of iced tea, those little boys came to me with both hands full of the pieces of colored tape which they'd methodically (and innocently of course) peeled off every piece of furniture! I thought I'd kill myself — or them!

We "airmailed" our children to Geneva. David, ten, and Tina, four, went to the country school in Onex, but Shanda, fifteen, went to a private boarding school. After a few weeks, we got a big kick out of visiting Tina's first grade. In a delightful conversation, the teacher told us, "We all got along fine around here until Tina learned to speak French and tried to organize the first grade." John, sixteen, remained in the house in Pacific Palisades, near Mother, to finish school at Santa Monica High before joining us in Geneva.

At this time Mother made a traumatic decision — she would divorce Daddy after 48 years of marriage. So upset, I called her from Geneva, and she said, "Oh, honey, I want peace in my old age." Daddy was devastated. Everything that had been stable in his life suddenly ended and he never really recovered. His heartbreak is apparent in these lines from a letter he wrote to Mother:

> **It was a tragedy that I was too busy and self-indulgent to realize and appreciate or even comprehend the strength, loyalty and great unselfish love I had in you. I'm deeply and profoundly sorry for all the heartaches I've caused you, sweetheart, because I was SO wrong. SO "selfishly" wrong. So, a warm embrace to you sweetheart, pray for me. I love talking to you.**

For my parents to divorce was so painful, such a heartbreak that it was incredibly difficult for me to turn around the next day and plan a special party for the Golf Club. So, when Germaine asked, "Would you like to have the 'Court Chasse'?"

I said, "Sure, let's have it." I thought "Court Chasse" was a kind of wine. (No holding back on this one!)

What sounded like "Court Chasse" to me, however, turned out to be The Corps de Chasse, a fabulous team of men and women on horseback, who dressed in black riding pants, stunning red coats, spic-

and-span boots and helmets, and carried brass horns to sound the stages of the hunt. They honored La Maitresse de la Maison (me!) by taking off their hats and playing the salute. For the guests, Bill, and myself, they performed their traditional ritual near a stone wall bordered by masses of red geraniums. What a picture the scene made for my bouquet of memories.

One thing which was not picture-perfect about daily life at Le Ranch, and which drove Bill out of his mind, was the furnace. All the labels on it were in French, and it was located in a crowded basement cubicle, I mean I'm talking disaster.

One evening, we were supposed to meet a friend of Bill's, Mr. Todd Hardeen, at the Gentilhomme for early cocktails and dinner. Because Bill was struggling with the furnace, he sent me on ahead with instructions: "Buy him a drink and I'll get there when I get there!"

I found Mr. Hardeen at the bar and we started to make polite conversation. He asked me about my background, and I told him I grew up in the theater. And he said, "Oh really! My father was in 'Hellzapoppin.'"

I looked at him, stupefied. "That's my line!" I laughed. "Who was your father?" "Hardeen, the magician. He did the magic act in 'Hellzapoppin.'" (Hardeen was the brother of Houdini.)

Well, we were off. After that opener, it didn't matter to me when Bill got there. I never got a chance like that. We talked show business — and maybe Bill joined us later, I forget!

Meanwhile, Bill was down in the small basement, trying to fix the furnace with the help of a Swiss repairman, who was clearly sorry that he had been the one who had to deal with this angry American. The air was blue with profanity, and Bill had asked our six year-old Tina to translate. She sat on the basement steps patiently trying to interpret what her Dad was raging about (while expertly editing the explosive profanity out of the dialogue!). Bill did finally fix "the fucking furnace"(his words) — thanks to Tina and and an obliging Swiss workman who had a sense of humor. In the end, Tina looked at Bill and said, sympathetically, "You don't have enough juice in your throat Daddy!" He grinned ruefully, giving her a hug.

□   □   □

From the beginning, John has been a superb pilot. Like his father, he was happiest in the cockpit of an airplane. So, right after he received his license for aerobatics flying, he took off from the Geneva airport in a rented airplane to stretch his wings. Although he knew there is a proper time and place for aerobatics, he decided to buzz his former school — Le Rosey — just about the time the kids were coming out for lunch. He did two low passes over the school, all the while watching over his shoulder as the kids poured out, looking up at his airplane. On the third pass he ran out of altitude and went into the ground — feet first, his face crashing against the control panel.

The phone rang at Le Ranch and I ran to catch it. It was Mlle. Schaub of Le Rosey in tears, trying to control her voice as she told us the horrifying news — and urging us to hurry. I said we'd be right there! We gasped the news to our guests, jumped in our car and burned up La Route Suisse on our way to the school in Rolle which was about 45 minutes from Geneva.

As we were nearing Rolle, we heard the sound of the ambulance coming towards us. The European siren has a sound totally different from ours in the United States. It isn't shrill and wailing like ours. It goes BAM-BOM BAM-BOM BAM-BOM and it struck terror in our hearts as we wildly wondered what had gone wrong. Bill, confident that John was a fine pilot (although Bill was very stingy with his praise), was sure John had lost an engine. We did a frantic, high-speed U-turn to follow the on-coming ambulance to Geneva, ready to do battle if the gendarmes tried to stop us.

When we got to the hospital, having practically climbed onto the back of the ambulance to get there, we couldn't see John. They'd already put him in Intensive Care. We were also frustrated because the doctors and nurses conversed with each other in French, and neither one of us was good enough to follow what they were saying. By the time we did see him, doctors had performed a tracheotomy so he could breathe, and his feet were bandaged, but not yet in casts.

Bill asked John if he could hear and John nodded. Because Bill was so convinced that John had lost an engine, it never occurred to him that John could have been doing a one-man air show over Le Rosey in a rented plane. When Bill asked John if he'd lost an engine, John shook his head. He was totally honest. The crash had been his fault. Then — instead of telling John that we loved him and not to worry about a thing — Bill, for some reason I have never been able to figure out, chose to take him to task saying, "What would ever persuade you to stunt an airplane that didn't belong to you?" he said. It wasn't a long speech. It didn't have to be. But this was the wrong place to make it.

Bitterness emerged from this incident like fallout from an atomic bomb. I don't think Bill had any idea how badly John was hurt, both physically and emotionally. And I don't think he ever understood how deeply sensitive John was, and how destructive the least bit of criticism could be, let alone his angry blast when it was still questionable whether John would live. John was painfully aware he had made a mistake and he didn't need his father to spell it out for him over and over again.

I hurt for John. For once in my life, it was hard for me to rationalize Bill's behavior. The story in La Journal de Geneve about the crash didn't help either. The story was very critical and cruel about "these irresponsible Americans." I wrote to the editor of the paper:

June 26, 1961

Dear Mr. Payot:

Because I'm a very proud mother — and a distraught one — permit me to take issue with your correspondent who wrote the account of my son's accident last Saturday.

First of all, flying is his business — he is fully qualified to fly single- and twin-engine aircraft in any kind of weather. He has his Commercial Pilot's License which means that he is able — after very strenuous training and difficult examination — to fly an airline if he so chooses. He will recover from his accident and live to fly again — and I would be comforted to know that such a precise and capable flyer had my life in his hands.

His one fault was to be eighteen years old and want to 'salute' his friends at Rosey!

He might be called upon to defend his country someday. He might inadvertently be able to protect the very writer of that article. I don't say that he was right, I simply am outraged because I have watched him suffer and he is not able to speak or defend himself.

Right or wrong, I would like to be put on record to say that he is not an 'inexperienced student pilot.' He is an experienced, well-trained pilot who was involved in an accident — to his own despair.

When I read John the letter I had written, he said "I wish my mother would write a letter like that." I answered, "John, I wrote that letter! I'm your Mom, honey (my tears were choking me), don't you know me?" He looked away. I figured that John's head injuries were so severe that he was suffering mild amnesia.

Instead of being a blessing for John, being the son of Bill Lear was difficult for him from the time he was fifteen. The hostility and anger just grew instead of dissipating. He felt the pressure to live up to his father's reputation as a high achiever. If his father could see him now, he'd be very proud.

Chapter Sixteen

One late afternoon in the early '50s, Bill had been standing out on the ramp at the Van Nuys Airport, in California, where we had just landed our airplane. It was a gorgeous early evening, the sun was setting, silhouetting a DC3 and a Lockheed Lodestar parked next to each other. Bill stood there for a long time studying those two airplanes, wondering why the Lodestar wasn't a better performer.

At that time, it was possible to buy all kinds of stuff that had been manufactured during the war, but had been sent out across the country after the war labeled, "War Surplus." Airplanes were included in these commodities, so Bill zeroed in on the Lodestars.

Before he was through, he owned several. The first was used for test-flying the autopilot, but the next one he stripped down to airframe, and used it to "cut his teeth" on the study of aerodynamics. (Somewhere, someone might even have a Learstar with Bill's "teeth marks" on the leading edge of the wing!) But trying to improve the Lodestar's performance became more than a hobby for Bill, his work placed him on the cutting edge of the corporate aircraft industry.

For his own comfort and amusement, he designed one of the first elaborate interiors: couches, big comfortable chairs, tables, a galley and — this blew us away in the '50s — a television set! But I'd get so irritated because we'd be watching. a baseball game — the bases would be loaded in the bottom of the ninth, the score tied 3-3, and Willie Mays would come up to bat — and we'd lose the damn signal. Bill, however, turned a deaf ear to my fussing about reception for my baseball game. "We have much more serious problems, honey —

shut up!" I shut up.

Unfortunetely, no amount of problem-solving could help Bill with Kelly Johnson — the finest designer of aircraft our industry has ever known. Kelly, who had designed the Lodestar for Lockheed Aircraft, heard that Bill was monkeying around with his airplane, and underlined his scorn by issuing a White Paper that spelled out the performance of the Lodestar, claiming nobody could improve on it. Bill not only showed that he could improve on the performance, but compounded the insult to Kelly by naming his airplane the Learstar!

A feud ensued. I heard the whole thing, chapter and verse, from my side of the bed. (Oh Kelly, wherever you are, remember Bill told this to me!) It went on for quite a while. And finally, inevitably, at an Air Force cocktail party, I found myself in the ladies room putting lipstick on in front of the mirror. Standing next to me was a woman I sort of recognized but couldn't place. (Aviation? Theater? P.T.A.?) I said, "You look very familiar to me."

And she said, "You look familiar to me, too."

So I said, "Well, does Mrs. Bill Lear mean anything to you?"

"Hell, yes!" she exclaimed. "I'm Mrs. Kelly Johnson!"

We went back to the party and got our husbands together, forging a friendship of mutual respect and admiration. Months later, Kelly called and said, "Bill, we need you to do something for us and we can't tell you what it's for. It could be a kite or a covered wagon! We can't even give you a contract — this is a handshake deal, OK?" Bill, enormously proud, said, "Sure, Kelly. It's a pleasure doing business with you!" That "something" was to design the guidance equipment for our country's U2 spy plane. It was a great coup for Lear, Inc. and put us in the Big Time.

Bill had proven something with the Learstar — there was a market out there for corporate aircraft, but the planes needed to be faster. The Learstar could only fly 300 miles per hour and it had a range of 3,800 miles. With its reciprocating engines, the Learstar could serve a purpose, but not for getting you to your destination as fast as possible.

Around the time Bill started doing business with Kelly, we saw a newspaper headline which had stunning historical importance:

"707 Streaks Across the Nation in 5 Hours!"

This headline was the first indication to the country that the jet airliner had been born. Bill put down his paper and said, "Wow! General Aviation is going to need a little private jet to keep up with that speed," and he ticked off his competition on his fingers: "Cessna can't do it, Beechcraft can't get out of their own way..." (Don't forget, modesty was not one of his virtues.) So, with great excitement, he called his Lear, Inc. board together and presented his views.

His idea, however, was met with less than enthusiasm by the board. Finally, after heated discussions, it was agreed that the executive committee should decide. A couple of days later, members of the committee came to Bill's office and said, "Listen Bill, we've decided you can't do this. First of all, Lear, Inc. is going like gangbusters. You're paying off investors, we're able to declare dividends and the company has never been in such good shape. Second, you don't know anything about the airframe business and they'll kill you out there." Bill was listening, his eyes changing from blue to steel gray. "So," our poor chairman of the executive committee continued, "We've decided that it would be unwise to commit Lear, Inc. to this insanity!"

Bill said calmly, "Gentlemen, you're mixed up. You've got 'ownership' and 'management' confused. You're fired!" After firing his entire board he sold the company to Siegler, an American manufacturer of electronic equipment, and the company was renamed Lear Siegler.

Subsequently, The Swiss American Aviation Company (SAAC) and our Learjet was born. This all happened in 1961, while I was learning to say "vacuum cleaner" in French!

Sometime during the first months, when Bill established SAAC at Altenrhein in Switzerland and the preliminary engineering was being developed, Bill Jr. told his dad about the P-16, a Swiss jet fighter. Bill Jr. had flown it. He said that even though the Swiss had mothballed it because they'd had fatal accidents trying to fly it, it was an excellent airplane. The wing of the Learjet was modeled after the P-16, with its eight spars, and that model continues to this day including the present Model 60. However, the similarity between the P-16 and the Learjet ended with that eight-spar wing.

Unfortunately, Bill hit a brick wall in Switzerland when he tried to accomplish things commensurate with his sense of urgency. Communication, for example, was a big problem, and not just one-on-one conversations with his engineers. International phone calls were a nightmare too. He got so frustrated! Even after we learned to spell in French, when Bill realized that he had to make an appointment with the overseas telephone operator in order to call Santa Monica, it was the beginning of the end! And then there were the numerous holidays. Gee, it seemed every time he turned around, there was another holiday for the workmen. Now, for a fella who has a problem when all his boys go home for the weekend (or try to!), he was really becoming unhappy with the Swiss system of one holiday after another on top of long weekends on top of centimeters on top of parley-vooing Francais! Anyway, as time ate itself up, we realized that Switzerland would not be the location of production for the Learjet.

Those early days in Geneva were a challenge for the children and me too. I was trying to run the household, keep help and market — all in French, which was never easy. And the children, David, for example, had to learn his times-tables in French. (Imagine, "six fois neuf egale cinquante-quatre" (6 x 9 = 54). Tina, however, learned her alphabet and how to read and write in French by the time she was in the first grade.

While we were living our busy lives, an intense interest, as well as a competitive one, was building in the United States over this exciting new aircraft that didn't even have a name yet. Finally, at the Reading Air Show in 1962, Bill announced that SAAC would move from Geneva to Wichita. The announcement shook up a lot of people, but with one stroke of his corporate wand, he sure tumbled my gyros!

I had known a move was in the wind, but I really wasn't ready to give up our wonderful home and way of life in Geneva. There were so many things, even little things I would miss like, afternoon tea at four o'clock with a pot of chocolate on the tray for the children. The children's lives would be changed a lot too. Because there was no television, they played outside until bedtime. They did their "devoirs" (homework), both Tina and David practiced the piano with Germaine standing over them counting, "Un deux trois quatre. Un deux trois quatre." I also loved being able to fly over to Paris for dinner, or to Majorca for the weekend, or to Rome, or to Athens. "Let's go skiing this weekend in Zermatt." (You should've seen Bill on skis — he couldn't control anything! He grumbled — on his back for the eleventh time — "I could enjoy this if I could put a goddamned autopilot on these fucking things"!) And then there was the market in Geneva, under the chestnut trees, where I'd found fresh vegetables from the little farms in the country, breathtakingly beautiful flowers, all kinds of mushrooms, fresh fish, and an incredible choice of 30 different kinds of cheese! "Please!" I pleaded, can't we commute from Geneva to Wichita?" "No! Get packed."

Well, the way I found out that I would be moving back to the States wasn't exactly like that. I was on a trip — driving to Athens with Daddy and the girl he had just married, Eileen O'Dare. Daddy had found a level of comfort with Eileen, who had great talent and a lovely sense of humor. She had been a fine dancer and a headliner at Radio City Music Hall before she joined Olsen and Johnson. They were married in Geneva with cartoonist Hank Ketcham ("Dennis the Menace") as best man. I was (with an aching heart for my mother) the matron of honor. As we dressed for the ceremony and I struggled with the hook at the back of Eileen's dress, I realized that I was a rare daughter of the groom, as I performed the duties of mother of the bride!

The next day we took off in our station wagon from Geneva — Daddy, Eileen and I, as well as Shanda and one of her girlfriends. What a cozy little honeymoon. The object was to drive to Athens and from there to our vacation home, which I had just furnished, on the Aegean Sea across from the island of Spetsai. Billionaire Greek shipping magnate Niarchos' island was Spetsai-Pula, a little satellite off the shore of Spetsai.

Everything went along fine until we got to Dubrovnik, Yugoslavia. We were in the dining room cooling off, exhausted from the long drive down from Trieste, Italy, when the concierge came running across the lobby into the dining room and said, out of breath, "Madame Lear! Madame Lear! There's a call for you from the United States!" It was a level of excitement equal to announcing that a UFO had just landed in the parking lot! I hurried across the lobby and picked up the receiver.

MOYA: Hello?
BILL: Hi, baby! Are you all right? How's the trip?
MOYA: I'm fine. The trip's spectacular and I'm so happy to hear your voice!
BILL: Listen, Mom. I've got something very important to tell you — can you hear me OK?
MOYA: Yeah — just go slow.
BILL: Blahblahblah. (I couldn't understand.)
MOYA: Didn't get it, honey — say again. (pressing the receiver closer to my ear)

BILL: (shouting) I SAID I JUST BOUGHT YOU THE MOST
         BEAUTIFUL HOME YOU EVER SAW IN YOUR LIFE IN
         WICHITA, KANSAS ... FURNISHED!

BLACKOUT

MOYA: (trying to keep the dismay out of my voice) Uh — won-
         derful, honey. Now what?
BILL: Well, here's what I want you to do — can you hear me?
MOYA: Yeah. Loud 'n' clear (my head spinning with the implica-
         tion of all he was saying).
BILL: Go back to Geneva, pack what you need, fly to New
         York, pick up your car (I forgot why it was in New York)
         and drive immediately to Wichita. We're all waiting for
         you!
MOYA: Uh — (stuff still swirling in my head)
BILL: And honey, be careful.
MOYA: Right!

Click. Either he hung up, or we were disconnected — whatever —
my whole life changed as I walked slowly back across the lobby to our
table. There was an immediate cacophony of, "What? What happened? What'd he say? Say something!"

I told them. We continued the trip. I knew I might not get another
chance in the foreseeable future, so we put the Oldsmobile on the
boat, sailed down to Athens and drove to our home which wasn't very
far from the ancient Greek Theater at Epidaurus.

We spent a few magical days. When we wanted to go out to dinner, we would light a lantern and put it out on the terrace so that the
fellow who operated the "cahique" (that's Greek for water taxi) would
see it and stop by on his next trip to take us over to Spezia. We'd climb
off the boat and into a horse-drawn carriage. Nothing's changed for
hundreds of years on that little island except maybe the music. We
clip-clopped out of the village along the coast to a little restaurant on
the edge of the sea called (are you ready?):

BLUEBERRY HILL

Can you believe the name? When we drove back to Athens,

Shanda, her friend and I boarded another boat, with the Oldsmobile safe in the hold. As the boat moved slowly away from the dock, I saw my wonderful white-haired Daddy standing alongside Eileen, and I yelled a running family joke:

MOYA: HOW MANY MEN DO THE ENEMY HAVE?
DADDY / EILEEN: TEN THOUSAND!
MOYA: HOW MANY MEN DO WE HAVE?!
DADDY / EILEEN: TWO OLD MEN AND A BUGLER!
MOYA: (leaning over the railing, yelling at the top of my voice)
         SOUND THE CHARGE!

We got off the boat at Bari, in Italy, and drove to Rome. During our time in Europe I had gotten pretty good at driving, reading maps and finding good places to eat. The three of us had spent a lot of time in Rome, so it wasn't a total sacrilege that we had to get up early the next morning and drive straight through to Geneva.

We pulled into our driveway at Le Ranch in Onex early the next morning and staggered out of the car. I slept a couple of hours, packed, and took the next flight out for New York, leaving the girls home. Germaine saw me off and we both had heavy hearts knowing that nothing would ever be the same again.

I thought I'd sleep on the plane. Ha! I never closed my eyes as I wondered about Wichita and about "The most beautiful home I ever saw in my life." "Furnished." I wondered how the children would handle MOVING AGAIN! Omigod, the packing!

A voice on the intercom interrupted my thoughts: **"Ladies and gentlemen, we are starting our descent into New York. Put your seats in their upright position."** (Just when we were getting comfortable!)

I mused, "One good thing: I can zip through customs. Don't have anything to declare. They can't lose my baggage 'cause I didn't check anything." I carried only a garment bag and a duffel. I rummaged around in my purse and found the telephone number of the folks who had my car. I'd just apologize for not socializing and crawl in bed, then leave at four in the morning. The only ones awake would be the milkmen and folks getting home late from a party. New York City would be yawning and I'd be scooting through Manhattan at dawn. Wichita, here I come in my trusty Oldsmobile. I drove straight to Wichita, stopping only to sleep between ten p.m. and four a.m. It's hard to believe it's been nearly 30 years since I made that trip!

Just as there was a world of difference between the cities of Geneva and Wichita, there was also one between our American-style ranch house in Geneva and our Wichita home at Two West Parkway — a lovely two-story home, on a half-dozen rolling acres, where we sat on the back terrace in the evenings watching fireflies.

Once we got the family and the household together in Wichita, it was fun getting settled in an American city again. John had just turned twenty, Shanda was eighteen, David was fourteen and Tina would soon be eight. Shanda was in high school and we put David and Tina in Country Day School, which became Wichita Collegiate. I found the way to the market, how to get to the plant, and we were in business. That first year was a blockbuster— we laughed, there was also heartbreak, stress, jubilation, and despair! I wonder how I survived.

Bill moved the Learjet project to Wichita because it had a built-in economy geared to aviation. He hired the engineers and started the program while negotiating with the city to build the hangar.

Almost to a man, there were naysayers in the aviation industry in Wichita. At Beechcraft, Cessna, and Boeing, they said, "What does Bill Lear know about building airplanes? And if he did build it, it wouldn't fly. And if he got it to fly, he'd never get it certificated. And if he got it certificated, he couldn't sell it because nobody would want to buy it." They didn't think he knew what he was doing, and they felt sorry for me too.

Bill knew better, because he watched the development of the Learjet from its inception in Geneva when he laid out the plans on the floor of our living room. "Here's where the pilot and co-pilot will sit," he told me, "and we're gonna put a seat here..." His engineers believed in the project — "Damn it, Bill, this is what we need!" From the beginning, the concept of the Learjet was exciting for everyone who worked on it. In any case, it didn't matter to Bill if they bet against him; he'd been going against naysayers throughout his career.

Once completed, the Learjet would sell for around a half-million dollars. It would have eight seats and a picture window for each seat.

Wichita had raised more than $1 million in revenue bonds for a Lear Aero Spaceway on a 64-acre cornfield, and Bill hired 400 workers, who were welded into a tightly-knit team. Bill, however, had to be in the middle of things all the time, and haunted the hangar every day with our little dog, Jet, scrutinizing drawing boards, his hands on every facet of the operation. He'd browbeat the engineers, even call some of them "idiots!" He worked seven days a week. After all, it was his airplane. Sometimes he'd even order design changes on the spot.

Bill also wanted the plane to weigh less than 12,500 pounds — calculating that it would fly one mile farther for every three pounds trimmed, and also because the FAA certification process was faster and simpler for a plane in that weight category. When Bill jumped on an employee who was installing a piece of equipment that "only weighed three pounds," Bill said, "Goddammit, that's too heavy. I'd sell my own grandmother to save a pound." After that outburst, employees started calling pounds "grandmothers." It all paid off. When it was finished, the Learjet could fly 560 miles per hour, and it sold for $640,000 — about half the price of its competitors.

I had a happy husband with a challenge. He was so excited, and the whole atmosphere in our house was alive. Even the children were a part of it. The general community rallied behind us. I'd stop to get gas and the guy who pumped it for me would lean in the window and say, "Hi, Mrs. Lear. We're so thrilled!" I'd go to the department store, and the girls would come from behind the counter and shake my hand: "We're so glad that you moved to Wichita." It was wonderful the way that whole town was behind us.

I bonded with the pilots, the engineers, and the other employees. I supported Bill in everything he was doing throughout the process, and I tried to keep peace in the house and food on the table, not to mention something in the refrigerator if he got home too late. The closer we got to the first flight, the more our adrenaline rushed. Everybody waited for the "baby" to be born.

John joined Learjet at the beginning and among other duties, he was editor of *Charge!*, our in-house publication. By this time, he was married and his first baby daughter — Moya II — was born (September 8, 1963) one month before the first flight of the Learjet She was a beautiful, blond, blue-eyed baby girl — the first of my 12 grandchildren. John roared out to the plant to pass out cigars, and he got arrested for speeding!

In honor of the baby's birth, a friend wrote the following lines which appeared in *Charge!*:

> **Another Lear is now in town**
> **Another Lear to win renown**
> **She's extra happy, warm and wet,**
> **'Cause she got here before the jet.**

The story of the final months before the delivery of the first Learjet, however, was recorded by John and given to his father for Christmas 1964, which surprised and pleased his dad so much. John had written the Learjet story in pen and ink in his own beautiful handwriting and illustrated it with stunning photographs of the first Learjet 23. He dedicated it with these lines:

> **I have assembled these memories for my Dad, so that in case he missed the little delicacies that make a venture so exciting (while worrying about all of the things he worries about), they will not have been lost to him forever.**
>
> **John Lear**

As Bill and I read the dedication and the story that followed, we were so deeply touched that we had to wipe our tears away, especially Bill, because he didn't expect such a magnificent gift from John. John's narrative, based on his journal entries, traced the steps leading to first flight from the first engine start, to the "bugle call" of the first edition — June 7, 1963 — of *Charge!*, to the "rumblings of unionization" that John ultimately discovered never amounted to anything.

John's journal recorded this entry for August 1, 1963:

> **The aft and forward sections of the fuselage were mated today, and it was interesting to note that almost everybody was not as happy with the fact that they were mated, as they were about how happy it would make the old man. He was out of town, expected back the next day.**
>
> **Another note—the plane looked much larger than everybody had imagined.**

Aug. 6, 1963:

> **With the mating of the wings and fuselage Monday, fewer than 7 days have elapsed during the joining of the three major portions of the jet.**
>
> **As soon as Charge! Volume 7, number 14 hit the stands, the skeptical industry jumped.**
>
> **Pete Bulban, Dallas editor of Aviation Week, called me and**

said, (in just as unexcited tone of voice as this excited editor could muster) 'Are you guys really. . . I mean is this what's. . . YOU'RE ALMOST THERE!'

"But, Pete," I said, "that picture is almost a week old, you ought to see it now!" Well, he did, and so did the industry, through the critical eyes of Aviation Week. In their following issue they printed three photos with an accompanying story.

Then, about a month later — as we approached countdown time — September 3, 1963, John made this memorable entry:

> It seems as though all the exciting things happened at night— like the mating of the tail to the fuselage! We really began to see an airplane. The crane slowly lifted the tail from the mating dolly that had held it for several days, and placed it on the aft of the airplane.

During the above period, the tension and excitement at home, as well as at the plant was almost indescribable. I'd hit the floor running every morning making sure there was food on the table, gas in the cars, the bar stocked, the coffee pot hot, out-of-town guests provided for, children picked up at school — a list as long as your arm.

When we got to the plant the morning after the tail and fuselage had been mated and saw our Learjet in all her glory for the first time, everyone wept to see Number One Learjet 23. She was so beautiful, none of us could believe our eyes! John's entry for September, 26, 1963:

> The excitement of the first flight had been building, of course, ever since the beginning of the program, but tonight, the flight test personnel, a few employees, and I witnessed the Learjet take its first breath. Bathed in the moonlight and silhouetted against the bright hangar lights, this silver tiger strained its anchoring chains as its turbines turned for the first time. The run was brief but triggered an excitement impervious to the stark biting cold of that Wichita night.
>
> The day of first flight, we all got up and got going. The children weren't excused from school, but it was a rite of passage for the whole family, so we took them with us anyway. Bill had a

heavy cold, and was very upset because the board of directors weren't going to let HIM fly the first flight by himself. They said, "Bill, we can't afford to lose you AND the airplane." But from then on, Bill flew every flight himself.

John recalls the day of the first programmed flight on October, 7, 1963:

> It was late afternoon on October 7, 1963, when all of the employees, half the city of Wichita, family and friends lined the runway to witness the first flight of the Learjet. It had been a highly-charged day from early morning; no one had slept and everyone's heart was pounding. Small problems had surfaced that had made the flight that day questionable, yet it HAD to fly. YES! We were going to fly! There was full press coverage, national in scope, and the world of aviation waited — many skeptics present and accounted for.

By early afternoon, there had been still one minor adjustment before the first programmed flight. John's diary records:

> The last straw came about two o'clock when engineer Bob Carter announced that before we could fly, the oxygen system would have to be purged and that it would take about two hours. Roughly ten seconds after our Great White Father heard this, things were rapidly being buttoned up, including Bob. A little after three, the jet was fired up, and taxied to runway 14. After a brief check at the end of the runway, a low-speed run to the other end was made. Turning around it headed back at a higher speed and lifted its nose for a second. Back on the Learjet ramp, it was refueled.

One of the incidents I witnessed and have retold with pleasure for years was how Bill talked our wonderful test pilot, Hank Beaird into test-flying the Learjet. Bill had brought Hank aboard in Geneva. He was a handsome, always-smiling, lanky pilot from Alabama. He joined us in Wichita some weeks prior to first flight so that we could get the benefit of Hank's engineering knowledge and he could familiarize himself with the airplane.

They were over in a corner of the hangar, hammering out an agreement on how much it was going to cost Bill for Hank to test-fly the Learjet. The world waited outside, press, employees, everyone in Wichita who could get out to the field. Even Edgar Bergen was with us for that incredibly important day. Finally (I breathed a sigh of relief, scared to death Bill would get fussy about something at the last minute), they walked toward the Learjet.

John's diary records:

> ... at 5:40, with 50 minutes of sunlight left, the Learjet taxied out for the first flight. ... the entire length of the runway was lined with employees, visitors and Wichitans. Highway 54 running perpendicular to the runway was lined with cars, who, having been alerted to the first flight on their radios, had pulled to the side.

Hank Beaird shook hands with Bill and, as he got to the top step of the airplane, he turned around and yelled, "Hey Bill, where's my parachute?" Bill grinned at him. "You don't get a parachute goddammit — I want this airplane back here!"

I was standing with Bill out on the ramp in front of the plant. We were holding hands. He was gripping mine hard. When the Learjet went up, both of us were weeping. It took off like a rocket. I don't know WHICH was the biggest thrill, being in the jet taking off or standing on the ramp watching it take off. It was one of the most emotional moments of our life together.

Co-pilot Bob Hagen took off and Hank — with his winner's smile — landed it. The crowd heard Hank's transmission from the cockpit over the loudspeakers — his excited reporting that all was well and, not long after, his cheerful news that the Learjet had outrun and lost the chase plane!

From John's diary:

> Nobody was prepared for the tremendous acceleration which rocketed the jet airborne in 1700 feet, and into the annals of aviation history.

There was great jubilation when they landed and Bill got his airplane back, plus a glowing report from Hank. The news ricocheted around the world and the industry held its stunned head in its hands and yelled, "The sonuvabitch DID it!" All of us were so high with excitement — the kind of euphoria we all felt was a lot like being in love.

There were many spontaneous celebrations that night. Bill had one at a Chinese restaurant near the plant. Tex McCrary, an old friend from New York, commented at dinner, "Now of course, you people are too close to this thing. You don't really know what you have." June Shields, Bill's great, irreplaceable secretary, has since remembered: "Bill, bone-tired — with the anesthetic of euphoria beginning to wear off — whispered very quietly, 'I know. I know what we have.' " We knew we had an incredible airplane, but, even so, we couldn't predict how successful its future would be. We had no idea at the time that there would be so many Learjets sold.

We scheduled a first flight Party on October 12, 1963, at the Cotillion Ball Room in Wichita, where all of us celebrated with delirious abandon. Joyous and proud, we sang, for example, Learjet parodies on old songs that Daddy had written the year before in Geneva. Although he had not lived to see the Learjet fly, I felt he was there when it first began to take shape. At that time, he'd written several song parodies (I resurrected his song book), one to the tune of "Dark Town Strutters' Ball":

> *I'll be down to get you in a Learjet, honey;*
> *Be ready for takeoff at half past eight.*
> *Now, honey, don't be late.*
> *We're gassed up, waitin',*
> *Ready for the takeoff.*
> *Breakfast—New York, London—lunch,*
> *Paris—Pernods with my honey bunch.*
> *It'll be a glorious day*
> *In route to Wichita, hooray,*
> *Where we'll have that good ol'*
> *Learjet Jesters' Ball!*

June Shields, wrote the following song to the tune of "I've Been Workin' on the Railroad," for the first flight party:

> *I've been slavin' on the Learjet*
> *A 25-hour day*
> *Haven't finished all the work yet*
> *(My feet are made of clay).*

Can't you hear the siren wailing?
Rise up so early in the dawn.
Don't you hear the boss's shouting,
"C'mon, the day's half gone!"

William, must we rise?
We've got bleary, sleepy eyes,
William, all our logs aren't sawn.
William, give us a surprise,
Listen to our plaintive cries,
William, we are weak and wan!

Someone's making a pitch to William
Someone wants to get rich, I know;
But if someone does a hitch with William,
He'll have to earn his dough.
Fee, fie, fiddle-e-i-o, fee fie, fiddle-e-i-o-o-o-o,
Fee, fie, fiddle-e-i-o, the Kansans, now they know!

The Learjet spirit, forged in the hearts of our employees and their families, never dimmed. We all went home from that party tired, but happy. The wives were probably thinking: "Now, maybe my husband will have more time at home!" Wrong, girls. No small jet had ever been built for general aviation, let alone "certified," so the next immediate challenge was to obtain certification.

I had no concerns. Bill never voiced any to me either. He knew it was going to be all right. But no FAA examiner had ever flown an airplane like the Learjet. Hank Beaird had to check out the FAA pilot before he could check Hank out! It required everyone's best to get the job done, and it was accomplished in 10 months — a record in the history of certificating a new jet aircraft.

Some of the funnier things that happened during the course of that certification process were Bill's telephone conversations with the regional director of the FAA in Kansas City. During one of these, when Bill was screaming his frustration over the telephone, the director (probably pulling the receiver away from his ear) said, "Geesus Bill, if you'd just open the window, I could hear you!"

The development of the Learjet involved a series of blockbuster achievements. The clamshell door was one of those achievements;

however, Bill disagreed with his chief engineer about its design. Unlike his chief engineer, Bill was convinced that the top of the clamshell door should keep off the rain and the bottom provide the steps. The engineer said, "Dammit, Bill, you take all the fun out of it when you insist on making all the decisions." And Bill said, "Well, I'll tell you what: if you put up half the money, I'll let you make half the decisions!" Bill's quote became famous all over the industry!

"You'll never get it certificated." Wanna bet?! Receiving our certificate for the Learjet was the next milepost after our historic first flight, and yet another cause for jubilation considering we received it in ten months. The news exploded in the plant — I mean literally exploded! I was so proud of Bill for pushing it and accomplishing everything so well. He knew exactly what he had to do, and he did it. Every time he did something like that, it just added to the dimension and the stature of a great man.

After the formal ceremony in front of the plant in Wichita, when FAA head Najeeb Halaby presented Bill with the actual certificate and they shook hands, everyone took off for the Diamond Inn (a local establishment that doesn't exist anymore), toasted our Certificate and dove into the pool — including, of course, the Boss! He dove in with his undershorts on. When he got dressed, he wrung out the shorts and hung 'em over one of the chairs around the pool. Someone picked them up, stitched "FAA Certification" in felt letters on them, and the boys ran 'em up with the flag in front of the plant the next morning!

What they did was symbolic of their sheer, unadulterated admiration for their remarkable, unconventional, warm-hearted, pain-in-the-ass Boss. Such a thing could never happen today — first of all, because the climate is a lot different in business today, and, secondly, because there aren't any Bill Lears around anymore.

□   □   □

Clyde Martin was a tall, gangly pilot who worked for Boise Cascade. He was easy-going, accommodating, and everybody at Learjet liked him. He had talked his bosses into buying a Learstar in the late '50s, which they were still happy with. But now, in 1964 or '65, a new age had dawned, and everybody wanted a Learjet. So the board of directors of Boise Cascade sent Clyde to Wichita to take delivery on their new Learjet. When he got there, he found that deliveries were slow, so he thought he'd better get back to Boise. But when he arrived back in Boise, his board said, "Get back to Wichita and don't return without that airplane!"

So Clyde came back and established a beachhead in the Pilot's Lounge. He got interested in the flow of the airplanes on the production line, found Boise Cascade's model number and started tracking it. Clyde walked around a lot with a cup of coffee in his hand. He sat and read magazines. He talked to the mechanics and got to know a lot about what was going on. Everybody knew him except You-Know-Who.

Well, inevitably, Bill was walking through the plant one afternoon with Buzz Nanney, one of his executives, when he spotted Clyde and said:

BILL: See that guy over there?

BUZZ: Yeah.

BILL: I want you to fire his ass outta here! He doesn't do anything but drink coffee and read magazines!

BUZZ: (nonplussed) But Boss! That's Boise Cascade's pilot. He's waiting for his airplane!

BILL: Oh. Well, in that case you better send him to my office and I'll buy him a drink!

□   □   □

Learjet earned $52 million during its first year on the market. By June 1965, there were orders for more than 100 planes and projected sales of 120 per year for the next decade. What's more, the company was going to make a slightly larger model, plus the Lear Liner, a 28-passenger jet. In view of this, it is hard to believe that not long before that, we were hocking everything hockable, including our home in Geneva, in Wichita, both in Palm Springs, as well as our home in Greece, to meet the payroll and fund the project.

As the Learjet operation moved into the organization and sales phase, producing the airplane at a profit and all that went with that process, Bill, who was best at creating, became restless and had trouble sleeping. He was, for example, on the phone all the time. It sure became difficult to live with him.

The corporation kept growing. Learjet, Inc. became Learjet Industries in September 1966. Learjet Industries included the Learjet stereo division which turned out 1,000 eight-track players (another of Bill's inventions) a day and 700,000 tape cartridges a month. There was also Learjet Avionics manufacturing aeronautical devices. But, at the same time, everything was collapsing within. Actually, problems had been building for some time. Bill's aggressive management style so intimidated subordinates they were afraid to let him know what the true picture was in the business world. While there was a worldwide slump in aircraft sales and the sales department couldn't find buyers, Bill still wanted to produce ten Learjets a month.

In the fall of 1966, the company underwent a reorganization of its management, and a new president was named. It was thought that Bill's strong hands-on style of management would inhibit the new regime, so Bill was persuaded to leave town to give his Wichita executives more direct authority. We bought an ocean-front home in Laguna Beach, California, and moved there on October 31 (Halloween!).

I knew it was wrong from the beginning. I went to church on Christmas Day and cried through the entire service. The news about the dissension in Wichita was disturbing. The man who had been appointed to take Bill's place was trying to alienate Bill's board members against him — which also made me feel uneasy. Piled on top of that, the children weren't all that happy with the move, either.

Real estate people will tell you how the sound of the waves lapping the shore is very calming! Uh uh, folks, where we lived, a Great Invisible Force pulled the waves out to sea, where they united into one enormous wave which rolled in and crashed on top of our bedroom — about every seven seconds!

When I got home from church, I walked into the room where Bill was reading the Sunday paper and announced, "Honey, we're in the wrong place!" He looked up from his crossword puzzle and said, "I think so, too!"

We called the movers Monday morning, and they said, "You're kidding, right? They had just moved us in two months earlier.

After five wild, happy days of packing to go back to Wichita, we were going to spend our last day at Twentieth Century Fox Studios! Our fascinating tour would include a visit to the set of "Lost in Space" and a meeting with actor Rex Harrison.

For some reason we had arrived at the Beverly Hills Hilton very early, at 7:30 the morning of our tour. We would not be picked up by the studio limo until 9 a.m. Nothing was open, not even the coffee shop, and we were all starving. The bell captain took us to the Wilshire exit and pointed toward Beverly Hills. "It's not much of a walk and Armstrong Schroeder's is not very far," he told us. This information was not received with very much enthusiasm by the assembled Lear family.

We were in a line (one in back of the other): Bill, Moya, Shanda, David and Tina (John was ferrying Cessna O2's to Da Nang as a private pilot contracted by the military). The family was walking through the lobby, wondering what to do, when David said kiddingly, from his next-to-last place in line: "Why don't we register, get a room, and call room service." Bill muttered, "Brilliant!", and went to the desk and registered. We paraded to the elevator, went to the room and called room service! "I want pancakes!" "I want waffles!" "So do I!"

We had so much fun that day! And the next morning, we all climbed into the Learjet and flew back to Wichita. Bill, Hank Beaird, the children, three dogs and I were happy to be going home!

□   □   □

Our Learjet had taken its place in the history of aviation. The accomplishment was exciting, beautiful and, in the course of its development, Bill had yanked the whole general aviation industry into the Jet Age. To Bill's delight, and to the consternation and confusion of his competition, all non-military jets became known as "Learjets." It was a generic name like "Frigidaire" or "Xerox."

However, it soon became evident that the Learjet was too fast for some pilots. We started to lose airplanes and lives. Bill immediately began an in-depth review of the Learjet's engineering, and intensified the education of pilots flying Learjets. By the Fall of '65, with 65 Learjets in corporate service and more than 11,000 hours of flying time on the books, not a single accident had occurred involving the aircraft.

Fate intervened at approximately 6:32 p.m. on October 21, 1965, near Jackson, Michigan, when a Learjet crash took the lives of Lear production test pilots Glen David and Larry Bangiola. Following months of investigation, the FAA concluded that the accident was the result of electrical problems — a finding that Bill refused to accept.

Bill was obsessed with finding out "why." He never slept, and with his boys, took the Learjet apart piece by piece. He stayed at the plant, didn't come home for days. Two more fatal crashes occurred, and he wept, "What is happening?" But he still couldn't accept the FAA's quick-fix explanation of "electrical failure." He continued to search for the truth, and everyone worked with him until they had "rebuilt" the Learjet.

After a thorough analysis, the theory that finally made the most sense was a logical one. Since the beginning of aircraft production it has been customary to drill holes in the horizontal stabilizer — part of the tail of the airplane — to drain moisture. However, if the Learjet took off in the rain, with its rapid climb and acceleration, those holes sucked the water in, rather than draining it. Then, when the plane reached a certain altitude, the water froze, causing "flutter," which is extremely violent and can be fatal if the pilot doesn't respond instantly.

Bill grounded his Learjets until he answered in his own mind what was happening. His critics (and there were many) said he knew the FAA would ground the airplane, so he simply jumped the gun. But I lived with the man, and I watched him suffer and search and analyze until he found the solution. The Learjet was his life, and if one pilot's life was lost because of his airplane, he wanted to know why, and to fix the problem.

So he did! Putting his own life on the line, he and his co-pilot, Ron Puckett, took his Learjet up in a driving rain to find out what was going on, and it became clear that the problem was exactly as he and his engineers had determined. As he achieved altitude, the freezing rain caused violent flutter that resulted in shaking the instruments loose from the panel. In a subsequent test flight, they discovered damage to the wing of the airplane — confirming his theory. All engineering changes were made, and our Learjet emerged triumphant.

□ □ □

During his research, Bill called Donald Douglas and asked him about the drain holes in the DC-8, and Douglas reacted immediately, grounding his DC-8s until the problem was solved. By that time, however, there had been three fatal Learjet crashes. With this devastating problem, a limp market and other factors, Learjet sales began to drop off. We had borrowed against everything we owned — our home, our paintings, our stock, everything hockable. The bank did all it could to help us. Ken Johnson, the bank president, was a prince of a guy, a hero. As Bill was slowly, but surely headed for negative net worth, the inevitable happened: Learjet was for sale. Bill didn't want to hear about it.

Spring 1967 was an agonizing time. It seemed like the end of the world for us. We'd been married 25 years, and after doing everything we could to avoid losing Learjet, the time came when Gates Rubber made a serious offer to buy the company. But that offer didn't come before Bill had reached the end of his rope and wanted to kill himself. Behind at the bank, he couldn't see his way out. He was watching what little money came in disappear. And he worried himself sick. But he didn't want to sell his company because he felt he would lose his identity, moreover he couldn't see his next objective.

We'd gone to our home in Palm Desert to get some R & R and perspective. Bill went to bed and didn't want to get up. He was truly suicidal. I was genuinely frightened and called Justin Dart, the brilliant CEO of Dart Industries, long-time friend and owner of three Learjets. His son, Steve, hearing the urgency in my voice, went out on the golf course and told his dad that Bill needed him.

Justin came over immediately and talked good plain horse sense to Bill for a couple of hours. Bill listened to Justin. For all kinds of reasons, it was right for Bill to sell, but sometimes your heart and your head aren't in alignment. He'd experienced the same sort of terrible downer when he'd finished the autopilot. Bill couldn't see the greatness of his accomplishment. He felt empty, drained, and depressed.

We flew back to Wichita on a Sunday afternoon. The meeting of the principals of Gates Rubber and Learjet was to take place the next day. When we got back to the house, Bill dictated his list of demands to me, seated at the typewriter. I sat there and cried. I thought, he wants the world with a big, wide red ribbon around it, and he'll never get it.

The next morning, we drove to the plant, and as he held my hand, he said, "Well, we had fun, didn't we, honey?" I gulped back my tears as I squeezed his hand and said fervently, "We sure did!" He really didn't need comfort. Not then. He was strong, he knew what he wanted and, by God, if they were going to take his Learjet away from him, it was going to be on his terms!

The negotiations droned on all day while he stayed in his office. At one point, late in the afternoon, one of his people called me at home and asked, anxiously, "Moya, is Bill all right?" I said, "Sure he's all right, what's the matter?" "Well, he wants to turn down the deal!" I had to laugh. "Listen, if he wants to turn down the deal, don't try to persuade him otherwise — I hafta live with him!"

What had happened was that Bill got impatient toward the end of the day, stormed into the room where the negotiations were taking place and said, "Listen, the deal is the way I stated it. If you guys try to take one thousand-dollar bill off the top, it's no deal. And you'd better hurry, because I'm slowly getting drunk in my office!"

Shortly after that, I got a call from a jubilant Charlie Gates. He said, "Well, Moya, would you like to shake hands with your new partner?" I said, "Everybody come home — I'll feed you and drink you!" I hung up and stood quietly in our silent home, looking around and thinking, Yes, honey, we did have fun and we grew and we'll never forget our five years in Wichita!

P.S.: Bill got everything he wanted and they piled more on top of that!

Chapter Seventeen

At the time Bill sold Learjet, our lives had begun to change dramatically. The children were beginning to leave the nest, and with them, many of my "Mommy" responsibilities were becoming unnecessary. No longer the Brownee Brown Dance Recitals, the Berkeley Hall School affairs, dressing up for Halloween parties, the thousands of Easter eggs we dyed and hid and lost until we smelled them the following year!

Around this time, I looked back on my 25 years with Bill. They were spectacular years crammed full of excitement and accomplishments, moving and raising children, and, above all, living with the man I loved. I had no regrets. None!

But there was always a lot of conflict in my heart — being torn between the children's problems in their young lives and Bill's constantly swirling activity — the quintessence of the fast lane. He wasn't close to any of the children. They could have called him any moment of the day, but they didn't know that. He never took time out to take them places on weekends. This is something, John, even now, is still bitter about. ("Dad never took me fishing." "John, come on, honey," I said, "your dad wouldn't know how to bait a hook but he did love you.") It was just that Bill didn't know how to do that — go on a picnic, pack a lunch and go down to the beach, throw a baseball. And more importantly, he didn't know how to communicate with them. He just didn't know how to be a father.

I tried to bring him closer to his children from his former marriages too. One day early in our marriage, Patti and Bill Jr. came to me and said, "Hey, Moya, Mom needs a washing machine and Dad won't buy it for her." I went to Bill and said, "What's the matter with you, honey? Why in the world won't you buy Madeline a washing machine?" She got her washing machine. Bill Jr. and Pat have grown into fine adults, and I love them both very much.

I also pushed — successfully — for a reunion with Mary Louise, Bill's daughter from his first marriage. She became an ordained minister of the Presbyterian Church and is a joy to know.

I always tried to bring Bill closer to his children, and succeeded once in a while, but I never thought it was often enough. Now, when I began to see the shift from "Mommy" to "Mom," it was evident in many ways that Bill and I were moving into the next phase of our lives. While David and Tina were still in school, John was a pilot in Los Angeles, and Shanda was about to find her own way.

As I watched Shanda test her options, searching for her place, I felt a special tenderness for her restlessness. She attended the University of Michigan, but didn't find what she needed. When she came home to Wichita for the funeral of my daddy, who'd died of kidney failure in January 1963, she never went back to the university. Shanda wanted to sing. Eventually she went to London to live and study voice. But her father wanted to see her continue her education, get good grades, and all that good stuff. And she didn't want to do that. It was particularly difficult for a man as focused, decisive, and determined as Bill to comprehend anything less in his children. He was hard on them.

Fathering a daughter like Shanda was a confusing issue for Bill. On the one hand he was proud of her great confidence, poise, and personality; on the other hand, he wanted to lock her in her room until she was 30, or give her a tank to drive if she had to leave! I took him to task about his attitude in a letter dated March 27, 1963:

> **My very dearest wonderful courageous and darling husband!**
>
> **These lines I write on my birthday morning, right off the top of my heart!**
>
> **It's so full — of so much — sometimes my tears spill and my heart aches unbearably. It's not always an unhappy moment. Sometimes I love you way beyond the bounds of mortal man. I know where you are — you're leaning over someone's drawing board, you're flying (exactly where you're the most comfortable**

— the most at peace — the proudest).

We have the most important thing in life; love and respect for each other. We take nothing for granted. Each day that our feet swing over the edge of the bed, it's a NEW DAY!

But remember my dearest darling, with all this success and activity, don't lose track of Shanda. I've listened to the recent discussions and I want to tell you something: Our Shanda is a talented, beautiful, spirited, sensitive girl. You can't talk down to her. If you do, you do it at the risk of losing her closeness.

Bill Jr. used to say, "I can't talk about my personal affairs with Dad." He couldn't confide in you and you'll have to work and wait for John to really tell you the deep things in HIS heart. Our Shanda's a wonderful girl — and she should have nothing but our faith and support.

This is the way parents lose their teen-agers — they don't try to see things in THEIR light for awhile. They don't ride things out — they don't RESPECT them (because maybe the kids have made mistakes and maybe the father or mother colored their acts with a stupid color and it was never erased).

Everyone loves Shanda — all heads turn when she walks into a room, she's such a beautiful girl. And she loves you. She wants more than anything else for you to be proud of her. But darling don't criticize her for being young. She argues like all your children will. DON'T ARGUE WITH YOUR CHILDREN. It will always end in disaster. You're too smart and they're too young and it will never benefit anyone. You suggest — you wait — you're patient — you're enormously grateful for the good, forgiving the mistakes. Remember Mother Olsen's advice for all of us: "Have a short memory for the bad and a long memory for the good!"

She inherited this beautiful personality and magnetism for people from all of us — from you and Daddy and me — and it's pretty high voltage. But don't forget that she's capable of handling it. She knows a dangerous situation when she sees one. She's aware. And she has principles. She'll have fun — she'll have sweethearts — and she'll escape and handle it by herself. And don't forget, my darling — this one thing: If Shanda likes 'em — WE LIKE 'EM!

Darling — it's harder for you to scale everything down to a

child's world. It seems so stupid to you — particularly when they're being stupid at the top of their lungs. But keep them all close to you — don't make the same mistakes other successful extraordinary men make who lose their children while they're making staggering material gains.

There's no one like you. You aren't like any other human being in the world. There's no pattern. You're YOU and I LOVE YOU WITH ALL MY HEART AND SOUL!

Chapter Eighteen

When I lost Daddy, I was overwhelmed with memories. He wrote some great letters that have become family treasures, and you might like to read them. Some of them are tucked in the appendices of this book. One was written to my baby brother Clem when he was two days old in May 1917. Another was written to his nephew Ronnie, three, after Daddy's brother died. Daddy's spirit and sense of fun will always be remembered. He loved children and loved having a gang of them around him. He loved to play.

Daddy's career spanned nearly fifty years, from the beginning of vaudeville in the teens through Theater in the Round, radio, and in the process he made eleven movies. Olsen and Johnson was the first comedy team on television, but "Hellzapoppin" at the Winter Garden in New York was the apex — it was the biggest, most famous show in the country at that time. It was one of the longest running musical comedies on Broadway with a run of more than 1,600 performances.

After "Hellzapoppin" ran its course, Daddy did shows for the Armed Forces abroad. He just always loved to entertain, always needed the audience. After Chic Johnson retired, Daddy kept entertaining on radio shows, playing Air Force bases overseas with a group of performers. In 1961, he was even profiled on TV's "This is Your Life."

Daddy didn't have a grain of sense about money or investments, and he was well-known as the softest touch in town. He just couldn't say no. Though he was a great star and made millions of dollars during his lifetime, he died bankrupt. Maybe it was because he was the softest touch in town.

Daddy's good heartedness sometimes led to disaster. One day while walking down Broadway with his newspapers and his apple and his Black Jack chewing gum in his pocket, Daddy met a friend — a midget from Russia — "How are ya?" Daddy inquired.

"Ole, we're in deep trouble. The circus closed and they're throwing us out of our apartment tomorrow. The immigration people won't have our visas back to Russia for two weeks and we don't know what to do!" (The little guy was almost in tears.) And Daddy said, "Hey, you don't have to worry. I have an apartment in the basement of my house and you can stay there until you get your visas!"

He brought home all the members of the Russian's group, all five of "The Mighty Atoms." And my mother (through clenched teeth) said, "How long are they going to be here?" Daddy said confidently: "Don't worry, baby, they'll only be here until they get their visas. The immigration authorities have promised them their visas in two weeks." Like gospel, right? He believed everybody. Like the countless people over the years who had promised earnestly to pay him back, "next week, next payday."

Two years later, "The Mighty Atoms" were still with us, and my mother protested: "I want those midgets out of my basement!"

It didn't bother my children like it bothered my Mother, they had a great time with the midgets. As a matter of fact, they taught Shanda to dance. And one time while we were visiting Mother in Malverne, the neighbors thought they had a banner headline: "Moya Lear let her children smoke cigars out on the lawn after dinner — I saw 'em with my very own eyes."

As I've already mentioned earlier in this book, when we were kids growing up, Daddy loved us to death. J.C. and I were so close we were almost like twins. We explored the theaters, went on hikes, played together, climbed trees. But we weren't alike. Mother and Daddy called J.C. "Stormy" when he was a baby because he had one of those Johnny Jump-ups, and when he got mad he'd bounce in that swing. As we grew up, J.C. excelled in his schoolwork. And he was very principled. He took Christian Science literally: "If God is all-powerful, why do we need insurance?" J.C. also displayed an unusual gift for research — for words — and for poetry. His sense of humor was delicious. He wrote funny stuff — such as the time I brought my friend, Henrietta, home with me one weekend. J.C., who was in his late teens, got a terrible crush on her and wrote this poem:

HENRIETTA

I 'fretta,' Henrietta
Ever since the day we 'metta'
By the fact that you no getta
The same feeling that I got.
Think I'll cut my throat
With my 'Giletta'
Or turn on the gas 'jetta'
Then there'll be no need to fretta
HENRIETTA!

J.C.'s senior thesis at USC was a monumental book report on the Los Angeles Telephone Directory of 1936! Who else but an Olsen would think up something like that? He called it, "Fun and Romance with a Telephone Directory." Toward the beginning, the thesis reads: "Although there is practically no plot, there are nearly 300,000 characters in this alphabetical novel. I say practically no plot, because the book does mention Home, Wedlock, Power, Fate, Anger, Fear, Profit, Fortune, Glory, Land, Liberty, Riches, Peace, Love, Comfort, Joy, Hunger, Cash, Luck, Honor, Money, etc., as other books do, but there is no story line." It's an incredible, massive effort that must be recorded before it becomes buried in dust in some file, and you can find a shortened version of it in the back of this book.

However, after all the fun we shared as children and teen-agers growing up, life for J.C. took a twist. When he graduated from USC, Daddy needed him. "Just for a few weeks, just come and take care of things for us," Daddy said. But it became a permanent arrangement. It was just sad that J.C. didn't get a job and do something on his own. Instead, he stayed with "Hellzapoppin." His only marriage was turbulent. And he lost his only child, Nanette, to leukemia in 1955. He carried that shock and sadness for the rest of his life, which — as it turned out — wasn't very long.

He checked out of the human race on his 40th birthday. He'd had a fight with his wife. He didn't fight. She did — and she left him. In the heartbreak of those last days, he had in his pocket her prescription for sleeping pills, because he was going to the pharmacy for her. All of J.C.'s humor and spontaneity, sensitivity, warmth, honesty and deep, basic raw intelligence — all came to a shocking, heartbreaking halt in

May 1956.

Bill and I had flown down to Nice, where we were met by friends who had invited us to spend the weekend at their beautiful old home in Villefranche. It was an elegant invitation and we were having a good time catching up on the gossip. We told them what was going on in Geneva — they told us who was in Monaco, Cap d'Antibes, and which yacht belonged to whom. Our host was the attorney for Aristotle Onassis, the Greek shipping tycoon, and we were invited to have cocktails on Onassis' yacht, the famous Christina!

The weekend was packed with things to do and people to talk to. I never noticed the ripple of unease. Bill was holding me closer than usual, but I just thought he felt as strange as I did with all these super-sophisticated people. Sunday came and as soon as we could we were out of there and up in our little Cessna 310 (ten years before the Learjet!). We took off and grabbed some altitude before soaring over the Alps to Geneva and home.

I was looking out the window at the Alps stretched out below us and thought I never in my whole life had seen anything so breathtaking. Anyone who doesn't believe in God should be required to look down from a Cessna 310 over the Alps and read His Handwriting!

After Bill reached cruising altitude and got things squared away, he said very quietly, "They found J.C." A wash of shock went through me at his tone — what he'd just said — the way he'd said it.

Bill had gotten the news, perhaps from a telex from his company in Los Angeles. Or maybe Mother had called. I never found out. Not wanting to believe what he was trying so gently to tell me, I choked, "What — are — you — saying?"

"Honey, they found him in the attic of his house."

I screamed. "No! No! No! No!" I pounded on the control panel. I completely lost control. I tried to get out of the airplane. Bill was on autopilot and reached over to hold me — firmly at first. Then, when the screams subsided, into tears and sobbing, we talked about things most people do under similar circumstances. How guilty they often feel. Bill suffered because he had wanted to (and should have) given J.C. a job in Bill's company. J.C. was broke and needed a job badly. But, Bill didn't know in what department to place him.

My Daddy suffered the most bone-wrenching guilt. The utter despair of lost time, of "Where was I?" and "Where did the time go?" and (the inevitable) "If only I'd . . . " He was haunted by these feelings until his own death in 1963.

They found J.C. in his attic "with a hat over his face" — when I later read that last part in *Variety*, I was rocked with pain and sadness. None of us ever really recovered from this loss. J.C. haunts us still with his humor, his pictures, his poetry and letters. But, we'll never feel another of his hugs or hear the sound of his voice.

Ironically, it was around the time of J.C.'s death that Bill began having even more difficulty reaching his own children, who were fast becoming teen-agers. About that time I wrote to him:

> **John will grow up next year. Hold him close in the process. Fabulous fathers who have sons have seldom been wise enough to love enough. Share with him. Don't separate yourself from him by telling him too many times what your problem was. Because it boils down to something like this: Daddy's a genius. He doesn't understand. He's not close.**
>
> **Don't look at him through your Lear, Inc. eyes. Look at him compassionately as a father looks at a son who is suffering with the excruciating pain of growing up. Be grateful that he doesn't have polio or some awful disease that we couldn't do anything about.**

Along with his shortcomings, Bill had that engineer's precision and orderliness. "If you put baggage in the trunk of your car, you put the handle on the outside so that you can pull the #!@^* suitcase out when you're unloading the trunk!" I recall some of his spectacular tantrums about loading the car trunk or the airplane efficiently, and putting bags where they'd fit. And anybody who brought more than two suitcases got on his "S" list forever.

Bill had a lot of weaknesses — impatience with mediocrity, immaturity, total impatience with clumsiness. Even with me — if I stumbled on a curb or something, it irritated him. But he was quick to forgive. He could blow up, go right through the ceiling with caustic sarcasm and get over it just as fast. The only one of our children he was good with was Tina. She was different. She had my sensitivity for knowing when to shut up, to get out, not to bring up a subject. A sense of timing.

Bill loved his children and wanted to be close. He just didn't know how. He had taken such delight in them when they were little. He loved to tell the story about eight year-old John and Shiner, our black-eyed white boxer:

BILL: John, I was so sorry to hear about Butch's dog getting run over. (Butch was a little neighborhood pal.)

JOHN: Me too, Dad.

BILL: And I thought with so many pets in this house, maybe it would be a very nice thing to do to give Shiner to Butch.

JOHN: (with tears brimming in his eyes) Oh Dad, I couldn't give Shiner away!

BILL: That's OK, John. Don't worry about it. I just thought —

JOHN: But I'll sell him!

BILL: SELL him?

JOHN: Yeah. Do you think eight dollars would be too much?

BILL: (trying to keep a straight face) I think that's fine, John, but why eight dollars?

JOHN: Well, with the 52 I have in the bank, that would make it an even 60!

But like so many successful fathers, Bill wanted his children to have the same values that had stood him in such good stead — values he had developed under very different circumstances. He didn't want them to grow up "rich kids." But our children didn't grow up like Bill. We did have money.

One time in his early teens, John tried to get a paper route, but the job went to a kid who "really needed it." John railed at the unfairness of that judgment: "I needed that job more than any of those kids!" And he did, he needed to be able to prove his worth to his father — in his own way. Like my father with my brother, Bill couldn't see John's special gifts.

John was the first of the children to experience his father's impatience. I'd loved traveling with my father, so it never occurred to me that our constant moving to be with Bill would be so difficult for John. Everybody else adapted, but there are people who can't adapt. John was one of them. He hated to change schools so many times, wanted to go to school with his friends. We were beginning to hear about teens and drugs, and, like all parents, we worried about this problem even though we had no reason to believe that John had tried drugs. Bill, however, had no patience with the kids with the duck-tail haircuts who hung around the garage while John was building his car. But, John wanted to be one of the bunch. He was fed up with hearing about how great his father was, and all he had accomplished. He wanted to have his own friends. He wanted to be one of the guys. He would do anything to BE one of the guys. But Bill had trouble with that. He didn't want John to simply run with the pack. He wanted his son to be a leader. I could see clearly how normal this was for children to want their own friends.

I wrote to Bill about John's grades, which he was concerned about. These are excerpts:

> Y'know, Lindbergh wasn't a good student either, sweetheart. He's a pretty nice man. Some kids can make fabulous grades and some kids can't. I don't think we should devil him about grades.
>
> I KNOW HE SPENT ALL HIS TIME ON HIS CAR! I KNOW! I KNOW . . .
>
> You wouldn't get him a car. So he built his own. We can at least ante-up the insurance. Sweetheart, you don't have enough patience to raise John. Or any respect for a little boy's heart that's in a young man's body — growing slowly and FULL of complexes. Please remember John's history. He needs guiding but encouragement. What he doesn't need physically or emotionally is a "good kick in the ass" — especially by you.
>
> That he needs good firm intelligent counsel. Yes! That he needs to get straightened out with regard to living in Geneva with his family. Yes. But I don't think you should be the one to do it, my darling. What I'd really like you both to do is to see Dr. Rose (a friend and psychiatrist from UCLA) not the company psychiatrist. I want you both to go. What I want to know — along with what's troubling with John — is WHY YOU CAN'T RAISE SONS! Why you insist on alienating yourself from them. Why with all the money we have, you can't relax and be generous with your boys and not quarrel over the impossible situation of them wanting things like a car (a set of wheels) — very normal and very practical (I've had one since I was fifteen) without you telling them the dreary details of how much it costs and how much the insurance costs and how much the upkeep costs, etc. They know that, darling. They also are filled with frustra-

tion because they can't get a job to earn it.

Either "too young" or "Lear!? I've got kids lined up who need the job . . . go get a job with your old man!!"

Don't try to force your early experiences on these kids, sweetheart. It's a different world, different atmosphere.

Bill saw his limitations and struggled with them. He wrote the following to me:

I hope and pray that I am getting closer to John and am following all of your exhortations and being real patient with him. I told him the other day that I was not always right and sometimes terribly wrong and that it was because I had a terrible fear of being poor because of having been so damned broke at times, owing everybody and with no apparent way to pay my debts and it makes me do things that I just shouldn't do. I explained to him how I wanted him to have an incentive in life and that I was fearful of providing him so many things that it would look silly for him to get a job and go to work, starting at the bottom when really he had more coming in from his estate than he could earn and that would and could destroy his will to take a job and earn only a small portion of what he got anyway. I told him I wanted his love so badly and in my desperation to reach him and help him that I over reached and was probably destroying the very thing I was trying to do, win his love, respect and help. I told him that I needed his love even worse than he needed mine and that everything I did was to aid and abet his future. I told him of the trust that I set up for him and for all of my loved ones because I wanted them to have something now when they are of age and not have to wait until I died to inherit it. That I didn't want to be a dead asset to him but a living asset to help him. I tried to explain why I divided his income so that he got part of it when he was twenty-one and part at thirty and the balance at thirty five. I wanted him to have something even if he spent all he got too soon so he would learn by his mistakes. I think I got through to him and I believe he will be closer.

Mom, we must never do a thing like this again, leaving a boy in his tender years without supervision and guidance —when he has the run of things with other boys, who no doubt tell him what to do and what to say. And the pity is that John does not want to stand out in the crowd, but to be a regular guy, a conformist and average fellow, doing what the boys approve of and not what he knows better about. It's our fault if he is this way and the natural result of leaving him in a situation that was bound to create the condition we got. We must never do it again. He must either be under our guidance and love or go to a school where he will be supervised and organized. He will kick up a fuss but his future is more important to us than his temporary ire or fussing. I know you will agree and we have to present a solid front, no disagreements that he can use to split us down the middle and then our troubles with John will disappear.

John hated being in Geneva, hated being in Switzerland — period! And, just as I had reacted to my own father's infidelities, he hated knowing about his father's girlfriends. He became nasty and critical of his father and full of black, dark anger. It is one of the tragedies of our family that the gulf between Bill and John never did narrow. Whose fault? They were both wrong.

Chapter Nineteen

After the Learjet deal was signed, Bill wanted to leave town that instant. I stood flat-footed in the living room and said, "No! We're going to wait until the end of the week when the children are out of school."

War was declared! That was Tuesday. Bill did crossword puzzles; he played the organ; he poured a drink; he fixed a sandwich; he spent hours on the telephone. He didn't say, "You stay until the end of the week. I'm out of here!" (Which wouldn't have surprised me.)

But by Wednesday, as I wondered if either of us would live through this, I read in the paper that the Governor of Alaska, Walter Hickel, was going to give the commencement address at the University of Kansas. My heart jumped! I read the story to Bill, and he said, "So?"

MOYA: Honey, (patiently) we'll get in touch with him and ask
           him if he'd like to have a Learjet Taxi Ride back to
           Juneau. We'll have a nice trip and fill in the days until
           Friday!
BILL: (grumping, inconsolable) He won't want to do that.

Guess what?! He not only wanted to, but the very next morning, Governor Walter Hickel came screaming up the ramp in front of the Learjet hangar with his motorcycle escort, and we were loaded and off to Alaska before Bill could say, "but . . ."

We had a blast. We went salmon fishing in Anchorage and I — *me,*

Moya — caught a 22-pound salmon, shrugging off all the guys want-ing to help! ("Here, let me!" "No, I want to!" "I can show you!") But I shrugged them off yelling, "Get outta my way, this is my very own fish, he's on my line and I'll pull him in!"

The next day, we flew our beautiful Learjet (which created excite-ment wherever we went) to Nome for lunch. And the great part of that lunch was standing on a promontory, looking through high-pow-ered binoculars mounted on a rock, across the Bering Sea at a Russian looking at me through his binoculars. Still looking, I waved, and he waved back! I looked away from the binoculars at my friends and asked, "Is that . . . ?" And they nodded, smiling at my astonishment that a Russian was looking back at me and waving. I passed the binoc-ulars to Bill and said, "Look! You aren't gonna believe this." Bill looked and said, still looking, "I believe it."

From there, we flew to Fairbanks, where Alaskans were celebrat-ing their Centennial. There were parades, flags, Boy Scouts, the town was on its ear! While we were at one of their colorful bars, we met a fella who told Bill there was some great land in Reno, Nevada, that was up for grabs and that he should look into it. Bill said something like, "Yeah, right!" and ordered another beer.

Anyway, we filled those three fabulous days to the brim, flew back to Wichita, scooped up the children and started another new life in Beverly Hills where we bought another beautiful home. I think it was the most beautiful of the thirteen homes we had lived in. It had tiger maple floors, magnolia trees, tennis courts, a swimming pool, and es-pecially, beautiful French windows. Leonard Firestone had been the original owner.

But Bill wasn't happy. He was fat in the bank with nothing to do. He had no challenge to overcome, no lofty heights to scale — he had only to sit in our gorgeous home and spend his money. That wasn't his style. His feeling of uselessness depressed him, and again I watched him and worried about suicide.

Three or four months after settling in Beverly Hills, Bill was trying half-heartedly to establish a base of operations. There were all kinds of ideas about what he should do with his time and money. Sam Auld, an associate who had been with Bill since 1955, said, "Hey, Bill, why don't you do something about pollution. Why don't you design an en-gine that burns clean?"

Bill wanted to know why it hadn't already been done. "What's the problem?" he said. Nobody knew exactly, but if it wasn't solved, the quality of life on our planet was going to deteriorate to a dangerous level.

Curiously, during one of these discussions, the phone rang and the conversation went something like this:

ALASKAN

FRIEND: Hi, Bill, this is Pete Lewis! (Not his real name.)

BILL: Uh. (No idea who this is.)

FRIEND: C'mon Bill, remember we met in the bar up in Fairbanks?

BILL: Uh, right. (Still no idea. Which bar? Who is this?)

FRIEND: Bill, I'm the guy who told you about the land up in Reno.

BILL: Oh my God, sure! I remember.

FRIEND: Well, I just called to tell you that if you're interested, you'd better move, because time's running out.

Well, Bill moved. He sent Buzz Nanney, our friend, negotiator, moderator, and fixer-of-whatever-needed-fixing, to see if there really was land up there. Sure enough, there were 3,500 acres out at the former Stead Air Force Base, and Bill bought the land.

His financial advisors jumped all over him. "Bill you're just going to piss your money away! Why would you want to buy land up in Reno, Nevada?" Bill answered, reasonably, "Well, I don't know anything better to do with my money than to buy land!"

So that's how it started. I couldn't believe my ears when I began to hear little conversations about Reno, escalating to a deadly serious level. I ignored them, writing them off as a result of his acute boredom. I figured he'd found a way to relieve the monotony!

I, on the other hand, loved being in Beverly Hills. Our home was beautiful. We had a lot of friends there, and I had all my family close to me, including Mother. Tina was home, going to school at Berkeley Hall, a Christian Science school. I was settled and happy. But we were only to live in that house six months.

Then Bill was invited to be guest speaker at a luncheon in Reno attended by everyone important in the state: U.S. senators, the governor, the president of the university, the editor of the newspaper, and other prominent people.

We both flew up for the event. Bill was at his best. He was a great speaker and held the audience, including me, spellbound. I was spellbound until he started to praise Nevada in general, "How great!", and about Reno in particular, "What incredible potential!" And when he closed by saying, "Moya and I are looking forward to coming up here more often!" Well, he got a standing ovation from everybody but me!

On our way home, after we had achieved altitude, I unbuckled my safety belt and stormed up to the cockpit and laid it on him! "You ought to be ashamed of yourself, letting those great people think we might move up to Reno... you know darned good and well we'll never move to Reno, Nevada! It's a one-night-stand, ferheavensakes!"

He said, "Well, honey, you don't have to. We have our Learjet and I can fly back and forth!" (Oh yeah, right. I knew that would never work. I looked around my gorgeous home, Mother and my whole family nearby for the first time in my married life, and, man, I started to worry!) In fact I wrote a note and put it in his brief case one day, which said in part:

I will never never never never move to Reno, Nevada.

But Bill became more determined than ever, and we made several more trips up to Reno, and dammit, my feet started to slip out from under me. Every time our Learjet clamshell door opened, I got this powerful aroma of sage and pine, and saw the most incredible cloud formations I'd ever seen. I was a goner, a dad-blamed goner. This all happened over thirty years ago and I've loved Reno with a passion ever since.

The day we moved into River House in Verdi, a little town which is just outside of Reno, was the first day of forever for me. I was home. I would never move again. And I knew Bill felt the same way. We dug in, we had work to do, and we were happy. Forget how I had fought him about moving to Reno. And when I saw the Sierra and Lake Tahoe! Where we would live on the banks of the Truckee River, the air was fresh — the sky was the bluest sky I ever saw, and it's the same today, and I'm home forever!

□   □   □

On Bill's birthday, June 26, 1969, I presented him with two volumes of his patents, dated from Jan. 9, 1934 to April 8, 1969. I had the leather distressed to look like old law books. The title was embossed in gold on a red leather panel on the spine of the books:

WILLIAM P. LEAR

vs

I N E R T I A

In the first volume, on the first page entitled "Prelude," I inscribed:

> I remember YOU, darling — quite apart from (yet closely integrated with) this very impressive statistical evidence of your philosophy of supply.
>
> Remember after World War II, when I was so worried about impending bankruptcy, and you took me in your arms and said confidently, "Don't ever worry about THAT Mom — because I believe there's an Infinite Source of Supply of ideas — so they can't bankrupt my mind!"
>
> The world will remember your brilliance.
>
> I will remember your warmth — your wonderful heart that Fortune Magazine missed by a country mile!
>
> The laughs — the free-roaring laughs we've had. The square MILES of needlepoint I've worked . . . waiting. Waiting. The Passing Parade of characters. The Swinging Door of Chief Engineers!
>
> The hot coffee and homemade bread consumed. The heads bent over drawing boards. The all-night phoning with me cross-eyed from lack of sleep! But not YOU! You are on your White Charger — with sword drawn — challenging the enemy:
>
> THEY SAID IT COULDN'T BE DONE !!
>
> I know it CAN. Because I've watched you do it. Again and again. And now. And tomorrow. Material for Volume III.
>
> So — the world will have your technical record.
>
> I have your sensitivity. Your warm spontaneous embrace on a street corner. Your surprise . . . your inspiration . . . your hearty laugh. The miracle that is you . . . your faith.
>
> With my whole beating heart,
> Mom
> Verdi, Nevada
> June 26, 1969

□   □   □

Despite all my efforts, a couple of years after selling Learjet, Bill would continue to battle depression.

One Sunday, I'd gone to church in Reno with Mother. I felt uneasy. We were going to get some ice cream afterward, but I said, "No, we'd better go home." We bumped right into Bill as he was leaving the house. He'd left me a note written on the back of an envelope it on my pillow: "April 22, 1968. To whom it may concern, to Moya Lear my beloved wife, this constitutes full power of attorney to act in every manner and this includes signing of checks on all my bank accounts and cashing all CDs when due. To pay our lawful debts and all expenses. William P. Lear" He admitted that he was going to get into an airplane and fly it out to sea until it ran out of gas.

I said, "You go to bed and pull the covers up and stop acting like a child. You've got so much to contribute and you've got so much character and you ought to be ashamed of yourself!" He went right to bed. It was the first time I really put my foot down when he was in one of those moods. I was angry; I could see what he was doing. By now I knew his true character, and I knew that no matter how down he was, he didn't really want to end it all. As the years went by, he hung on to me more and more. Needing my strength, he knew I was the best investment he ever made.

□   □   □

Our move to Reno finally led to a new challenge, fighting polluton. Bill's task was to invent a steam turbine engine that would burn clean! The news media carried the banner that labeled our efforts:

BILL LEAR'S STEAM CAR!

I battened down the hatches and we were off again! Bill was totally absorbed and committed and fascinated. He was fired-up; he had a new challenge, a fevered commitment to clean up air pollution!

During the engine research and development years, we went through a lot of difficulty and setbacks but also had some stupendous highs. Bill had taken on a task the magnitude of literally moving a mountain, a mountain of inertia. There's a very, very short list of men who have taken on Detroit and the United States government with such gusto.

Bill predicted that the practical steam turbine engine would make him known as "The man who cleaned up air pollution," and that Lear Motors would make steam engines for manufacturers of cars, buses, trucks, boats, and helicopters.

The challenge was to make the engine small and light, and yet to get good gas mileage. He also needed to find a safe, inexpensive fuel that would not freeze at low temperatures. Of course, I'm greatly simplifying the problems they ran into, but from my side of the bed, these were the problems I heard about the most.

The problems involved in building a steam turbine engine soon became very clear. It wasn't easy, and Bill learned something new every day. And because it was virgin territory for him, he was vulnerable to every smooth-talking con artist who came out of the woodwork. Anyone who knew the buzz words like "cleaning up pollution" and some of the language of engineering found his way out to Stead and into Bill's office — to the dismay and despair of a small cadre of genuine engineers and good friends who loved him and hated to see him waste his time and money on every slick, rip-off scheme known to man. For example, once he got off-track, building a race car that we were going to enter into the Indianapolis 500! He even started to build a race track out at Stead. My heart sank.

Along with whatever else I was born with, is a strip of hair at the back of my neck that sticks straight up when I meet a phony. The sound of a voice, the way someone shakes hands, eyes not straight— something tips me off. And I'd say to Bill, "Watch out for him (or her or them)." Most of the time he listened. When he didn't, I never said, "I told you so." I didn't have to. I could almost always depend on my intuition.

Looking at the bus with the steam engine installed, I didn't have the same feelings as I did for the Learjet. I knew what the steam engine was supposed to do, and that if Bill proved his point, it would be great. But it was nothing like the excitement of the Learjet. A bus was a bus. It was a big bus, and it had a big engine, and it was smelly, and dirty — oil, grease and dirt — and there was nothing exciting about it. The two projects were totally different.

Building a steam-driven car was exciting. Bill learned a great deal and we made many new friends. Ed Cole, the president of General Motors at that time, recognized what Bill was trying to do and helped by sending him two buses and a lot of moral support. I got to know

Dolly Cole and we became good friends, eating peanut butter sandwiches on the banks of the Truckee River, while waiting for our husbands to come home. She's one of the stars on my list of great,
genuine people I know.

Frequently, during those years, we traveled in our Learjet back
and forth from Reno to Washington and New York. At one point in
the early '70s, we were invited to dinner in New York by Pat and Dick
Nixon — the President and first Lady. After having flown from Reno
to Teeterboro, New Jersey, we were met by Herb Fisher, our pal with
the New York Port Authority. It was an exciting and prestigious "date"
with the Nixons, and we loved the whole adventure, including our
stay at the Carlysle.

We had arrived so late at the hotel however, that we quickly
checked in and went up to our suite. Bill jumped in the shower while
I unpacked and laid out our stuff on the bed. When he stepped out I
jumped in. As I was dressing, I noticed Bill's black leather belt —
hand-tooled with the three views of the Learjet and all his lucky numbers (4, 7, 11, 13). It had a big silver buckle with his initials in gold. I'd
had it made for him for his birthday when we moved to Reno. I didn't
anticipate the problem I'd have getting it off of him! So, thinking he
really wouldn't try to wear it with his tux — but who knew what he'd
do given the opportunity — I removed the "opportunity." I rolled it
up and hid it under a pillow in a closet. This all took about ten seconds. As I was nonchalantly putting on a hasty makeup, I watched
him through the mirror looking for his belt.

> MOYA: (innocently) What're you looking for honey?
> BILL: My belt. I just had it.
> MOYA: Dad! You've got your tuxedo on and your red
>   suspenders. You can't wear that dumb belt."

(I went to the door.) "Now stop acting like a four year-old!

> BILL: (sitting down in a chair) Not going without my belt!
> MOYA: You'll be a cartoon. (Shoulda saved my breath.)
> BILL: Don't give a damn.
> MOYA: (so mad at him I could've killed him.) All right — be an
>   idiot. (I gave him the belt.)

We left the suite and walked down the hall to the elevator. I was furious, but he was grinning happily.

BILL: (putting his arms around me) Don't be mad at me,
          Mom. I yam what I yam — why'd you marry me?
MOYA: (grumbling) Damn if I know.

□ □ □

But after a few years went by, it became clear that we were going to need some money. A lot more money for this steam project. We'd just about exhausted our personal funds. We were getting down to a scary level. He broke my heart walking up and down the corridors of the U.S. Senate and the House in the early '70s trying to get someone to listen. I followed him with my heart aching as I watched him courageously and persistently pressing for help in Washington.

"Listen to him, goddammit!" I was screaming silently, "he's sounding an alarm. He's trying to clean up pollution in our cities. He's trying to build an engine that will burn clean for our buses. He really does have something to say. Why won't anyone listen?"

They listened, patronizingly. (Get him out of here — he's a nut case.) What he was, was totally impatient with and scornful of the lack of basic intelligence in our Congress, the waste of time, the passing of the buck. They sent him here, they sent him down there. They insulted him in such an oblique way he didn't realize he was being insulted — but I did. And I wanted to put my arms around him, drag him out of there and take him home. He had so much to say and no one was listening.

Senator Barry Goldwater of Arizona was (and is) a loyal friend and a staunch supporter. I loved him for standing up and being counted in Congress, paying tribute to Bill. The following is what he said, and it was printed in the Congressional Record:

A STEAM-POWERED ROAD VEHICLE
February 4 in Reno, NV, I had one of the greatest thrills of a lifetime that has literally been packed with thrilling events.

I had my first ride in a steam-powered road vehicle. I was not only thrilled because of the ride, but thrilled because once again, one of the geniuses of our time, Bill Lear, has overcome what many experts said were insurmountable odds. He has created an engine of simplicity and power that I feel will revolutionize the automotive industry in the same way his earlier discoveries affected the electronics, communications, and aviation industries.

This engine not only produces power and does it quickly and efficiently, but the exhaust emissions are approximately 50 per cent of what the official standards will call for in 1976. He is installing the invention in a conventional car, and having sat in the driver's seat, I can attest to the fact that it will not carry any more instruments than the present automobile. It will operate in precisely the same way as do present automobiles and will start in 6 seconds after the engine has been turned on. Engineers for years have dreamed about using the simple power of steam to provide combustion for land vehicles and now Mr. Lear has come through again as he has on so many occasions in the past when technology seemed stalled.

Even with this incredible support from Senator Goldwater, no one helped financially. Bill finally, reluctantly, threw in the towel in 1974. It was a major event in Reno, because it was the end of an era. The headline read:

BILL LEAR'S STEAM CAR BITES THE DUST

Before he threw in the towel though, we had put nearly $17 million into the project! It wasn't only lack of financing that crushed Bill. After all his research he still didn't have the solution. He hadn't found the right fluid for the steam turbine engine, although research had been exhaustive. He also concluded the steam turbine engine would be too costly to mass-produce, too hard to maintain and impossible for an average mechanic to repair.

Bill told an interviewer, "If I'd just read a book, I would've known it couldn't be done the way we tried to do it." No waffling. No excuses. It was hard for him to just flat out admit that it couldn't be done, but he did. Someone will do the job, but not with a steam turbine engine.

Our money was almost gone. Bill was getting very worried. He'd go to the market and go slowly up and down the aisles, picking out what he thought was nourishing and inexpensive (like powdered milk!) — he even tried to teach me to market that way! I could see what he was trying to do, and it broke my heart to see him suffer like that — it was so unlike him. (I had no intention of drinking that powdered milk!)

We didn't go to the movies because it was five bucks apiece! We had dinner at Bill Fong's, his favorite Chinese restaurant, and ordered chow mein with two forks! He was scared to death he was going to depart this world with nothing left for me and the children.

I said, "My darling, our lives will be rich — just remembering! Don't worry."

He needed me so much during this period; he wanted me with him all the time even at the plant. But I was sure everything would work out fine. There was a payment due from the sale of Learjet, and that payment, plus some money he had put in an investment portfolio for me, was our safety net.

Most importantly — Bill still had his Infinite Source of Supply of Ideas.

There aren't many people in the world today who can take a $17 million kick in the teeth, pick themselves up, dust themselves off and mutter to the world at large "All right, you bastards, we'll build an airplane. That's something we know something about!"

Chapter Twenty

Bill literally did "pick himself up and dust himself off," and started all over again when he began serious work on the Learstar 600, which became the Canadair Challenger.

The concept of a large executive jet that could also be configured as a jet commuter or a freight carrier had already been born during our last years at Learjet, the Lear Liner, Model 40. Extensive engineering had been implemented, a mockup built, and contracts on the Lear Liner sent to the following companies for signature:

Aircraft-002   Rexall Drug and Chemical Co.
Aircraft-003   Mead Johnson
Aircraft-004   Aerojet General
Aircraft-005   El Paso Natural Gas and Oil Co.

A presentation to Ozark Air Lines had been scheduled and Alaska Airlines had approached Learjet with the prospect of a major order for Lear Liners to service their short-haul routes. In spite of all the above, the entire project was dumped by Gates after the company bought Learjet in 1967.

I think Bill was out there by himself in the mid-'60s, with his vision of the approaching need for the commuter jet. All that's left of our beautiful Lear Liner (as I record this in the '90s) are some dusty engineering files in storage someplace and a couple of models. Brian Barents, our fine president of Learjet (and we can thank our lucky stars for him!) has one in his office, and Don Grommesh, who worked with Bill from the beginning of Learjet (bless him!), rescued the other one.

Now, let's fast-forward to 1974. Bill commissioned gifted engineer and good friend Richard Tracy to help assemble a team of hard-working key engineers. They started serious, detailed engineering on the Learstar 600. By that time, the concept had started to flower and Bill was off on a new and exciting program, hindered (as he was during most of his career), by the ever-present need for funding — a lot of it — quickly! Once again we were flat on our butts. Because of our negative net worth, Bill borrowed, sold, and did whatever else he had to do to get that airplane, the Learstar 600, established.

It was during this time that Fred Smith, president and founder of Federal Express, dropped in to see what Bill was up to. (I'll never forget this!) And Fred, after listening to Bill and seeing the mock-up, told him he wasn't interested in buying a Learstar 600! Bill's heart nearly stopped with the acute disappointment he felt. Fred added, "I'm interested in buying fifteen!"

This conversation with Fred Smith confirmed what Bill had envisioned, and although we weren't ready yet to tool and fund production for fifteen"Learstar 600s," Fred's interest validated the work already accomplished, and encouraged and excited Bill and his small corps of engineers.

Bill respected and appreciated the new aerodynamic development of the aft-loaded wing, coupled with high-bypass ratio turbofan engines. Early on he envisioned the exciting potential of combining these two elements together in one design: the Learstar 600. It would be faster, with much longer range and, best of all, it would have much more economical fuel-consumption characteristics. Matter of fact, the publication *Business and Commercial Aviation,* in February 1979, stated candidly that the Learstar 600 was the first commercial coupling of these two advanced techniques, and commended Bill for his farsightedness.

Finally someone was listening. Canadair was also listening. Canadair needed just what Bill was ready to sell, however reluctantly. His reluctance stemmed from not wanting to lose control of what he felt was his last airplane. Canadair was in a difficult place, economically, it needed to lay off hundreds of workers. Almost ready to close down, they needed a big project to put people to work, and Bill had the Learstar 600, plus priceless experience and background in the business-jet world.

He knew how to get things done — how to get them done quickly, efficiently and (because he always worried about where the next payroll was coming from) economically. He had designed, built and marketed equipment for pilots in the 1930s. His remarkable work on the design and manufacture of the autopilot (which pilots bless him for to this day) had put him in the category of a man who knows what he's talking about. And if you challenged him, you'd better have your facts straight.

He knew the market and the people in it. And along with all this, he had an uncanny ability to look into the future and fathom what kind of product was going to be needed ten or fifteen years down the road. So his gifts were two-fold: depth of experience in general aviation, particularly with the business-jet, and true vision.

His was not an ethereal, off-the-wall vision, but a vision based on his intuitive ability to anticipate trends before anyone else had a chart! He stayed on top of the latest technology and knew all the people who could feed him that information.

The Learjet had been designed and flown at a cost of ten million dollars in one year's time and, don't forget, without the help of computers. This was achieved because Bill was there directing traffic. He had the control and the authority to say, "This is what we're going to do," because it was his ten million dollars, and because he had a gang of great engineers who respected him and they had the kind of total confidence in him that was necessary to build the airplane his way. If they ever questioned one of his moves and backed it up with their math, he'd say, "Don't mix me up with your education. This is the way we're going to do it!" They'd laugh when they found out he was usually right! And, very significantly, the airplane he insisted on (day and night, weekends and holidays!) came out on its first flight not one pound overweight, not one single pound.

Fred Kearns, president of Canadair, knew about Bill's abilities, his remarkable genius, and so believed Bill could save Canadair time and money. In a meeting where minutes were kept in November 1976, Fred said, "I have to have Bill Lear in this program for it to succeed."

Bill was convinced that his 90-inch fuselage was the key to the performance of the Learstar 600. When Canadair increased it to 106 inches, Bill heatedly challenged Harry Halton, the vice president of engineering. Harry, who had authorized the change, explained, "Well, for each inch you increase the diameter, the range and speed fall off really very little."

Bill said, "Well, if that's absolutely provable, go ahead, make it 106 inches. Take a big bite!" He didn't believe in nibbling at a problem.

Despite having increased the diameter of the fuselage, there was reluctance to lengthen the airplane to preserve the "fineness ratio" (the relationship of the length of the fuselage to its diameter). Seeking to draw attention to the problem, Bill dubbed the airplane "Fat Albert." It was still his airplane, but to Bill it looked like someone putting on weight, full of pizzas and Snickers bars. He told me, full of despair, "It's getting too heavy. It won't meet its performance specs. And it's sure as hell gonna get more expensive."

In all fairness to Canadair, they just didn't know how to deal with Bill. There was a tangle in their top management that resulted in them saying, in substance, "Mr. Lear, if we need you, we'll call you." It broke his heart, but not his spirit, because he later went on to begin work on the Lear Fan.

After all this agony, the Learstar became a great airplane. Canadair has renamed it the Challenger, but they can never remove Lear from its bloodstream. I'm proud of it. It was born in Bill's heart. He spelled it out, and he foresaw its remarkable place in the executive jet realm, as well as its logical application to the commuter routes.

During all of this friction, understandably, I was physically and emotionally suffering and I went down in flames with severe back pain. I mean, it was an agony to turn over in bed, let alone go to the bathroom! I heard Bill come in the front door whistling, and I thought, "What a sweetheart he is, to come home in the middle of the day to see how I am!"

Wrong. He was on fire with excitement. He said, "Get up, Mom, I have something to show you!" I didn't care if he had the Thunderbirds (the U.S. Air Force aerobatics demonstration team) out there standing at attention, I couldn't get up!

He said, persistently, "I'll carry you," leaning over me to lift me out of bed. I said firmly, "Honey, I'm in severe pain. (I was talking to the wall.) I can't move without it hurting. Just tell me about what you want me to see." It was like trying to stop a flood with a picket fence. "Just hold on to my shoulder, we'll go very slowly."

I clenched my teeth against the pain and let him carry me out the front door. And there in the drive was a four-door white Audi, with a matching, but plain interior. He said, "Get in and drive it. You've never driven such a car in your life!"

I gave up trying to get through to him. I slowly and painfully got into the driver's seat. Once seated, I looked at the dash, then down at the gear console, and for once was grateful for an automatic transmission. I have always preferred stick shift because I could accelerate faster, and with smart driving, get better mileage. To humor him, I drove it up our hill, over to the gas station and back home. "Dumb car," I thought, "just a nice, ordinary car. How can I tell that beaming face, 'No! Bring me back my own car!' "

But I did. I told that beaming face, "No! Bring me back my own car," which was a classy little white Mercedes 280 SL with "MOYA" plates. He could not believe his ears, that I would turn down his four-door Audi with its modern engineering, automatic shift, up-to-the-minute technology — for that little two-seater, with its stick shift, and, for air conditioning, a fan on the dash that plugged into the lighter! (His idea when I had asked for an air conditioner!) I inched painfully out of the car, and totally blew him out of the tub when I said, "Honey, it's a nice ordinary car. Go bring me back my own MOYA car. I love it. It's mine. Don't monkey with me and my car!"

He said, "OK, Mom, I won't try to reason with an idiot."

Guess what, folks! I never knew this until months later. He had sold my Mercedes, so sure had he been that he was doing the right thing, and he had to go back to pay the dealer to drive my car off the lot where they'd put it up for sale! He had even forged my signature (not an easy thing to do) on the title. However, with all the fuss he made about my car being old-fashioned, he was later overheard to say, "Why can't they design seats for airplanes like Moya has in her Mercedes?"

I still drive that Mercedes to air races. But she's a little cranky now, and so I bought the beautiful Mercedes 500 convertible and added about 20 years to my life!

Chapter Twenty-one

Bill never wasted time with regret, with the Steam Project or anything else. He never brooded over his losses. And he never looked back. He was creative, innovative, mad, restless, difficult, brilliant, passionate, moody, unpredictable, outrageous, exasperating, explosive, impossible, funny, and sometimes, a lunatic!

He was like an incredible piece of tapestry — woven on an ancient loom — multi-colored, multi-textured — with a solid gold cord slashing through the whole gorgeous work just for brilliance. A little pure wool for integrity. A little polyester and denim because he was so practical. A little cashmere for his gentleness and tenderness (which very few people saw, except me).

You hold this piece of work up to the light and say, "Oh, yeah, it's beautiful all right — but — it has flaws!" Right. He had flaws. A lot of 'em. But he was mine. And I dealt with them. And if anybody tried to pick on him, I'd scratch their eyes out!

I was always close to the people who worked for Bill. I kept track of the wives and the birthdays and the parties. I loved to do that. And that united the whole bunch.

One Sunday afternoon years ago in Grand Rapids, I was driving with a man who worked for Bill. Also in the car was a wonderful guy from the Air Force who was in Grand Rapids to supervise a military contract. We were going to go see some dogs, and while we were driving, Bill's employee commented: "You know what we have to do — we have to lock Bill in a closet so we can get production out." He continued in this grandiose way about these plans and added, "if we could just eliminate Bill Lear we'd be OK." I was in the back seat and got steaming mad as he talked over me as if I weren't there, or as if he had enlisted my support for the benefit of our military guest.

When I met Bill at the airport the next day, I told him, "You've got a rotten apple in this barrel and you'd better do something about it. He's not loyal and he's not doing the job he should be doing." But Bill took care of that man a couple of days later in our home in Grand Rapids. Bill came back unexpectedly from out of town and found all the engineers sitting around the table talking, while "Bad Apple" sat at the head of the table offending everybody. Every night at dinner, there he was, presiding over Bill's dinner table and Bill's boys, who out of love for Bill were trying to tolerate this interloper. One night during dinner, Bill walked into the dining room unexpectedly and said, "Hi, everybody!" Bad Apple said, "Hi Bill, have a seat." "Don't mind if I do," Bill replied, and he promptly dumped Bad Apple out of the chair onto the floor and sat down. Those guys just loved it.

Maybe Bill WAS difficult. Maybe he did have a couple of girls besides me (couple?) — but the way I felt about all this was captured in a little verse of a song from "South Pacific" (give me some freedom of gender) and when I give my talks, I sing:

> So supposin' he ain't bright
> Or completely free from flaws
> Or as faithful as a bird dog
> Or as kind as Santa Claus
> It's a waste of time to worry
> Over things that he is not —
> Be thankful for the things he's got!!

Take gifts, for instance. After I'd had Littlejohn, even with the difficulty, nothing could shake me from the sheer bliss of having my first baby. And to celebrate, I wanted something pretty. So I asked Bill to find me a beautiful nightie and negligee.

Guess what? He came home with a huge box from Orbach's full of dumb little nighties, pajamas and a bathrobe, nothing special. I could see just how it happened. Jerry Ohrbach was a pal. Bill must've found a cute little sales girl and got a discount from Jerry. Such a deal. I had Elizabeth Arden in mind. Handmade lace, chiffon, pale pink. Oh, well.

The other gift disaster was the Christmas before Shanda was born. I was huge with my pregnancy (she was born in January) and Bill had asked me what I wanted for Christmas. I said, "Well, if you really want to know something I'd love — it's one of those alligator leather cosmetic cases with all its matched fittings, pretty little crystal bottles with silver tops." (Pause.) "You can get it at Elizabeth Arden."

Well, he asked me, didn't he?

Y'wanna know what I got? He went tearing out Christmas Eve to got it at the drug store — an Evening In Paris set! Gaudy blue bottles, in a silver box, cologne, bath powder, hand lotion, bubble bath! I don't remember what I said. But I thought, "That ain't it, honey!" And I groaned.

I loved everything about Christmas — still do. Shopping, decorating the tree, wrapping presents. The music, the carols. I even designed all our Christmas cards (still do) and so loved hand-addressing them. One Christmas, my mother said to Daddy and J.C., "Why don't you do a Christmas card for Moya?" What they did was a masterpiece which was, "Written by J. C. Olsen, Illustrated by John Olsen, Inspired by Lillian Olsen," and titled simply, "Noel."

An excerpt:

NOEL

'Twas the night after Christmas and all through the house
There were bills from McCreary's and Abraham Strauss.

The stockings were hung by the chimney with care
But were empty 'before' and 'after' Santa got there.

(Because we always forgot to fill the stockings!)

The children were nestled all snug in their beds
We'd just put lumps on their dear little heads!

It just isn't proper and it don't seem right
Santa staying out with a bag all night!

If and when Santa had anything for us
We had to discuss it with William Morris!

Bill hated Christmas. He was depressed. He drank. He shut out the joy. I was dismayed by his attitude. Part of it, I finally figured out, was his rebelliousness. He hated to be forced into anything, to be obliged to do something because it was expected of him. (Like show up for Christmas or Thanksgiving dinner!) He couldn't stand being expected to buy me a present just because it was my birthday or Christmas. Forget our anniversary! But one time, he came home with a gorgeous mink coat over his arm, just because it was a Tuesday evening in January.

And then, in the summer of 1967 (just to keep me off balance), he told a jeweler in Beverly Hills, "Well, I've been married to this dame 25 years, I'd better buy her a diamond." When we were married he had sent me to Tiffany's to buy my own wedding ring. I bought a little gold band for $11 and had our initials and the wedding date engraved inside. So Bill bought a 10.14-carat pear-shaped pink diamond for me (we lived at 1014 Laurel Lane) and I walked with a limp for weeks, wearing that gorgeous ring.

His gifts always had some kind of little drama attached to them, like what took place a week after he bought me the ring. He called me away from the dining-room table: "Mom, I have something I have to get your opinion about." I looked at him with my mouth open. He hardly ever asked me for my opinion. Dumb struck, I followed him into our little library. There were two jewelers with an enormous display of beautiful jewelry — sapphires, rubies, diamonds, everything: pins, bracelets, rings, it was all there! He said, "I want you to pick out something you like." At that moment, he was called to the telephone.

As I examined their display with astonishment — and dismay — I explained to the two gentlemen, "I very much appreciate my husband doing this for me, but I really don't care for this kind of jewelry." I added, "And I'm sorry that you had to go to all this trouble to bring this very impressive collection for me to see." (Security men had been placed around the perimeter of the property.)

Then one of the jewelers said, "Mrs. Lear, before you say no, I'd like to show you this piece." And he opened this long, flat, box. Inside was the most beautiful diamond necklace I'd ever laid my eyes on — made of graduated, pink pear-shaped diamonds!

I said, "That is the most beautiful thing I ever saw in my life! I'll have that!"

Bill walked in the door at that moment and said, "Did you find anything?" and the man said, "As a matter of fact, she just found this," and he held out the box.

Bill said, "That's beautiful, how much is it?" The man answered, "Seventy five." And Bill said, twinkling, "Oh I guess I can afford $7,500 for this woman!" and made out his check, adding a zero. He loved to see me wearing that necklace.

The funniest part to that story was that Tina had walked into the library and backed out suddenly, blanching, scared to death that her dad was in cahoots with jewel thieves!

Another time, in Paris, we had a date for cocktails with some friends at the Ritz Bar. While walking down Peacock Alley (the very elegantly appointed hallway that houses the display windows of the finest shops of Paris) toward the Ritz Bar, we stopped to look at the jewelry in the windows. I said "Honey, if you ever want to buy me a present and you don't know what to buy, there it is. That string of pearls." They were beautiful creamy pearls. He didn't say a word. I sighed, "Well, someday."

We strolled toward the bar hand-in-hand, loving Paris. We met our friends and ordered drinks. I had started to tell a story when George, the elegant Majordomo of the bar, came over and said, "Madame Lear, this is for you." I looked up at him and, smiling, took the little box of chocolates. "Thank you." I put the box in my lap and continued my story.

Finally Bill said, "Don'tcha want to open the box?" (And I thought, "Oh, he wants one of these chocolates!") I opened that box and simply could not believe my eyes when I saw the very string of pearls I'd admired only a little while earlier! He had magically fished it out of that window, had it wrapped, and presented to me. It seemed impossible to me how, but he had done it. And I loved it. That was just yet one more instance when he picked his own time and place to give me something absolutely beautiful.

In listing these little glimpses of Bill, I have to include the time we were attending a white tie reception for the astronauts at the Hilton Hotel in Beverly Hills. I was standing at the door of our room waiting for him with our tickets in hand, ready to rush because we were late. He was sitting on the edge of the bed watching television, and I wondered impatiently what in the world had captured his attention. I couldn't believe it and you won't either. He was watching

Sesame Street.

I will always feel his presence at the National Business Aircraft Association, and ache to walk beside him once again checking the action up and down the aisles.

Bill was very proud of me — and proud to show me what he was doing. For so many years we would walk through the plant, hand-in-hand, with him explaining to me (in Brownie terms so that I could understand the principles) — the gyro (what is roll, pitch and yaw?); the workings of the autopilot; the Learjet and the leading edge of the wing ("get that body-repair guy out here with his gunk!"); the cruciform tail as opposed to the T-tail; what went wrong with the steam engine.

And in spite of all his impatience, if I got upset with something or somebody during the day and called him, he took time for me. One day during the steam turbine engine program, I called him fuming about something, and he said, "C'mon out to the plant, honey." He closed the door behind him, shut off his calls, put his arms around me and asked, "What's the matter, sweetheart?"

My tears spilled because of his tenderness and his immediate response to my problem. He listened to me. We discussed it quietly for a few minutes. He didn't hurry. He solved it. Then he said, "C'mon out in the plant, I want to show you something."

So much wonderful fascinating stuff he discussed with me — just exactly as though I knew what in the world he was talking about! Matter of fact, one time when there was a lot of turbulence going on, he said, "Honey, if I couldn't come home and tell you about it, I wouldn't give a shit about anything!"

Chapter Twenty-two

By mid-1977, Bill was suffering major back pain and did everything he was told to do to alleviate it, including seeing a chiropractor, exercising, even trying acupuncture. He could no longer lean over drawing boards or even get in and out of his airplane. Finally, he had a myelogram, which indicated a nasty wedge in his spine. Surgery wasn't an option, it was absolutely necessary — and urgent.

Before we left for the hospital in San Francisco (for the first time in his life he didn't want to fly), we went to the plant at Stead where the Lear Fan project was going full-bore. It was a pusher airplane with two turbine engines and a single propeller mounted on the tail. It would be made entirely of graphite.

He had a great, heavy heart when he said goodbye. On our way, I held his hand and said (reaching for anything that would take his mind off what was happening), "I'll bet you don't remember what 'obedience' is? And that day in March of 1978 he said quietly, looking far away:

TO BE OBEDIENT
IS TO DO WHAT YOU'RE TOLD TO DO
RIGHT AWAY. LOVINGLY.

What he recited had been written on a piece of second-grade lined paper in crayon during the '40s and was pasted on our refrigerator! I looked at his wonderful face with so much pain in it, and wondered where in the world he had stored that little bit of wisdom from our kitchen in Santa Monica.

When we arrived at Stead, we went through the entire plant to say goodbye to his gang with sadness and great affection. Finally, it was time to go, and I settled him in the Audi (yeah we bought one) because it not only was a great car as Bill had always maintained, but it had a seat that could be adjusted all the way back. We sped to San Francisco watching in the rear-view mirror for the highway patrol. My mind was in a whirl of apprehension and terror. I reached for his hand and held it all the way. He slept fitfully the entire trip, and woke up just as we were crossing the Bay Bridge.

"Let's go to Trader's," he said. "Oh my darling, are you sure?" "Yeah." So we went. He ordered a beer, but only managed a few sips.

Milt Weilenmann, a trustee, and Sam Auld had waited in Reno for Bill's Will and Trust Agreement to be typed with Bill's final revisions. Both friends were disturbed by the gravity of the situation. After Bill had been admitted and settled in his hospital bed, they arrived troubled and concerned. Bill ran everybody out except Sam and me — asking Sam where he should sign.

SAM: Bill, you really have to read this.
BILL: The hell I do.
SAM: Bill!
BILL: Godammit, is the Lear Fan project protected?
SAM: Yes, but Bill, please let me read it to you.
BILL: (persisting) Is Mommy provided for?
SAM: Yes.
BILL: Are you and Milt and Fran appointed trustees?
SAM: Yes, but Bill —
BILL: All right, give me a pen!

Sam groaned and looked at me for support.

MOYA: Honey, it wouldn't take long for Sam to just hit the highlights.
BILL: I just heard the highlights. Sam, thanks. Don't worry. I'll be OK.

I walked out of the room with Sam to say goodbye, and to thank him and Milt and hug them. They were concerned about the Notary and I said, "What in the world difference does it make? Maxine can notarize it when you get back to Reno. Isn't the job of the Notary just to authorize that it's your signature?" (Boy, did I learn a major lesson in legal procedures in the years that followed.)

After everybody left, I stayed to kiss Bill goodnight and tuck him in. It broke my heart to see the anxiety in his eyes. "It's all right my darling," I said. "Dr. Saunders will be with you and watch you every step of the way." He smiled sleepily, comforted to remember that John Saunders, his good friend and doctor, would be there. "And don't forget Nano's prayers, sweetheart, and all the pals you've got out there who love you."

I opened the door and left. Then I turned around, opened the door again and stuck my head in. "And remember the one who loves you the absolute most." Then I said very quietly: "Goodnight, my darling."

The day of the surgery, my cousin Louise and I went into Intensive Care and the nurse said, "Mrs. Lear, Mr. Lear is saying something and we can't understand him." We leaned over him and listened intently to his mumbled words, trying to encourage him to speak more distinctly. I laughed and cried at the same time when I realized what he was saying:

"Do you know why mice have such tiny balls? (No, why?)

"Because very few of them like to dance!"

It was a crack-up for the nurses who dealt with death and dying all the time — but they'd never had Bill Lear in Intensive Care!

I stayed at the Metropolitan Club, and started the long, heart-breaking final siege of waiting for him to come out of surgery, waiting for the doctor's report and the X-rays. Sitting with him. Feeding him.

Those last days in the hospital he talked to me with such urgency in his voice, "Mom, don't let this project get away from you. I want you to FINISH IT! It's very important. It's the way they're going to build aircraft in the future."

"FINISH IT" became the battle cry! On the walls of his hospital room he had all the blueprints of the Lear Fan 2100 — " a new plane for a new century." He had a WATS line hooked up from his hospital room to his boys (his engineers were always "his boys") who were working on the Lear Fan project at our plant out at Stead.

As Bill was healing from back surgery, we received the shattering results from a blood test which indicated that he had advanced leukemia. The prognosis was devastating: he had only about two months to live. I leaned against the wall of the hospital corridor and my heart pumped, but my brain wouldn't accept what I had just been told. We had both been informed, but neither of us wanted to tell the other.

Then, of course, we clutched at straws of hope, at every tiny shred of improvement. ("The white count went down a little." "He ate a little better today.") I prayed. I tried to put him safely in God's arms and KNOW that Life Is Eternal. But I wanted him in MY arms. In a last-ditch effort to try everything, we went to the City of Hope hospital in Duarte, near Pasadena. But he hated it and wanted to come home. Clay Lacy and Al Paulson, our old friends in aviation, picked us up and flew us home to Reno. It was his last trip in a Learjet.

And the doctors were right. He had almost exactly two months to live. His surgery had been on March 12, 1978. His wonderful, warm, vibrant body, full of mischief and brilliance, left us on May 14, 1978. But his strong spirit is still present in hangars and airplanes all over the world. And it has never left my heart.

When we lost Bill, the girls in the plant sent out the word that the funeral would be held on May 17, 1978. This heart-breaking news ricocheted around the world. It was comforting to me that so many friends in aviation came out to Reno. They wanted to be here, and they wanted to tell their stories about Bill — funny stories, inspiring stories, moving stories.

The church selected for the funeral was a Mormon church because it was the only one that could contain the enormous crowd of family, friends, and employees. But, most importantly, it was chosen because of one of the trustees, Milt Weilenmann, a Mormon who comforted Bill during those last days. Milt had also been extremely helpful with the painful funeral arrangements.

I was lost in myself. I couldn't focus. I had all my children with me, and they were dealing with grief in their own ways. I wanted to hold them all in my arms, but we just kept moving. John was the one who took charge. He got us to the church on time and kept everyone together. I loved him so much for that.

Several of Bill's friends and associates eulogized him, and most of the eulogies were very moving and touching. However, when one of them stated that Bill had become "born again" before he died, and NOW he would walk with God, Tina jumped to her feet, walked swiftly to the podium, and pointed out that her Dad had walked with God his whole life — he didn't need to be "born again" to validate his faith.

After the services, we all went outside to the church parking lot which had filled up with the large number of mourners and overflowed and spilled into the street. Everyone waited for the "fly by" of Learjets in the Missing Man Formation, which the pilots — all friends — were going to dedicate to Bill. Clay Lacy, our very dear old friend, had jumped in and organized the flyby. Clay flew one Learjet, Dee Howard's pilot, Al Ackerman, flew another, and our dear friend Len McIntosh's plane, piloted by Dunham Seaton, was the third.

"Here they come! Here they come!" Everyone saw the three specks in the sky and our hearts pounded for Dad, for Bill, and all that he had brought to that assembled bunch in the parking lot, knowing that there were thousands around the world who would miss him.

When the Learjets roared overhead (I'm sure the FAA turned the other way), all our heads turned to follow them, and we watched the Learjet flown by Clay peel off and fly out of sight, leaving me in that parking lot sobbing, along with everyone else who was shattered by the flyby.

"G'bye, Dad."

2 West Parkway, Wichita, Kansas. Home to the Lears during the Learjet days, 1962–67.

Bill wrote "Don't tell me it can't be done" on this photo of him jumping on the new stressed acrylic windshield material for the Learjet. Watching are Paul Mantz, famed stunt pilot, and Captain Mike Sutton.

October 7, 1963, the maiden flight of Learjet Moxel 23, N801L, at Wichita, Kansas. Pilots were Hank Beaird and Bob Hagen. (Learjet Corp.)

Former vice president, and future president of the United States Richard M. Nixon, visiting Learjet, Wichita, Kansas on May 11, 1966. From l. to r., Allan K. Higdon, Richard M. Nixon, Moya, and Peter de Koszmovszky. (Learjet Corp.)

Learjet Board of Directors, August 4, 1965, from l. to r., David Van Alstyne, Jr., A. Gilmore Flues, Moya, Bill, Fran D. Jabara, Daniel I. Sargent, Harold R. Boyer, Elroy McCaw. Note on chair reads: "Dad – my wonderful one – we never had so much fun – and the future with this gang is exciting! – I Love You – Mom," in Moya's handwriting. (Learjet Corp.)

John Glenn and Bill. (Lear Avia Archives)

Round-the-world record setting flight of 1966 in a production model Learjet 24. Eighteen world records were set during the 50 hour and 20 minute flying time. L. to r., John Zimmerman (observer & record keeper on board), Bill Sipprell– V.P. Learjet, John Lear – pilot, Bill, Hank Beaird – pilot, Moya, Rick King – pilot. (Lear Avia Archives)

Bill panning for gold. This photo was symbolic of his move to Reno, Nevada and the purchase of the decommissioned Stead Air Force Base just north of town. It was here he envisioned a planned industrial and residential community, Leareno, and began work on the steam vehicle project in the late '60s.

The Lear Motors Corp. and Learjet Service Center (circa 1970), located at former Stead Air Force Base, Reno, Nevada.

Moya and Bill and dogs at their home, River House, on the Truckee River near Reno, Nevada, in the early '70s.

"STEAM IS BEAUTIFUL" — the Lear steam powered bus on its inaugural run, February 11, 1972. Moya at the wheel with Bill at her side. The first run occurred at the Stead Airport, headquarters of Lear Motors Corp. in Reno, Nevada.

Senator Barry Goldwater and Bill with prototype steam powered race car, January 1972 at Lear Motors Corp., Reno, Nevada.

Bill worked tirelessly to develop the steam turbine engine. (Photo by Baron Wolman, San Francisco.)

Buckminster Fuller, Moya and Bill at the dedication ceremony of the Pioneer Auditorium in Reno.
(Lear Avia Archives)

Test pilot, Clay Lacy, Bill and Danny Kaye rehearsing for maiden flight of Lear-Liner.
(Photo by Art Alanis)

Gerald Ford at a celebration in
Grand Rapids, Michigan, with Bill
and Moya, 1962. (Lear Avia Archives)

Frank Sinatra with Moya and Bill at the Learjet plant in Wichita, Kansas, 1964.
(Learjet Corporation Photo)

Eddie Rickenbacker photo inscribed by him, "To my good friend - Bill Lear."
(Lear Avia Archives)

"Learjetters Fly-in" — Bill's surprise birthday celebration June, 1975, Lear Avia facility, Stead Airport, Reno, Nevada.

Bill hamming it up in Hawaii. Two of Moya's favorite photos.

Bill at a Lear Motors company picnic at Riverhouse in the mid-'70s. A similar photo appeared in an article in the Smithsonian Institution's magazine. Another favorite photo of Moya's.

Bill and Moya at the Plant, 1977. Plane models are the Learjet (left) and the Lear Allegro.

Bill and Moya in a tender moment at River House, August, 1977

Moya and Bill at River House, near Reno in the mid-'70s, going for their early morning swim.

Flight of Learjets at Bill's funeral service in Reno, Nevada, May 1978, just prior to center plane pulling up creating the moving missing man formation. (Photo by Harry Upson, Reno.)

Bill's last great design, the revolutionary all-composite, pusher airplane – the Lear Fan 2100. Moya courageously promised Bill that she would "Finish It." First flight of N626BL (Bill's birthdate) occurred in Reno, Nevada at Stead Airport, December "32", 1980.

Moya receiving Honorary Doctor of Laws Degree and delivering commencement address, Pepperdine University, California, April 16, 1983.

Moya at River House. A favorite photo taken by a close friend during a winter visit (mid-1980s)

Moya today, at the computer, writing her book.

Neil Armstrong was Moya's seatmate on record-breaking race around the world in a 747 with Clay Lacy at the controls and 100 passengers, 1988. (Lear Avia Archives)

Lady Margaret Thatcher with Moya, Las Vegas, October 1995. (Photo by Cook's Photography, Reno.)

Moya with President George Bush. (White House Photo)

River House, 1995. (Photo by Jack Bacon.)

Moya and children on the occasion of her 75th birthday, March 27, 1990. Clockwise: Moya, David, Tina, Shanda, and John. (Photo by Bob Goodman, Reno.)

BOOK THREE

Moya Olsen Lear

(1978 – Now and Beyond)

Chapter Twenty-three

We all deal with grief in our own, personal way. While some of us rock in a darkened room, some of us can't shut up, can't stop re-telling the story of how it happened — the hours, days, months in the hospital. There are as many variations of grief as there are souls that hurt and grieve as they deal with the hopelessness and despair that accompany the excruciating loss of a loved one.

I loved Bill almost from the moment we met, and, as I write this, we would have recently celebrated our 53rd wedding anniversary.

Some things made his loss more painful than others. Our bed-room with the door shut when I was alone! The bathroom — with his shaving kit in its prominent place. Years ago, a friend had given him some great big, sticky block letters, and Bill stuck his name on that black leather shaving kit:

BILL LEAR

I didn't move that kit for nearly ten years. I don't know how long it took me to empty the closet. I used to wrap my arms around his jackets and sob as I felt him there and heard him laugh, as he told me a story.

The place where I'd feel the most immediate grief was in the car. He used to hold my hand in the car. Now I'd put my arm out and he was not there! I'd pull to the side of Interstate 80 and scream, scream until there was no sound, just my agony.

Having to get up in the morning, needing to get to the plant —

addressing myself to Lear Fan — saved my life, literally and absolutely.

You don't know what your capacity for achievement is until you've been challenged. And if you aren't challenged, you kind of "go along" in life; you don't move around or think very much. I was challenged in a very remarkable way: "Be sure our Lear Fan is finished and flown. FINISH IT!" "Right, honey " (positive that he was hallucinating).

But as he persisted from his hospital bed, I thought, What is he talking about? He knows there's no possible way I can do anything about the Lear Fan. But he did know. He knew I was going to need this work to do. He knew that I would be there, and that my "being there" would help keep the team together.

I certainly didn't understand that at first. In fact, I had made up my mind that I wasn't going to "be there" after I lost him. It wasn't a morbid decision; it was practical.

All our kids were married with families that I didn't really feel a part of because I had always been so close to Bill. For once in my life, it was devastating to have been so totally centered on him. And now I had lost him, and I was out there alone with no place to go.

Although I wasn't really thinking clearly at the time, I tried to consider options. I didn't know how to play golf or tennis. I didn't know how to play bridge. I didn't have a lot of girlfriends — didn't have a network. What I did have was enough sleeping pills left from Bill's illness, to put away an elephant. My big problem was how and where to take them. How do I get out of the house alone? I was planning that.

When you're down on your hands and knees groping around with that kind of a problem, you better have some kind of a faith. You have to believe in something to get you through this kind of agony. I don't know how you do the job without prayer.

A couple of days after the funeral, I went out to the plant. I sat down in Bill's chair — at his desk , in his office — and felt him there. His presence was so immediate in that hangar — at the desk — with me. I heard his voice, "Finish it, Mom. Don't let this project get away from you." He was there.

I sat at his desk for a long time. And the longer I sat there, the stronger I became. It was our Lear Fan now. Resolve and determination helped fill the emptiness within me where an unspeakable sadness had lodged itself.

The combination of hearing his voice and really wanting to try to help, got me through that dark time. And the loyal little gang of engineers cheered when they knew that I was going to see it through. Their faith stunned me. I thought, "What do they see that I don't see? What do they think I know?" So much was made in the news media of this "little housewife who became chairman of the board overnight" — it was overwhelming for me.

When I was patiently trying to explain to a *Time* magazine reporter what happened, he was writing furiously as he said, "Wait, Mrs. Lear, you're blowing me away!" I was also interviewed by *Fortune, Newsweek,* and the *Washington Post,* followed by appearances on shows such as "Good Morning America" and the "Today Show" with Jane Pauley. The best of all was the "60 Minutes" interview with Ed Bradley. (He was my favorite.)

When I give speeches, young women ask me, "How did you train to be chairman of the board?" I didn't train to be chairman of any board, I was just there. I was Mrs. William P. Lear. I just stood there and it fell in on top of me. And don't forget, I came from great stock and strength of character.

My mother, Nano, as she became known to all of us, was a rock to me. I remember once, calling her when she was about 85-years-old and asking, "Hi Mom, how are you, what are you doing?" And she said, "Oh, I'm keeping busy honey, I'm chauffeuring senior citizens to their appointments!" And five years later, she was stopped by the highway patrol, driving from Visalia to Reno, cruising along at 90 mph.

The arresting officer, glancing at her license, leaned in the window and asked incredulously, "Mrs. Olsen, do you realize how fast you were going?" And she said "No sir, I have no idea how fast I was going." And he said, "Would you believe you were driving your age?" She gulped when she realized it was her 90th birthday that very day, and this rare and kind highway patrolman gave her a great birthday present, he didn't give her a ticket.

I started going to the plant right after Bill passed away. One of the trustees predicted, "Well, she'll be chairman of the board, but only a figurehead." I surprised him! I kept a high profile. I was a one-woman public relations juggernaut and didn't even know it.

It was just convenient, I guess, to make me Chairman of the Board. Particularly since they didn't expect me to come to the plant every day. Nobody had been elected. They all wanted me there. They all had confidence in me.

Bill Surbey, who became vice president and chief engineer of the company, said I was their Secret Weapon! I traveled with key personnel and gave speeches for Lear Fan. He used to say, "We wind her up, press start, and away she goes." Bill Surbey or Hank Beaird or Don Madonna or Richard Tracy or Torch Lewis would give the technical details, the performance figures, the real scoop on our Lear Fan, and then I'd tell the story of the spirit, the love affair. We sure kept 'em awake!

I was Chairman of the Board of Lear Avia, the parent company of Lear Fan. They stood up when I came to the table. I didn't ask them to do that, they did it because they loved and respected me. I'd been a member of the board of directors since the days in Grand Rapids with Lear, Inc. This added to their confidence.

I conducted the meetings. I never knew that I could conduct a board meeting and I conducted it my way: "This here meeting will now come to order!" I did it with a gavel and a sense of humor! — but I did it. The board met at least once a month, in my office at Stead. We had an agenda developed by an executive committee and we discussed it. I loved doing it. I'd stay out at the plant till four or five p.m. unless there were tests I wanted to see in the evenings. Engine tests. Stress tests. So much drama went on with this new airplane. It was fascinating. It certainly helped me through my devastating grief.

I didn't run the company, folks. What I did was motivate the work force. I kept them all together, kept their spirits high. I went to all their meetings, including the eight a.m. status meeting. I met with the engineers. I listened to what was going on. I settled some problems. Personality problems — friction between engineers — not engineering problems. I helped expedite some critical policy decisions, and made sure they had what machinery they needed.

Bill had assembled a really fine team of maverick engineers. They came from all over the industry to work on that plane because it was HIS airplane. Because it was a remarkable project, they were fascinated and challenged by it. The whole theory behind the Lear Fan was revolutionary and visionary and it inspired everyone who worked on it.

I built morale and kept it high. One day, I looked out the window of my office in the hangar and thought, "Hey, we don't have a flag!" So I called Glenn Knowles, our maintenance man and said, "Hey

Glenn! I want a flagpole right there." I pointed out the window to the place on the ramp where that flagpole still stands. Then I called Washington, D.C., and got the United States Senate, and said, "Hey, Barry! We need a flag for the tarmac in front of the hangar!" ZAP! The very next day we had a flag that had flown over the Capitol Building. I wanted it for good luck. (I loved you so much, Barry, for that!)

Well. You don't run up the flag like an idiot, you call the Governor and the Mayor and a high-school band and the Marine Honor Guard and notify the work force to bring their families. THEN you run up the flag! That's what we did. Barry Goldwater had sent a letter with the flag. I hadn't had time to read it, so I just opened it at the podium and read it to those assembled:

Dear Moya

Today for just another time in the history of man, the genius of your husband and my friend Bill, will be shown to the American people. As you raise the flag above the hangar, know that with it go the admiration, respect and love of millions of Americans who remember and will always remember the great contributions Bill made to our country and our way of life and of peace.

Love,

Barry Goldwater

I wept because the letter was such a great tribute to Bill from an old friend.

❑   ❑   ❑

At the plant, I just helped out. I co-signed the purchase of our first autoclave. I helped with down-payments on some of the employees' homes. I had teas for the employees' wives — all of 'em, not only those of the engineers and executives. They all came to my house. I had a pot-luck lunch for the secretaries once or twice a month. (And if you ever want to know what's going on in your plant, just get all the secretaries together!) I validated everybody's place in the organization; I let them know they were all important to the project, even the little guys. And they were! I talked to them and had them up to my office. I looked after them like a den mother. They were great.

One day, I was marketing in town and as I bent over a freezer bin a girl patted me on the back and said, "Way to go, Mrs. Lear!" They hailed me on the street and in traffic. "Hi, Mrs. Lear!" It was a remarkable time in the industry and especially for me.

Nobody really expected the Lear Fan to fly. No one had ever built an entire airplane as revolutionary as this one. "C'mon, give us a break! No chance!" But guess what? There were mysterious ingredients: The Bill Lear mystique; my dedication to Bill's dream; plus the commitment and passion of the team and intense excitement in the vortex of pushing the frontier.

I got there at 8 o'clock every day. That was something stable. They knew I was there. I interacted with everybody. If they needed something, I'd get it. I helped solve their problems so they could do their jobs. There was no big problem in Lear Fan with bureaucracy. If there was something they needed, I got it for them or I wanted to know why they didn't have it. One time the fellas came to me with a problem.

CREW: Mrs. Lear, we need a consultant on composites who's with McDonnell-Douglas. We don't need to hire him, we just need to consult with him. D'you know anybody who could make that happen?

MOYA: Well, how about Mr. Mac? (Mr. Mac was the President and C.E.O. of McDonnell-Douglas. He and Bill had been friends for a long, long time. They used to talk on the phone for hours.)

CREW: Yeah, well, gee, if you know Mr. Mac . . .

(So I called McDonnell-Douglas in St. Louis and — bam — I got Mr. Mac right away.)

MR. MAC: Moya! What're you doing? It's wonderful to hear from you. Is there anything I can do to help?

MOYA: As a matter of fact, Mr. Mac, we need a man who's name is John Hart Smith. He's with your El Segundo branch. We just need to consult with him, we don't need him to join our force.

MR. MAC: You got him, but I thought you sold that project to Canadair.

MOYA: No, that was the Learstar 600. This is the Lear Fan, Mr. Mac. All graphite, twin turbine engines buried in the fuselage and a pusher propeller in its tail.

MR. MAC: (mournfully) Oh, I wish I had a propeller in my tail!

The first big challenge we had to face was raising capital. Even with the six million dollars Bill had already committed to the project, it was painfully evident, early on, that we needed a massive infusion of capital. In spite of Bill's success with Learjet, bankers and investors weren't much help.

Many of the business trips I had made with Bill in the '70s involved following leads for sources of potential funding. Bill and I had made lots of good friends trying to raise money for the Learstar 600 before Canadair bought it. We were always trying to raise money. He was such a renegade, and he had a terrible reputation for being difficult, but I saw a different Bill. And I was sure I could help other people see the Bill I knew and loved.

It's difficult to realize just how quickly money is spent to build a new aircraft. The fact that Bill had built and certified the Learjet for ten million dollars was a remarkable feat, an unbelievable feat. You can't do that anymore, ever, in any company. Now, twenty years later, we were facing a similar challenge — and we didn't have Bill.

We searched for partners for the Lear Fan. Sam Auld worked on nearly 50 prospects, among them McDonnell-Douglas. At one point in the negotiations we had a delightful lunch with Mr. Mac and his associates in St. Louis. It was the day they were announcing the American production model of the Harrier to the public. The original Harrier was designed and built by the British.

We had our mockup there, and after lunch, Mr. Mac climbed in and sat in the cockpit until they politely dragged him out to attend the press conference for the Harrier! He said "Moya, that's a great airplane and I'll get back to you."

We were terribly excited because his reaction to our Lear Fan was so enthusiastic and positive. But in a couple of days he called and said reluctantly, "Moya, I hate to tell you this, but my young management has persuaded me that we can't get involved in the Lear Fan because we can't reasonably mix general aviation and the military — and all our business is related to the military."

I said, "Mr. Mac, I certainly understand, and of course we're disappointed, but we've been very much encouraged by your interest, and we'll let you know how we get along." If a fella can give a girl a hug over the telephone, Mr. Mac gave me one. I'll never forget him.

Right after the Fourth of July, Lear Fan, with the help of Sam Auld, our president, made contact with the British government in Belfast, Northern Ireland, through Bob Adickes, a TWA pilot who had known Bill. The British believed Lear Fan would bring a good industry to Northern Ireland and put the people to work. They were impressed by Bill's accomplishments and his record in the industry.

The British already had one Northern Ireland/American manufacturing agreement — the De Lorean sports car — and at that time it still seemed promising. Initially, John De Lorean's agreement with the British helped Lear Fan; but later, as that government became disillusioned with De Lorean's extravagant use of their money, we experienced ever-greater scrutiny. But the British always recognized the distinct spirit and excitement that permeated our company. And the people of Northern Ireland became as devoted to the vision of Lear Fan as we were here in Reno.

One of the conditions for British backing was for us to raise a $30 million "high-risk stake" before they would come in with an additional $50 million. Oppenheimer, the Wall Street investment capital specialist, created a prospectus for a Lear Fan Limited Partnership.

For months in 1979, Richard Tracy, Bill Surbey and Torch Lewis traveled the country presenting the plans and specs in cities such as Chicago, San Francisco, New York, Atlanta, Dallas, Denver. With each presentation to Oppenheimer's brokers and major customers, the excitement and enthusiasm grew. Finally, it seemed clear that the $30 million private offering would be fully subscribed. But just as we seemed to be approaching the end of the extensive negotiations of the Oppenheimer R & D partnership, a big rock rolled into the road.

Well, let me paint the picture for you from my point of view. We were all sitting around an enormous table a half-mile long and about ten-feet-wide (remember this was from my point of view). Present were the British attorneys, my attorney Hal Hertzberg, the Lear Fan attorneys, the tax attorneys — the whole roll call — trying to make sure everything was all set to go. We were entering the final stretch, and only then did the tax attorney look up and want to know, "Who's the general partner?"

Everything got very quiet, because suddenly things got very

tense. No one had thought about this, perhaps because it was assumed. But now, the moment of truth. The problem was: who could qualify? Who had enough net worth to put up a guarantee of $3.4 million? It was a requirement imposed by the Internal Revenue Service.

Hal Hertzberg, my protector and savior, didn't want me to do it and carefully spelled out the risk. As he likes to put it, all of a sudden everybody was looking down a tunnel and there was only one person at the end — ME! I could NOT refuse and watch the whole Lear Fan program go down the drain. It was my personal decision. It did not involve my children in any way.

After I insisted on going forward, Hal figured out a way for me to meet the net worth test by means of a guarantee without actually having to lay out any cash, thereby at least preserving my liquid assets. And I felt, riding the wave at its peak, I would never need to pay that $3.4 million — because the Lear Fan would be an enormous success. The British, the Oppenheimer partners, and I would certainly get all get our money back, put a lot of people to work, and launch a great new airplane!

I signed all 200 of those Oppenheimer partnerships with absolute confidence and put a lot of people to work. The British took a three-month option, then another 30 days, then another, and another. Finally, on Valentine's Day, 1980, they picked up the option, coming in with a package worth about $50 million. And when those pages came in over the telex — ticka-ticka-ticka — with Bill Surbey, Torch Lewis (the head of sales) and I hanging over the machine shouting: "Come on!" There was just no doubt in our minds that we were going to do it.

But the agreement with the British gave us less than a year to put the Lear Fan in flight. Their two stipulations were that the Lear Fan would fly in 1980, and that we would manufacture the plane in Belfast.

Chapter Twenty-four

As far back as 1958, Bill had visualized his Lear Fan. He delivered a paper to the Society of Automotive Engineers in which he presented his views on the "Single Twin" — a twin-turbine, centerline thrust airplane with a single pusher-propeller that he felt would fill a major need for business aviation. However, by 1959, Bill switched gears, having discovered the enormous, mind-blowing power and future of jet engines, which propelled us to Geneva and planted the seeds of the Learjet program. But, it was the basic concept of the "Single Twin" that evolved as the Lear Fan — 30 years later! (And gave me the ride of my life!)

Bill's first love was always aircraft for general aviation, not for the military, or the airlines. He loved the little guys, the private pilots, the business pilots. He wanted his equipment to work for them. Bill treasured, for example, letters that he received from the bush pilots in Alaska thanking him for their T33R 3ABs (the first small transmitters and receivers).

Engineers in aviation are always trying to improve the performance of the airplane. They say that Bill drove his production guys crazy tweaking the design to achieve results, but everyone in the industry does it — it's the name of the game. It's just that Bill had the freedom that comes with owning your own company.

His earliest concepts and drawings for the Lear Fan showed twin engines mounted inside the fuselage with two drive shafts, one gear box and a single propeller. I kept hearing "centerline thrust" in relation to the engine design and asked my pal, Hank Beaird what it meant. And he said, "Moya, with a conventional twin-engine airplane, if you lose an engine on takeoff — and the pilot isn't on top of it instantly — the other engine will take you right down to the scene of the accident! But with our Lear Fan, because of its centerline thrust, that other engine can take you right up to 25,000 feet and you can fly until your fuel gauge registers empty — if you're dumb enough! The single engine performance is remarkable."

The entire wing structure is one piece and the fuselage rests on top of it. The wing is called a "wet wing" because that's where the fuel is stored. After going through major design changes, the first tail design was an inverted V, which was proven unstable; it was, in turn, modified to become a cruciform tail, which had high drag. The wind tunnel led to the final determination to use the Y-tail. All these changes required wind-tunnel time and cost a lot of money. And we didn't have a lot of that either.

But along with the design problems, by far the most controversial aspect of the Lear Fan was the material from which it was made: molded graphite and epoxy. The new buzzword in the '70s and '80s was "composites." A few such parts had been used by the military, but no one had made an entire plane from composites. Bill had made a fascinating trip once to Oshkosh — home of the Experimental Aircraft Association and a great air show — where he was first exposed to the incredible potential of composites, which launched him, thanks to his energy and vision, into a New World — into the Lear Fan program. So, let's do it!

Originally, because of the weight and strength of graphite, it looked as though the ultra-lightweight Lear Fan would carry eight passengers at nearly jet speed, while consuming a quarter of the fuel! That's what excited everyone. But we had a very long way to go. We had three big challenges:

One, a limited supply of time and money to build and fly ANY new airplane, let alone one with such a revolutionary design.

Two, establishing a team to deal with the enormous technological innovations necessary to construct a twin-turbine engine, pusher-propeller aircraft designed without rivets or seams.

Three, a limited body of knowledge about composites. Nobody knew everything composites could — or couldn't — do in 1979.

Those who worked on the Lear Fan also received a virtual "college education" in composites. Before he died, Bill regularly invited composites experts to visit and share their knowledge and opinions of these new materials. As the industry came to realize that Bill Lear was serious, the best in the field were eager to come and see for themselves.

Bill Benjamin, an engineer from Boeing, had written a book about composites tooling. He was one of the first who saw the feasibility of using plastic tooling for high-volume aircraft construction. Boeing had been researching composites for airplane fairings, non-critical parts and interiors, and to reduce weight throughout their aircraft. Bill Benjamin was one of the prophets of these advanced materials at that time — 1976–77 — and my Bill hired him to head up our manufacturing.

They created a Materials-and-Processes Lab where they experimented with shaping the composite materials. They molded and "cured" composite pieces in a small autoclave to study their characteristics. Graphite came in rolls similar to fabric. This was part of the whole exciting process that fascinated me. The graphite was rolled out on a table and cut with Gerber computerized knives in patterns established by engineering. Technicians working on these materials wore gloves and masks. That type of rigid control was necessary for all critical structural areas of the airplane. We also established a Clean Room for this division, and we were very proud of everything we were learning about this new frontier.

Like fabric, composite materials have different textures and can be woven for special applications. For example, for the outer skin of the Lear Fan we worked with the Fiberite Company, which supplied our composite material to develop graphite fabric with interwoven, fine aluminum fibers.

As demonstrated by tests for the FAA, should the aircraft ever be struck by lightning, these aluminum fibers would serve to disperse the charge over a large enough area that the conductivity of the carbon fibers would be able to handle major lightning strikes. That was just one example of a development that came from Lear Fan research.

Composite material was twice as strong as aluminum and about half the weight for a given thickness. The way the fibers in the materials were woven, and how they were oriented in the lay-up sequence, determined their structural characteristics. They could be multilayered with the fibers all running in the same direction for one type of strength or application, or with the fibers running in another direction for a different kind of strength — and that was the magic of this material. Even a few layers could be incredibly strong because of the way the fibers were bonded, so layering could be very thick or very thin. Using this process to bond parts of the airplane that eliminated rivets and created the very smooth surface of the Lear Fan, improving its performance. (Aren't you impressed with how much I learned on this project?)

To emphasize the remarkable function of this graphite material, one day a worker in the hangar was filling a tire with compressed air near the airplane. The gauge was defective, and when he looked away briefly, the tire exploded with a force so strong it went right through the roof of the hangar and landed out on the tarmac.

It was a stroke of incredible good fortune that the worker was only slightly injured. The metal gauge he was using bounced off the fuselage of the Lear Fan, leaving a slight dent. Everyone was very concerned. No one had seen a problem like that before. Ultrasonic tests showed absolutely no damage to the structure. It was still perfect. That accident became one of the selling points of the airplane.

Yes, things were really beginning to roll by the spring of 1978. Already, while Bill had been hospitalized at the City of Hope, Richard Tracy had been in Pasadena finalizing the airplane's configuration at Cal-Tech's ten foot wind tunnel. Richard determined that the most aerodynamically efficient design was the Y-tail and a low wing. So, Bill knew what the airplane would look like before he died.

Meanwhile, the company was growing. We had added more engineers, more people in composites, mold makers, tool makers, and support staff. People would come in to work on a particular part of the plane, and many, instead of going on to another manufacturer, stayed. Everyone wanted to be part of Lear Fan. By then there were maybe 100 people on staff. People so dedicated to the project that, when Bill died and we faced the question of whether to go forward, they made a commitment to stay, regardless of whether it looked like there was going to be any money. Their faith in the project was unshakable.

So, although there were many questions to be answered, there really was no question that the project would continue and that encouraged me. I wouldn't let them down and I couldn't let Bill down. It was a tough time, but not as tough as it seemed because we all felt his presence. There was never any question — he was there with us.

At one point there was a major meeting of the engineers in the corner offices of the hangar where they were thrashing out the pros and cons of composite structure. It was a head-to-head argument over sticking to composites and going for it or staying with the principles of conventional aluminum structure — "We've always done it this way so let's stay in familiar territory." A huge thunderstorm had been rumbling outside during this debate, and suddenly lightning struck that corner of the hangar, which scared the hell out of those engineers! And one of 'em said, "OK, Bill, we hear ya!"

We all learned as we went along. We were dealing with a material that nobody except the military had used for substantial pieces of aircraft structure — and even they were just beginning their first production application, such as the AV8B "Harrier II" wing at McDonnell-Douglas. The manufacturers told us as much as they could, but they were learning, too. Home builders, skiers, and surfers had used wet-lay-up fiberglass for a decade or more, but these applications were not suitable for production of a highly loaded FAA-certified structure.

We were already so far out in unexplored territory with a new design and composite construction that the decision was made to utilize a conventional structural arrangement. Frames and stringers — the interior "bones" — inside the skin of the aircraft. Would it have been better — or worse — if we had taken a bolder approach with these new materials? Some future project may provide that answer.

We built a wooden mockup — a full-scale model of the aircraft fuselage — to work out the cockpit interior as well as the seats, windshield, instrument panel and door. We took the mockup to St. Louis to exhibit it at the enormous annual National Business Aircraft Association.

December 1979 found us, a small bunch of believers with pounding hearts, celebrating Christmas around our mockup and a Christmas tree in the hangar. Two months later we had our funding — and ten months to build and fly an airplane that wasn't completely designed yet!

By the time the first fuselage was mated to the wing, my mind flashed back to 1962 in Wichita when we saw the first fuselage of the

Learjet. It was really incredible. Here in front of us was the Lear Fan we had imagined — a very sexy airplane. Really sexy — just like its mother, the Learjet.

A sales force was also in place and the first sales brochures had been issued. We had started to sell airplanes. (By the time Bill died in 1978, nearly 20 had been sold.) The sales reps had all known Bill, some of them from Learjet. Bill Jr. was one of the best. They were all very well known in aviation and had been involved in it all their lives.

When the news finally got around at the Stead plant in February 1980 that the British were going to fund Lear Fan with $50 million, our pride and joy was indescribable. We were proud that our Lear Fan project warranted this huge investment. It validated our faith and gave us an enormous boost. But it did something more. We met and began to know our friends in Northern Ireland — people with great skills and latent talents — who were waiting for just such a project.

The program escalated quickly. Our friends in Newtownabbey were quicker than we were. They implemented sophisticated, up-to-the-minute financial and manufacturing control systems using a Hewlett/Packard 3000 computer. They installed very advanced autoclaves. They established excellent training programs to teach people to produce carbon fiber parts, and also to implement high-volume composite production.

The exchange of talents between Northern Ireland and Reno was a good mix. The Irish were proud of our Lear Fan, and we were proud of our alliance with the great people of Northern Ireland.

The problem, in retrospect, was gearing up for production before we had an FAA-certificated airplane to produce. We knew we were deep in research and development. What we didn't know was the magnitude of the problems we were going to encounter before we could achieve our certification. We were also up against the FAA, which had never certificated an airplane like ours. And that single factor doubled and tripled the "issue papers."

We went to air shows, first with just the mockup and later with the mockup and the flight-test aircraft. Our son David had created an excellent promotional film on the Lear Fan. We actually had a traveling two-story theater that we could assemble in one day. The first floor was the screening room. On top there was a deck where, as a buyer, you negotiated with the sales force and walked out with your position in the production line! Now, this format has become very elaborate and is commonly used at NBAA, but when we were marketing the Lear Fan we literally stopped the show. With our spanking-new airplane, people wouldn't go anywhere else. They wanted to see the Lear Fan. It was so unique.

The buyer we targeted was not only someone who could afford to buy a Learjet, but who appreciated the efficiencies of this new design as well. The Lear Fan, with two turbine engines, approached the speed of a jet aircraft with significantly lower fuel consumption. That was part of Bill's innovative genius — to realize that by designing a clean, pusher turbo-prop aircraft to operate at jet altitudes (41,000 feet), the fuel consumption would be very low because the plane would be much lighter. Furthermore, composites of graphite and kevlar were impervious to corrosion and had great resiliency against wear.

The buyers were an interesting group of people. Some were fly-by-the-seat-of-the-pants pilots who really loved Bill Lear's airplanes and would buy anything he designed. Others were investors. There was a doctor back East who bought three airplanes and paid the deposit by signing over to us checks written to him by his patients. Other buyers were people like the man who raised all the chickens for Campbell's Chunky Chicken Soup, the people who grew the potatoes for McDonald's and a large leasing company which signed an order for 50 planes. They were very independent, entrepreneurial types. The Rockefellers weren't buying Lear Fans; our buyers were people who'd made it on their own. Mavericks. And I loved meeting all of them, from all walks of life, from everywhere in our nation.

We received firm orders with deposits for 295 Lear Fans. We had also, of course, a huge backlog, a tribute to the sales force, who called themselves "Bounty Hunters." They were seven great, professional aircraft salesmen: Torch Lewis, Bill Lear, Jr., Ed Chandler, Bob Graff, John Tucker, Ernie Phillips and Jack Prior. But no one stood up and said, "Hey, wait a minute! We haven't certificated this airplane yet!"

Chapter Twenty-five

Once the British funding was in place, it was full speed ahead. As I mentioned earlier, the two stipulations made by the British government were that we would manufacture in Belfast and that we would fly by 1980. The last part of this commitment was the key. We would lose our funding if we didn't get that Lear Fan in the air before the last day of 1980 — and that deadline was in just ten months!

In the U.S., the "license plate number" of an aircraft is its "N" number. That means it is registered in the United States by the FAA with that number. The "N" numbers we chose for our first airplane were N626BL. "626" stood for June 26, Bill's birthday, and "BL" for Bill Lear. While we chose N626BL for Lear Fan #1, the prototype aircraft, the second airplane was N327ML — my birthday and initials.

From the starting post on February 14, 1980, when the agreement with the British was signed, the Lear Fan team labored against time. By the closing days of 1980, everyone on the team had worked, literally, around the clock. The tension built daily. Ten months to tool, build and fly a prototype was an incredible challenge, and remember, we were also advancing the state of the art for such a project. We had set the date for first flight for December 29, 1980.

On December 20, 1980, in the middle of all the stress, strain, pushing, worrying, and excitement, we had our big Lear Fan Christmas Party! There were nearly 800 of us at Harrah's Hotel in Reno, including employees, and their families, as well as friends outside the company and their families. Teen-age children even had their own tables. Oh man, we had fun! I had told the party committee that after the door prizes were given out (of course, one of the prizes was a door!), I wanted to provide the finale.

When I walked up to the podium and looked out over that wonderful gang of friends and employees, I said, "I'd like to sing a song for you that I dedicate to your real boss, who couldn't make it tonight because he's out there in the hangar, working on his airplane!" And I sang to the music of "If They Could See Me Now":

IF BILL COULD SEE ME NOW JUST THINK HOW PROUD
   HE'D BE
THE WAY WE TURNED HIS DREAM INTO REALITY
I WISH THAT HE WERE HERE TO JOIN IN THE FUN
AND LAUGH AT THOSE WHO SAID IT COULDN'T BE DONE

ALL I CAN SAY IS WOW! WHAT A TERRIFIC HIGH
AS ALL TOGETHER NOW WE'LL WATCH OUR LEAR FAN FLY!
WHAT A FEELING HOLY COW — HE'D NEVER BELIEVE IT
IF MY BILL COULD SEE ME NOW.

IF HE COULD SEE ME NOW — MY DARLING DEAREST DEAR
AND VIEW THE FINAL CHAPTER OF HIS GREAT CAREER.
HE'D UNDERSTAND WHAT ALL THE SHOUTIN'S ABOUT
IF HE COULD SEE THE WAY HIS LEAR FAN TURNED OUT!

ALL I CAN SAY IS WOW! TO THINK IT'S REALLY REAL—
THE STORY OF JUST HOW WE SIGNED THAT FINAL DEAL!
   (with the British!)
WHAT A FEELING — HOLY COW — HE'D NEVER BELIEVE IT!
IF HE COULD SEE ME — IF DAD COULD SEE ME —
IF BILL COULD SEE ME NOW!

During that countdown time, with the days slipping by, both shifts of workers refused to go home. They slept in sleeping bags on the hangar floor and ate sack lunches their wives brought in. (I wonder what the union would say about that?) To surprise me on Christmas Eve, they even painted the Lear Fan overnight in the hangar after the mechanics and engineers left. It was painted white since Bill always felt airplanes should be white, so they wouldn't get so hot. Their effort was a Christmas present for me, and I have never in my life received such a magnificent gift.

By Christmas Eve, it began to look impossible that we'd meet the deadline, and, of course, the men insisted on working through the night. No one wanted to go home. We brought their families into the hangar and set out a potluck Christmas dinner on improvised tables put together with lengths of plywood set on saw-horses. The gang had placed a Christmas wreath on the beautiful nose of our Lear Fan for me!

We gathered around the Lear Fan, the families and their children, holding lighted candles (Dear FAA: We blew 'em right out!) and dipping our heads in prayer for the American Embassy hostages in Iran. Then we sang Christmas carols as the engineers and mechanics continued to work while singing along with us! I was choked with tears.

The next day, we had the first ground test of the complete engine-propeller installation, but it wouldn't turn over. They hot-wired the starter and got a run, then they took her back into the hangar to work on squawks and continue final assembly details. The next day she was back out for more tests. The work continued feverishly until, time had finally run out. The day had come! It was on top of us, with everyone feeling they'd left something out!

It was December 29, 1980, the scheduled day for FIRST FLIGHT! All of us felt Bill's presence. It was such a great day out at the old Stead Air Force Base in Reno. The Air Force personnel who had been out there during World War II never would've dreamed that someday a bunch of fellas who spoke fluent "airplane" would literally give birth to a brand spanking new aircraft.

The airfield was haunted by every spirit who loved aviation. And the people of Reno turned out as if the event were a combination of the Nevada State Fair, Reno Rodeo and Reno Air Races! The spectators included Governor Bob List, Mayor Bruno Menicucci, all the news media, newspapers, aviation press, TV crews, half the city of Reno, the Lear Fan families, and interested friends from all over the country. I mean, the world was there.

The tension was crackling in the air like electricity. We rolled the Lear Fan out of the hangar and a huge cheer went up. Hank Beaird, who had been our test pilot for Learjet, was our illustrious test pilot for Lear Fan, and we were very proud that he had joined us again.

As we all held our breath, Hank started the engines. The left engine refused to start! Our hearts stopped! The engine builders from

Pratt & Whitney jumped in, but by the time they fixed it, it was too late to fly. After a long, painful story, it was a no go. Everyone went home except the faithful gang of mechanics, engineers, and pilots. They went back to work.

The next day, December 30, everyone came back: the Governor, the Mayor, half the city of Reno, and the press (they didn't give up)! Then, a starter generator malfunctioned; a fuel leak surfaced in the wing; and the ignition system was giving everybody fits.

At the microphone, on a platform that had been erected for the occasion, was our talented, faithful friend, aviation writer Torch Lewis. He helped by filling in the painful time of waiting with a steady stream of entertaining aviation history. We had a generous supply of sandwiches, coffee, and sweet rolls for the spectators.

But — agony — December 30 rolled by, inch by inch, and we couldn't fly that day, either. Now we were getting very nervous. Everyone was worn out, but still terribly excited. Fate had turned the ratchet of suspense up another four or five notches.

When December 31st arrived, we knew we'd have to fly or the British Government would pull the rug out from under the whole project! Everyone came out to Stead AGAIN! The day was packed, dealing with endless details from the Squawk Sheet, speed tests and final weigh-ins before the FAA gave its approval to fly. We compressed several hours of high-energy, high-temperature brake tests into a few minutes. Finally, Hank started up the engines. Dennis Newton, a part of the Lear Fan team from the early days, was flying co-pilot. Clay Lacy was circling the field in his Learjet, waiting for Hank to take off, at which time he would fly "chase." (All first flights of experimental airplanes have a "chase" plane to observe the performance of the prototype.)

Hank executed some low-speed taxis (what an exquisite thrill it was to watch our Lear Fan take its first steps!). He did two high speed taxi-and-brake tests, then radioed to Clay that he would take off at the end of that final taxi — but suddenly, smoke puffed from beneath the plane! I whispered, "Oh dear God, now what?" The Lear Fan came to a screeching, smoking halt at the end of the runway.

Because we had repeated the high-speed brake tests too quickly, the brake linings caught fire and ignited the tires causing a "melt-down." The team jumped in like an Indianapolis Speedway team: changed the brakes, changed the tires, and once again, they prepared to take off to the music of lusty cheers from the diehards! The pilot started to climb into the Lear Fan again, and I yelled, "Hey Hank! All you have to do is take off, fly around the pea patch and land, and we'll have honored our commitment to the British!"

Hank grinned, gave me the "thumbs up" signal and closed the door. Due to intense pressure and the fading daylight, as Hank and Dennis did their cockpit check, they accidentally flicked the switch that activated the FIRE EXTINGUISHER. The engines were covered with foam, and it was all over at sundown on December 31, 1980.

They towed the Lear Fan back to the hangar, and everyone went home except the determined team of heroes. Well, we didn't go directly home. A bunch of us celebrated New Year's Eve and said some more prayers for a successful flight. It wasn't a late night. When I got home, I pulled the covers over my head and thought: I'm too old for this. I've got eleven grandchildren and I can't even remember their names!

New Year's Day 1981 was bright and clear. Another unbelievable windless 70-degree day. Very early, the runway was again lined with hundreds of workers and people who had come to cheer us on. I got out to the field and found the team in full force, with a "drop dead" agenda. The crew had been up all night and had worked that agenda down to the last possible hitch. I found out I was probably the only one who had gone to bed that night! John, our son, had been with the engineering team all night, and filled me in with late bulletins. David and Bill Jr. recorded our excitement with their video cameras. Barry Goldwater sent Hank a telegram:

BILL WILL BE FLYING YOUR WING.

Hank waved at me as he climbed into the plane. And at 11:56 a.m., we flew our beautiful, spectacular Lear Fan. Hank took off, and at mid-flight (by mutual agreement) they switched seats so Dennis could make the first landing. There had been concern that when the Lear Fan rotated, the tail would hit the ground; instead the beautiful craft simply ascended for a flawless 17-minute flight.

Every single employee, from the men who mopped up, to the girls who managed the switchboard, to the president of the company, cheered his head off as if the Lear Fan were the personal property of each of them, and, in a sense, it was. Ours was truly a love affair with an airplane, and none of us who was present at that moment in aviation history will ever forget it.

Because it was New Year's Day, we had ordered 65 cases of champagne. Shortly after the spectacular landing of the Lear Fan, the corks started to pop, and tired but happy employees, including the pilots and engineers celebrated. Hank remarked to me: "You said the Boss was flying my wing. He was standing right behind me. I heard him."

We had another reason to celebrate. Derek McVitty, of the Department of Commerce of Northern Ireland, endeared the British Government to us forever when he took the microphone and said:

"Today is officially December 32nd, 1980."

□   □   □

Although we had successfully flown the Lear Fan, there remained a race of time against money. We still had to achieve FAA certification before we could deliver airplanes to customers. While the Lear Fan team continued to meet the daily technological challenges we had to solve, there were other challenges, too, not only for the plane, but for me. And it was during the backstretch that the dream unraveled. But no one can take away the vivid memories of our own special Camelot out at Stead.

Chapter Twenty-six

During Bill's final illness, while he was confined to River House, our business and trial lawyer, "Spike" Wilson, came to me and said, "Moya do you know that Bill's giving away half of his company to his gang?" And I answered, "If he's doing that, he's trying to keep them together, so he's giving them a piece of the action."

When our estate and tax lawyer drafted the trust agreement, Bill wasn't worrying about what his kids would think. In his mind there was no reason to notify everyone about what he was doing — including me. He wanted to do it. The trustees had nothing at all to do with that. It was his decision. But the revisions to the actual trust agreement protecting the Lear Fan project were drafted at the last minute. This act fueled the suspicion of our children that the men Bill had named as trustees (very old and good friends) had gotten together and influenced Bill while he was sick and sedated for pain. They had nothing to do with it. Bill spelled out what he wanted and the attorneys drafted it.

I wanted to fulfill Bill's last dream of building and flying the Lear Fan, and whatever it took, we were going to do it. When I said, "I stand four-square with these trustees to get this job done, because that's what Dad wanted us to do," it was interpreted by the children as meaning I was in cahoots with the trustees. It looked to them as though I had been manipulated.

Also questioned was Bill's bequest to my sister, Joy — had she manipulated that? When Bill and I had discussed his will, he said, "Joy's going to need some help because she's going to have to send those five kids to college." That was so dear! I put my arms around him and said, "I love you for that!"

There were mathematical errors in the will and questions about the last-minute trust agreement, as well as questions about whether Bill had really known what he was signing and about how the trust agreement was notarized. All those questions were answered, and the answers weren't evasive as has been suggested. They might have been incomplete, but the whole business was horrendously complicated.

At the time of Bill's death, both our daughters lived in Europe. That distance only increased the dissension and suspicion. John had been disinherited many years earlier and was so incensed he didn't care. (I believe Bill would have changed that, too, but he died before he could.) That left only David, who chose not to contest. Eventually, the Lear Fan project was separated from the real estate and personal property; however, the resulting lawsuits locked up the estate for thirteen years and cost almost one million dollars in attorney's fees.

The real cost of the trust agreement and will disputes was not financial, but emotional, and fragmented our family. Unfortunately, the content of the documents was twisted and misused as black-and-white, dollars-and-cents evidence to "prove" that Bill had loved his airplanes more than his family. It took every ounce of patience, fairness, and objectivity I had to get me through this heartbreak.

I went to both my daughters' homes in Europe, determined to pull my family together. I listened to their positions, the reasons for their mistrust and anger. I saw the tragedy through their eyes, and we finally brought it to a conclusion. Once I waded through their emotions, and they finally understood that I was on their side, but that the Lear Fan project was uppermost in their Dad's mind in those last agonizing days, and that he had truly provided for the project in his will, we began to heal. I certainly never dreamed that my position on Lear Fan would alienate my daughters to the extent that it did.

But when you get a mix of a major will, trustees, a battery of attorneys and suspicious, disillusioned children, you've got trouble. This was part of Bill's legacy to us all: the challenge of forgiving and forgetting — of healing — and loving each other through it all.

□   □   □

After first flight, we stepped ahead of ourselves believing everything would go forward. Almost overnight we became a big company. We had nearly 500 people working for us at the Reno plant alone, and we had set up the operation in Northern Ireland with nearly 500 employees there as well. Training, tooling, engineering, and manufacturing were all gaining momentum for a 1982 production startup. We had a big payroll — and the Lear Fan had not yet been certificated. Everybody wanted to be part of this exciting project, which was nice, but that was part of the problem. We continued to take orders and deposits for airplanes, but spent it just as fast as it came in for working capital.

We searched constantly for money. Sam Auld kept meticulous records of 50 different potential funders. We got to a point after first flight where money was going out faster than it was coming in; things got so tense that we actually shut the company down and everybody took a voluntary week off without pay. These true believers were a work force who loved Lear Fan.

More than a wonderful company, Lear Fan was a "family" whose degree of closeness is scarcely imaginable. We had the sort of bond you'll never have again in your life, but it's awesome to experience once. There was such incredible camarderie — people were willing to work till midnight, no problem! You could close your eyes and feel the air crackle with an incredible intensity. And it was the same in Northern Ireland, with both people who purchased the aircraft as well as the aviation media. It was a magic time.

But magic doesn't replace good management and realistic planning. We couldn't control the economic difficulties that swamped the entire aviation industry in the early '80s. And we didn't have Bill's superhuman genius for steamrolling obstacles and bulldozing a project he believed in into a rousing success. What we needed was Bill. The man in total control of the project (the president, CEO, and chairman of the board) was light-years behind Bill in every way, especially with respect to his spirit, his philosophy, and his brass-tacks intelligence.

Three Lear Fans were flown, but right in the middle of the certification process, while we were running out of time and money, we were shot down in the pattern by a poorly designed gear-box. This was too critical a problem to be piled on top of all the other problems facing us at that time. We would not be able to continue. It was heartbreaking for me to watch the Lear Fan project come to a screeching halt and not be able to do a thing about it.

We had launched a great new airplane and put a lot of people to work. What we couldn't do was get our money back when the project failed. Along with all the debris left in the wake of the Lear Fan bankruptcy was my personal note guaranteeing the $3.4 million. Again, my attorney Hal Hertzberg came to my rescue and was able to negotiate this amount down to $1 million, which he arranged for me to pay over a period of several years.

No matter what, we'll always remember, with great affection, Lear Fan's beginning years. We also thank the British, the Northern Irish, all the Oppenheimer Partners who put up their money, and the Lear Fan gang in Reno and Belfast who have provided memories we all share and will never forget.

But even in the death of a dream can lie a kernel of good. Bill's belief in a composite aircraft has been proven. We did the homework for the industry in composites. Around 1983–84, other companies became adventurous enough to follow what Bill started in the '70s.

The late '80s saw the incorporation of composite structures in almost every aviation manufacturer's designs, thanks to lessons learned from our ground-breaking and back-breaking work on the Lear Fan. When they manufactured their own composite airplanes, they did so with many of Lear Fan's "pioneers" as well as the technology and innovations we developed. Aircraft companies are now using composites to a much greater degree throughout general aviation.

The Lear Fan will never fly again. But I kept my promise to Bill. We built and flew three Lear Fans. And it was a total labor of love — in many hearts — not only mine.

It was hard to shift gears after it all came down, hard to find my way — "Now what would I do?" Well, don't forget, I not only have our four children, I have twelve grandchildren and one great granddaughter. And along with having kept track of them, I've traveled around the country giving my talks, sharing my life with hundreds of women who want to hear what happened and how I dealt with it. I've been busy in my community too and help where I can. I've kept track of my friends and other relations. I've read a lot and love going to the theater, of course.

□   □   □

During the Lear Fan days, I received six honorary degrees: Doctor of Humane Letters from National University, San Diego; Doctor of Laws from Northrop University, Los Angeles; Doctor of Humane Letters from the University of Nevada, Reno; Doctor of Aviation Management from Embry-Riddle, Daytona Beach; Doctor of Laws from Pepperdine University, Los Angeles; and Doctor of Laws from

Clemson University in South Carolina.

I loved the whole experience of giving the commencement address at each of those fine universities and meeting all the young people. It also made me remember being 17, graduating from Valley Stream High School and wondering what life had in store for me!

WOW! What life had in store for me was — everything! A man I loved who loved me back. Wonderful children and grandchildren. A life full to the brim and overflowing. And of course, heartbreak and tragedy and loss.

I read about these girls declaring war on their men. And I'm so grateful that I never let that particular emotion get in my way. I did the laundry, made the beds, went to the market and put dinner on the table. (I also put the cap back on his tube of toothpaste — I didn't know you weren't supposed to do that!) I loved my babies and my husband to death.

Later on, I usually had someone help me with the housekeeping because, along with my days getting busier, I traveled a lot with Bill. In recent years, I have found that the children needed me more than I realized; so here I am, at end of the 20th Century, dealing with "damage control!

I'd like to share a little advice with the girls who are "out there" struggling with problems in the work-place. In the world of aviation, when a test pilot wrings out a new aircraft, he tries to achieve more speed — more range — better performance at altitude. It's called "expanding the envelope." And that's what these girls are trying to do as they work to achieve their potential. And I say right! — go for it! — but don't forget to be mothers and lovers in the process! I think it was television host Jane Pauley who said, "Hey, we can have it all, girls — just not all at the same time!"

It's hard to release this book without one more story, and I can hear, "hey, you forgot what happened when and that story about Bill" — but, here's the book. It's not all there, by a long shot, but I had to let go at some point.

Before I do close, I want to say a few words about each of my children. I am overwhelmed with love for my children and fiercely proud of the way they've grown up, especially since their growing-up years were not only turbulent, but at times lonely. Bill and I were absorbed in Learjet and the many projects that came before and after, like the steam engine program and the Learstar 600. In any case, one of the strong family traits that helped all the children cope when life in the fast lane got too turbulent was a healthy sense of humor.

John is a superb pilot. One of the best. The only professional pilot in the family. His favorite place to be, besides home, is in the cockpit. When he flys, his movements are smooth, almost poetic. Several years ago I sat on the jump seat behind him on a trip from Cairo to Tel Aviv and was stunned with pride at his command of that cockpit! He is also a gifted artist and writer. But probably because of his extreme sensitivity and deep tenderness (which very few people are aware of) he had the hardest time growing up in the shadow of his father. Along with everything else, he is an acknowledged authority on UFOs. John, married to his second wife, has four beautiful daughters. Moya II (who has just presented me with my first great-grandchild, Alexandra Tsatsos) and Jill, her sister, from his first wife Marcelle; and Alli and Jacqui from his current wife, Marilee.

Shanda has emerged into a talented entertainer with all her grandfather Olsen's genes alive and well in her. She is an authority on breast-feeding, and when she lived in Europe was the founder and president of the Italian La Leche League. She is a loving, caring human being who has overcome personal tragedy, and that has helped mold her into the wonderful person she is today. She was married to Italian businessman Gian Carlo Bertelli and has three children: Vanessa, Mara and Valente.

David is the founder and president of his own company, Lear Vision, which manufactures and sells innovative eye-wear. He is the gentlest of all the children; the one everyone in the family goes to for comfort and encouragement. He is married to his third wife, Jan, and has two daughters: Celeste, from his first wife, Merlene; and Erin, from his second wife, Sally.

While all the children are gifted with musical and artistic talent, Tina is full of poetry and music, lyrical movement and art. She also has, in her complicated genes, business ability and a sense of order. She is now happily married to Halim Dunsky. She was married for 20 years to Harry Jackson, the renowned sculptor, and has three children: Jesse, Luke and Chloe.

Mary Louise is the daughter of Bill and his first wife, Ethel, who has one daughter. I wrote about her earlier in the book. William P. Lear, Jr. is the son of Madeline. He was about eleven when I first met Bill and I defended him, like I defended John when they had trouble with their Dad. I drove up from Piqua, Ohio to Howe, Michigan where he was going to a military academy, thereby endearing myself forever in a little boy's heart because: A, I got him out of where he didn't want to be, and B, I let him drive in the left seat down the country roads on the way home! He served five years in the Air Force. He's married to his fifth wife, Brenda, and has five children; two from his second marriage and three from his third. He is semi-retired. Both Bill and Brenda fly their own airplane, and they live in San Antonio, Texas.

Patti has been married three times and has three children. She ran twice for Congress, then in her early sixties she decided to get a law degree and was graduated from Pepperdine University. She passed her California Bar and her Nevada Bar and lives and practices in Reno.

Oh, I've dealt with heartache, agony and tragedy — a lot of it! Bill left a lot of emotional wreckage behind when he left this world, but he also left a brilliant record of immense accomplishments against all odds which set many benchmarks for the aviation industry!

My friends have often asked me why I don't date or have a "significant other," and the reason is very simple: I gave everything I had to Bill. And when he left, he took it all with him! I will love him forever, and intend to find him someday (I truly think he'll be waiting for me). And y' know what he's gonna say when he puts his arms around me? "What took you so long!!" Then, we'll continue in the next world where we left off in this one and — on into eternity.

Afterword

Lear Fan N626BL is refurbished and displayed in the Museum of flight in Seattle as a part of aviation history.

Lear Fan N327ML has been purchased by the Experimental Aircraft Association in Oshkosh.

The FAA has the third Lear Fan at its headquarters in Atlantic City.

A Learjet hangs in the Smithsonian Institution in Washington. Bill was awarded over 150 patents in his lifetime. One of the first was the design for a device which made the automobile radio possible, dated January 16, 1934. For an excellent detail of Bill's career I refer you to Richard Rashke's book, "Stormy Genius" (Houghton Mifflin Company, 1985).

Bill's ashes were scattered over the Pacific from our Cessna, which carried our children, with John piloting, and myself. Hank Beaird, who was also on board, said, "They'll have to suspend shipping in San Francisco Bay for 24 hours because the water will be so turbulent."

Appendix A

A typical Olsen and Johnson route in the early '30s:

Sept. 27 . . . . RKO Theatre, Cincinnati

Oct. 4 . . . . Palace Theatre, Chicago

Oct .11 . . . . RKO Temple Theatre, Detroit

Oct. 19 . . . . RKO Theatre, Youngstown, Ohio

Nov. 1 . . . . Shea's Theatre, Buffalo, New York

Nov. 8 . . . . Shea's Theatre, Toronto, Canada

Nov. 16 . . . . RKO Theatre, Grand Rapids, Michigan

Nov. 23 . . . . South Bend, Indiana and Rockford, Illinois

Nov. 30 . . . . Davenport and Cedar Rapids, Iowa

Dec. 7 . . . . RKO Orpheum, Des Moines, Iowa

Dec. 14 . . . . RKO Orpheum, Madison, Wisconsin

Dec. 20 . . . . Riverside Theater, Milwaukee, Wisconsin

Dec. 27 . . . . Fordham, New York

Jan. 3 . . . . Madison and Chester Theatres, New York City

Jan. 10 . . . . Keith's Theatre, Syracuse, New York

Jan. 17 . . . . Keith's Theatre, Rochester, New York

Jan. 24 . . . . 105th St. Theatre, Cleveland, Ohio

Jan. 31 . . . . RKO Theatre, Akron, Ohio

Feb. 7 . . . . RKO Theatre, Toledo, Ohio

Feb. 14 . . . . State-Lake, Chicago, Illinois

Feb. 21 . . . . Hennepin-Orpheum, Minneapolis

Feb. 28 . . . . RKO Palace Theatre, St. Paul, Minnesota

Mar. 9 . . . . Capitol Theatre, Winnipeg, Canada

Mar. 21 . . . . RKO Orpheum, Vancouver, British Columbia

Mar. 28 . . . . RKO Orpheum, Seattle, Washington

Apr. 4 . . . . RKO Orpheum, Portland, Oregon

Apr. 15 . . . . Golden Gate, San Francisco, California

Apr. 22 . . . . Orpheum Theatre, Oakland, California

Apr. 30 . . . . Hillstreet, Los Angeles, California

May 8 . . . . RKO Theatre, Long Beach, California

May 20 . . . . RKO Theatre, Salt Lake City, Utah

May 29 . . . . Orpheum Theatre, Omaha, Nebraska

June 6 . . . . Mainstreet Theatre, Kansas City, Missouri

June 13 . . . . St. Louis Theatre, St. Louis, Missouri

June 26 . . . . RKO Theatre, Oklahoma City, Oklahoma

July 3 . . . . RKO Theatre, Fort Worth, Texas

July 10 . . . . RKO Theatre, Dallas, Texas

July 17 . . . . RKO Theatre, San Antonio, Texas

July 24 . . . . RKO Theatre, Houston, Texas

July 31 . . . . Orpheum, New Orleans, Louisiana

Aug. 8 . . . . Birmingham, Alabama

Aug. 15 . . . . Atlanta, Georgia

Aug. 22 . . . . First half week open

Last-half week, Charlotte, North Carolina

The twelve page book I made for Bill as a Valentine in 1944:

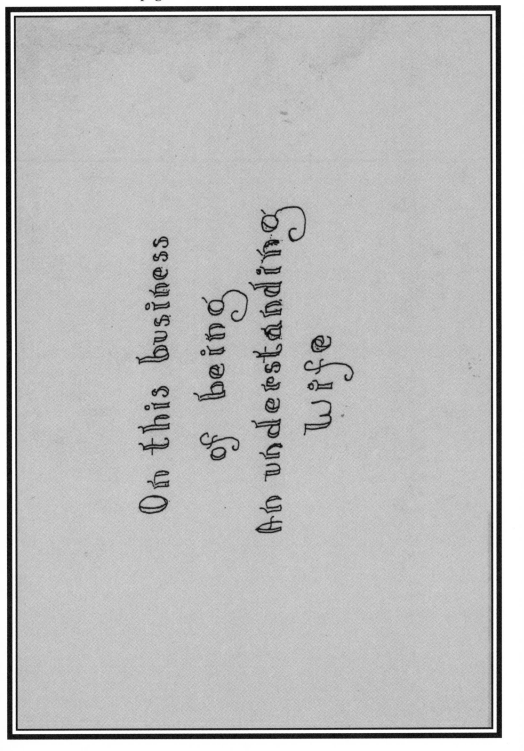

On this business

of being

An understanding

Wife

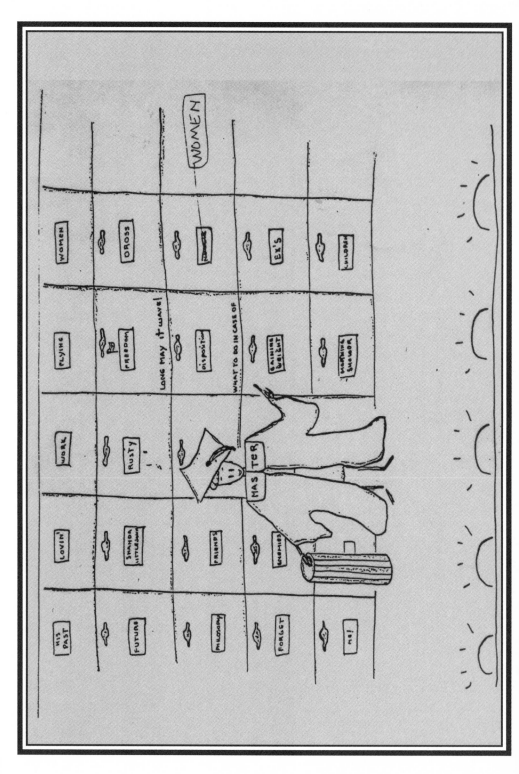

To My Girls !!

this will be our last meeting before I send you out into that ecstatic grim tumultuous exquisite turbulent delightful world of Marriage.

I am assuming that you have Married the Man you Love. this, then, is the accepted premise upon which I base my teaching.

there is a course for Beginners covering the Basic Principles of

How to Get the Man you Love – which meets in Rm. 307 – Mon, Wed, Fri, – at 9 a.m.

I will give you a few fundamental things to remember. You will find these axioms precious to cling to should you fall by the wayside – should your steps falter – should your hearts become faint...

A: Develop and cherish your Sense of Humour. Cling steadfastly to it in time of need. Let it establish the tone and color of your relationship. Let it form the foundation of a healthy normal adventure.

B: Establish and put into operation a Bureau of Weights and Measures. Let the workmanship be simple, logical, and understandable. The mechanics should be perfectly smooth and decisions reached with the least possible friction ...

If he loves you, he will help you work things out. If he doesn't love you, you should visit the nearest psychiatrist and have him explain why you're living with the guy! (get away from me, boys, y'bother me!"

C: A very important warning!:
DON'T BUILD FENCES!!
HAPPINESS
FUN
HOME SWEET HOME
THESE ARE CHAINS
IF HE HAD THE WINGS OF AN ANGEL
THE GREAT OUTSIDE WORLD

D: Watch your triangle behavior !!
this point is tremendously important
~ extremely difficult ~ requires vast-
intelligence ~ great tact, patience ~
in short, it takes a Straight-A student
to be rewarded with a Good Behavior
rating !!
First of all, you can't with. If
you're noisy about it, you're you-know-whichy-
If you're quiet about it, you're hurt ~
and he shouts 'he yi's wat he yi's'!!

If, in your naïveté, you figure maybe you could make friends with the enemy ~ you're soooo wrong!! You will be accused of hypocrisy ~ or of playing some sinister game of Cat and Mouse ~ and for some reason or another, you're always the Cat ~ she's never the Cat ~ she always manages to be the little Mousey~Wousey!

STAGE DOOR

Ziegfeld Follies

Remember ~ love and I had the wit to win, we drew a circle that took him in'!" Well, here's the only circle he knows ~ And you may as well know it now !!

I see heads! I see your anxious faces ~ what do we do now? ~ you say! ~ how do we handle this, you say! ~ I say ~ and this comes from your sage advisor ~ TAKE UP STAMP COLLECTING ~ all men are the same and they're all no good !!

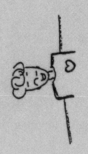

except mine ~ he's different ...

Appendix C

One of Daddy's letters, which became a family treasure, was written to my baby brother, Clem, when he was 2-days old. It was post-marked from Portland, Oregon, where Olsen and Johnson were playing at the time:

May 5, 1917
Dear "Son":

Well, I'm glad to hear that you have arrived on this "war-stricken" universe safe, sound and apparently healthy — 'twas a tedious trip no doubt, for you, and your fortunate ignorance of the trouble you were emerging in probably prevented you from turning back and hibernating yourself until some opportune moment when this world would be rid of Germans, high-cost of living and handed-down clothes.

I mention hand-me-down clothes as I feel that you are destined to become the unwilling but fated recipient of those that "Are too small for Moya" or "J.C. outgrew those so quick" — thus becoming the "Melting Pot" for "odds and ends" that can be "made over" — in other words a martyr to "Efficiency" or "Making Everything Count" — But such is fate and I know you won't say anything about it just now.

You are surrounded, or I might say bordered on one side by your older brother J.C. and on the other side by your still older sister Moya — neither having a better chance to "succeed" than you. You are all three ready to start and your Mother and Daddy are playing no favorites so now it is almost up to you.

We (Mother being 3/4 of the We) will be constantly instilling in your little lives to be truthful, upright, alive to your responsibilities, courteous to all, industrious. We will do our utmost to give you a good education. We will try to clothe you to our and your satisfaction.

We shall ALWAYS advise — and NEVER compel where we think that you should be entitled to your own opinion. Of course, My Son, always bear in mind that your mother and father have lived long before you — we have seen life from your own age up-up-up through the years that you have yet to see. So THAT is why we might appear unreasonable at times, but I know you'll LEARN sometime of the reasonableness of our criticism, and that is why we'll no doubt overlook your objections and remain firm in some of our views.

You are now two days old. Nothing but a mass of fingers, chubby arms, toes, cheeks and eyes. Nothing but a wonderful little bit of humanity that has been placed in our hands to mold into a useful life — a credit to society and worthy of your father and Mother.

Your father, my boy, will probably be the object of your scorn or admiration someday and it is he who is now penning this little effort. It is HE who looks forward to your future and it is HE who is attempting to make HIS future, in order that it may in some way assist you to achieve a future to be proud of.

I can't aspire for you. I can't work for you and I can't think for you. But I can provide you with means to teach you to think. I CAN show you why you SHOULD aspire—and THAT I intend to do.

Your Daddy at present is at the threshold of a varied career and possibly a varied future. In you, your brother, your sister and mother lies the incentive for all of his hopes of success. His ultimate success means your happiness and contentment and THAT automatically means HIS happiness. So you see that inadvertently, we all mean something to each other's happiness.

YOUR Mother, Boy Dear, is the finest of the finest. She's all I could want in a wife and I know that as a mother she'll stand alone. Absorb her goodness, listen to her advice and hearken to her wants, for they all are for your own good and I know she loves you and has given her life to bring you forth and teach you. And I shall always expect — yes I shall DEMAND that you obey your mother at all times — she will be your guiding hand — she will be your "refuge" as a child and at all times your counselor. Follow her teachings and I know you will fare well. And I will have ample reason to be proud of you.

Some day, you'll probably look back from the age of 25 or 30 and say "Why didn't I take advantage of my youth?" "Why didn't I listen to dad and mother" and OH, if I could only live it all over again." Don't! Don't say that you won't, for I know you will. I have done it, my father did it, his father did it — yes it will always be done so long as there IS life. I can only warn you and attempt to encourage "Right" at the very beginning.

Cultivate punctuality, saving and truthfulness, absorb all the education possible, refrain from the "Eternal Triangle" of Youth: Cigarettes, Bad Companions and Pool Rooms—for each means the other and all three breed crime, discontent and break your father and mother's hearts.

Devote your thought to "Character building," train your mind to THINK — and learn to READ your fellow man.

I can't emphasize too much the Value of Saving. Bitter experience has embedded that trait in your father and the folly of extravagance is evident everywhere. Frugality, my lad, is a virtue to be proud of. So I say: SAVE, SAVE SAVE if you would be happy and successful.

Improve your time. Never be idle and make every minute count, for a minute gone is a minute never to be seen again. Industry carries its own reward and idleness is a scourge.

Have some aim in life — some ambition. Always have something to work for and once you obtain your object — set your "ambition" further on and keep on plugging. By all means don't drift, don't seek the way of the least resistance. BATTLE. FIGHT and push yourself where you belong — IN FRONT and once there, BATTLE to stay there.

Success is Wonderful. Your soul tingles with satisfaction and the world is one beautiful song. So Boy o'mine — try to be a man, try to achieve. Create and don't copy. Build up your inner self and pay homage to 'Him that is All Power' to that one-power who alone holds our destiny. For 'tis He who IS LOVE and TRUTH and is Life Itself.

I will say good bye for this time, my son, and will continue this letter at some future date. Take good care of yourself and remember that I am always

Your Devoted

Daddy.

□   □   □

Daddy's younger brother, Ole, died of a ruptured brain tumor in Los Angeles in 1946. Daddy was playing Buffalo when he was notified. During the flight back for the funeral, he dealt with his grief in a wonderful way. He wrote a letter to his brother's 3-year-old son, Ronnie (we called him Butch when he was little).

Daddy wrote it as if it came to Butch from his daddy right straight from Heaven:

Nov. 1946

Hi Butch!

This is Daddy.

How's my boy?

'Spose you've been missin' me lately and wonderin' why we wasn't rasslin' and havin' fun and playin' together, and why Mother wasn't laughin' and cookin' and growlin' about our makin' too much noise. Well, to tell you the truth, it was a 'sprize and all of a sudden for me too — to leave so unexpectedly.

Remember the day I went to the hospital with that funny eye that was swollen way down to here? Well, the doctor fixed me up and I didn't have any more headaches and I came back home to play with you and work on our house that I was trying to build all by myself as a little hope chest for you and Mummy and then one night I was a-thinkin' and a-dreamin' and a-plannin' when all of a sudden a glow of radiant light swept through the window and I felt a lovely warm tap on my shoulder and I turned around and there was a beautiful angel who gave me a wonderful smile and told me what a lucky fellow I was — that out of all the daddies in my neighborhood I had been selected to go up and help God straighten things out in Heaven and I had to leave at once. It seems that during the war things had been kinda neglected — everything was run down and now that priorities had been lifted, Heaven could be put back into pre-war shape.

So the angel said, "Ole, He likes you 'cause you're so handy at everything and 'cause you've gone all through life doin' good. He prefers you 'cause you're a giver and not a taker."

You know Butch, the world is made up of two kinds of people — those who give and those who take. That's what He meant when He said I was a giver and not a taker — 'cause I guess I always tried to help my neighbor — my fellowman. I tried to know that Life is Infinite.

Anyway, that's what the angel said.

And I kinda blushed and hemmed and hawed.

And then came a rumble of heavenly music . . . A million angels broke forth in tingling harmony. A stairway of stars (bright shiny ones just like those in your eyes when you giggle) — moving just like an escalator — loomed up at the window there by the driveway. The angel lifted me up and put me on a step marked, "RONNIE AND RUTHIE'S DADDY" and away I floated . . . Up and UP and Up. Millions, billions and trillions of miles. The music grew fainter and fainter and in its stead I heard the murmuring of an avalanche of whispers. It was millions of other daddies chanting in rhythm, "WELCOME OLE!! WELCOME RUTHIE AND RONNIE'S DADDY!! WELCOME TO THAT PEACE BEYOND ALL UNDERSTANDING!"

You see they whispered because they didn't want to wake you and Mummy up.

God had a chariot and eight white horses with white fluffy clouds for wings to meet me and take me to my office which was on a great big water lily, nestling in a little pond filled with the milk of human kindness. The warmth of constant friendship seemed to prevail. There was a lilt of love in every face. And then two dewdrops trickled in from nowhere and told me what God expected me to do: Every evening we help put the Sun in the garage and then we hang out the Moon and sprinkle the sky with twinkling Stars.

'Member how we used to blow soap bubbles that spotted Mother's clean tablecloth? Well, we make stars the same way and it sure keeps us busy! I also have charge of one of the rain barrels and help turn the wind machine. So the next time it rains, just know that it's your Daddy helping to bring a drink of water to the flowers and trees and wheat and animals, just like I used to get up in the middle of the night and get my Ronnie "a dink."

And when a soft summer breeze ripples that silky brown hair of yours, just remember that it's your Daddy blowin' you a feather kiss. I also work in the Smile Department. We have to see that everybody smiles and has joy in their hearts. So when you see Mother smiling or Littlejohn laughing or Little Moya grinning, just say, "My Daddy's doin' that!!"

But what keeps me busiest of all is the Paint and Technicolor Department. First we have to keep the sky a deep blue during the day, but at sunrise and sunset we "doodle" a little bit and mix up some blending colors. And you know how we was gonna have a red barn? Well just watch our sunsets and you'll see where I always use lots of red.

Rainbows are a lot of fun. Then we swing our brushes and dib-dab in every color we have.

Flowers are always our homework. It's my job to be careful to get all the roses red . . . the violets blue. . .the lilies white . . . and the jonquils yellow. And, GUESS WHAT??? Just yesterday they put me in personal charge of all the petunias!!

Tomorrow we're going to start re-silvering all the clouds, re-bluing the sky, mixing the fragrance for all the flowers, putting a new coat of gilt on the Golden Stairs, and last and most important, trying to instill in all human hearts the fact that Life is Infinite! Eternal Life is Truth!

In other words, it's an eternal job, and Daddy is gonna be busy for years and years and years! So here's where you come in, Butch. I'm making you my right-hand man down there. You are my Stand-in. You are me. I am you.

Let's see if we can't work together along with Mother. Be good. Be kind. Be understanding. Reflect Love and Tolerance. GIVE, and don't always take. Acquire wisdom. Acquire unselfishness.

And if there must be wrinkles, make 'em laugh wrinkles. For at all times you are God's image and likeness and now that I am working personally for Him I want to be especially proud of the job you're doin'.

I won't be seein' you and Mummy now for a long time. And

I'm sorry I won't be there to cuddle Penny★ in my arms. I bet she'll be wonderful just like her Mother. But I want you to grow up and take care of her and Mummy, and, knowin' you, I ain't a-worryin'. So keep your chest out, chin up, and eyes straight ahead, for God is Love and all my Love is you and Mother and Penny. HUGS AND KISSES to you and Mummy constantly.

It's late now so I guess I'll have my usual cup of coffee before I turn in and dream about that day when we'll all be together again — you and Mummy and Penny and me. And hand and hand we'll walk into everlasting happiness.

Fondly,
Daddy

P.S. Wish you'd say a little prayer every night and include Daddy who kinda wishes God hadn't needed him so soon.

★Butch's Mummy was carrying a baby when Ole, Jr. died. They'd hoped it would be a little girl, and if so, they planned to name her Penny after the song "Pennies from Heaven." Happily, the baby was a girl, and her name, you guessed it!

Appendix D

J.C.'s Senior Thesis at the University of Southern California was a book report on the Los Angeles Telephone Directory of 1937.

What follows is a condensed version, The Author's Note reads:

This great book, which is the latest directory issued by the Southern California Telephone Company, is the most fascinating saga ever compiled on the phone owners of the Los Angeles Extended Area, an area that is one of the greatest playgrounds of the nation and the heart of the Motion Picture Industry.

Although there is practically no plot, there are nearly 300,000 characters in this alphabetical novel. I say PRACTI-CALLY no plot, because the book DOES mention Home, Wedlock, Power, Fate, Anger, Fear, Profit, Fortune, Glory, Land, Liberty, Riches, Peace, Love, Comfort, Joy, Hunger, Cash, Luck, Honor, Money, etc., as other books do, but there is no storyline.

This book contains everything from A to Z under the headings of humorous characters, famous personages, and interesting situations. It will please and enlighten everyone of ANY trade, calling and profession. For instance, medical students will find it a good substitute for Gray's Anatomy as the following terms are mentioned: Hair, Head, Brain, Memory, Temple, Pore, Sweat, Eye, Cheek, Lips, Tongue, Chin, Beard, Body, Lung, Back, Arm, Pulse, Hands, finger, Thumb, Nail, Palm, fist, Limb, Bones, Marrow, Knee, Foot, Sole, Livers, Kidney, an Ache, three Cramps, a Gut, Life and Sex.

Weather Experts will read, to their astonishment, the following names: Fair and Warmer, Clear, Sunshine, Pleasant, Nice, Mild, Sun, Bright, Warm, Fairweather, Grey, Hazy, Cool, Wind, Gale, Blow, Gusty, Foggy, Dew, Rain, Showers, Thunder, Jack Frost, Hail, Crisp, Dry, Cloud, Snow, Blizzard, flurry, Freeze, a Chill, and three Shivers!

Cooks will find practically everything they want to know mentioned: Waffle, Weiner, Bacon, Beets, Pickle, Sandwich, Bran, Calories, Sugar, Salt, Pepper, Fudge, Hershey, Gum, Clove, Ginger, Spice, T. Kettle, Coffee, Strain, Corn, Maize, Barley, Rice, Ham, Parsley, Honey, Hash, Garlic, 54 Beans, Kitchen, Ovens, fish, Apple, Olive, Kraut, Veal, Plate, Fork, Spoon, Glass, Grace, Dine, Chew, Passover, Lent, Dessert, Eclair, Tart, Wafer, Cake, Bakewell, five Meals, Mustard, and Custard. Among many of the respected phone owners in Los Angeles there are the following, shall we say quaint names: Cork, Stein, Glass, fillerup, Straight, Swallow, Belcher, A. Joynt, Booze, eighteen Beers, Champagne, Sherry, Port, Rye, Punch, Drinkwine, Stout, Hops, Brew, Brandy, Bourbon, Licker, Ginn, Mix, Soda, Martini, Tom Collins, Cherry, Bitters, Probst, Iva Brewer, Fred Guzzol, Lloyd Staggers, 50 Benders, High Full, Blind, Blotto, Stiff, three Sheets, a Wind and only one Sober.

There are enough romantic ingredients and pet names for the happiest lovers in the country. Are you in love? How could you possibly do without the following: Moon, Porch, Parlour, Bench, Park, Rumble, two Arms, Lips, Hug and Kiss, Lovit, Date, Young, Shy, Coy, Bliss, Love, Younglove, Mate, Sex, Yen, and Woo, Noble Loving (a man's complete name), Lamour, Caress, Darling, Dear, Dovey, Doll, Chick, Dearie, Honey, Darlin, Hon, Lamb, Lamkin, Lover, Lovelady, Lambie, Sweet, Truelove, Bride and Groom, Wedoo, Rice, Wedlock, Paradise . . . and Reno.

Wouldn't it be amusing if the following ladies (and they are all listed in the Los Angeles Phone Book) were all in the same graduating class of a swank young ladies' finish school: Helia Boozer, Meta Footman, Minnie Whims, Tempie Doolittle, Vera Batty, Iva Butler, Violet Green, Sarah Boop, Queenie Commons, Prudence Beers, Bell Dings, Meta Team, Margaret Foohey, Jesta Mole, Xilda Zo, Mattie Bonebright, Netta fish, Cleantha Jungles,

Verbie Bias, Emma Belcher, Belle Wrinkle, Ida Hell, Burdetta Snuffing, Etta Gourd, Lydaries Gland, Faith N. Ford, Valeska Frankenstein, Lillian Woodhead, Rosalie Mustachio, Lucretia Spie, Nannie Nuckles, Nellie Boxer, Dora Stab, Nellie Gunlock, Minnie Bangs, Iva Hurt, Maggie Gory, Nannie Corpus, Pearl Gates, Hazel Leavenworth, Burnie Bills, Jesse Few, Delia Mizer, Orpha Hoofer, Woopendra Ghosh, Fannie Shover, Laura Rubottom, Lobelia Rugtwet, Pearl Dunks, Nina Drips, Anne Howe.

There are names in the book a lot more famous than the movie stars you know so well. How would you like to meet Robert E. Lee, Francis Drake, George Elliot, Benjamin Franklin, Andrew Jackson, Samuel Johnson and James Boswell, florence Nightengale, Francis Bacon, Duke Wellington, Helen Troy, Alfred Tennyson, Robert Browning, Columbus, William Pitt, Zola, Hannibal, Caesar, Nero, Abraham Lincoln, Erasmus, Steve Brodie and most illustrious of all, Napoleon Plato, Tom Sawyer, Jack Horner, Hamlet, Neptune, Romeo, and Alice N. Wonderland. (Her real name.)

The following trios of names are made up of residents in Los Angeles as are all of these items, but of course they are not actually affiliated with each other. Hook, Line, and Sinker; Ready, Willin and Able; Speed, Officer and fine; Judge, Jury and Justice; Good, Goodenough and Toogood; Back, Seat and Driver; Tall, Dark and Hansom; Ding, Dong and Dell; Hipp, Hipp, Hurray; Deese, Dose and Dem; Roadhouse, Roulette and Gamble; Daniel, Lions and Den; Gabriel, Blow and Horn; Inch, Foot and Yard; fist, Punch and Shiner; Spies, Dawn and Shotwell; Spring, Sprang, Sprung; Sniff, Hankey and Blow.

For the fans of horseracing there is a Stall, Stables, Paddock, Booker, Favorite, Bettin, Wagers, Horseman, Horsey, Hoof, Race, 17 Furlongs, Post, Theroff, Canter, Gallop, Horsefall, Stretch, Win, Place and Show. Or are you a fight fan? You might be more interested, then, in Mr. Arena, Brawn, Strongman, Braveman, Braverman, several Box, Three Boxwell, fite, Bell, Punch, Mrs. Beezer, Biffer, Bonebreak, Sock, fist, Haymaker, Knock, a Ko, five Counts, Victor, Winner, Champion, Champ, Title and Shiner.

Would it interest you that Mrs. Lillian Turner Van Der Sluis is the longest private entry in the book and M. Oi is the shortest? Or that there's one guy who will be broke all his life because his name is Paul Broke: Does it interest you to know that the first entry is the AAAA All American Auto and Airplane Ambulance Association? (They weren't taking any chances). Does it amuse you to find out that firm with the name Aabb was 283rd in the book? (Imagine their chagrin!) Or that the last name is Orton Zzatz? Or that whoever You is You is listed in the Los Angeles phone book? (His whole name is Lew You.) Or that there is only one Name in the book? (L.G. Name). I'll bet he has trouble filling out applications.

Imagine the furor it would cause if the Weddings of any of the following pairs of Los Angeles families were announced in the usual newspaper style (a dash between the last names). Honey-Moon, Bride-Groom, Baby-Boy, Hang-Over, Good-Bye, Izatt-Nice, Pell-Mell, Tick-Tock, See-Saw, Lacks-Brain, Lillywhite-Hands, Off-Nutt, Shim-Sham, Cheap-Scates, Goings-On, Fallin-Love, Mr. Hunger-Miss Meals, Knock-Knee, Catch-Cold, Hitchin-Post, Walkin-Home, Slave-Driver, Shell-Shock, Fair-Warning, Wilt-Collar, Double-Chin, Both-Nutty, Gota-Tan, Lotta-Bunk, Cooks-Dayoff, Constant-Companion, City-Slicker, Perley-Gates, Hang-Nail, Bent-Fender, Polo-Player and Nice-Horsey, a double wedding: Hay-Stack with Mr. Needle as best man, and Wada-Gum with Mr. Chew as best man. Can you imagine a double wedding of Litoff-Bomb and Lotta-Blood or one between Haw-Haw and Ho-Ho with Mirth and Hilarious as best men? Or a triple wedding between Fallin-Line, Forward-March, and Keepin-Step? And believe it or not, a Goto-Hell wedding!

The following couplet poem is made up of Los Angelesians:

> *Finder and Keeper, Apple and Core,*
> *Castle and Moat, Proud and Poor.*
> *Work and Slave, Dine and Dance,*
> *Sink and Swim, Gamble and Chance.*
> *Lavender and Lace, Shoe and Sock,*
> *Blot and Blotter, Key and Lock.*
> *Former and Latter, New and Old,*
> *Sunshine and Shade, Warm and Cold.*

Rank and file, Ball and Chain,
Roof and Leak, Sink and Drain.
Arms and Lips, Young and Shy
Stitch and Pearl, Hook and Eye.
Bee and Stinger, Black and Blue
Salt and Pepper, Munch and Chew.
Rough and Ready, Might and Main,
Hurry and Scurry, Lose and Gain.
Street and Ditch, Bridge and Toll,
Troop and Trench, Drum and Roll.
Dance and Sing, Actor and Stage,
Pipe and Slipper, Book and Page.
first and Last, Large and Small,
Blond and Brunette, Short and Tall.
Chin and Beard, Razor and Hone,
Friend and Foe, Stick and Stone.
Carlock and Carkey, Board and Rent,
Poet and Rhymes, Easter and Lent.
Rose and Thorn, Wig and Pate,
Seat and Tack, Chalk and Slate.
Buyer and Seller, Workman and Boss,
Stocks and Bonds, Profit and Loss.
Bannister and Stair, High and Low,
Gavel and Raps, Plant and Grow.
Bank and Teller, Teach and Learn,
Rod and Reel, flower and Fern.
Apple and Magazine, Hands and Muff,
Hook and Crook, Huff and Puff.
String and Kite, Rope and Hang,
Bell and Clapper, Ring and Rang.
Judge and Jury, Gentile and Jew,
fine and Dandy, Many and Few.
Doctor and Nurse, Ache and Pain,
Fair and Warmer, Thunder and Rain.
Adam and Eve, Paradise and Bliss,
Hamburger and Onions, Hug and Kiss.

Last of all are the hybrids and misfits which do not fall in any distinct class but are in a class by themselves. Some of them

sound so strange that they sound unbelievable but I assure you again of their absolute existence in this year's phone book of Los Angeles. I close this article with Mr. Mister, Rose Bush Rose Blossom and Bud Blossom. Standfast, Playfair, Doctor Dock, Dr. Gum and Dr. Grab (dentists, not associated), Doctor Blind (an eye specialist), Doctor Stork, Doctor Lawyer, Lawyer Lawyer, Lawyer Argue, Lawyer Law, Bent Auto Service, Godbehere, June Garden, Bumgardiner, Ivastock, Misses Bonds and Rob Banks, Goforth, June Glory, Tinkle (a plumber), Burn Lumber Company, Elmer Bulgey, Percy Cowherd, Peter Barnicle, Harold Garlick, Lloyd Reeks, Philbert Pew, Faith Victory, C.D. Battles, three Husbands, two Faithfull, B. Bold, B. Bright, I.M. Bright, Longnecker, Handloser, Mrs. Hands, Orville P. Gripe, William Zilch, John Crumb, Clarence Clever and Paul Perfect. There's no Stella Dallas but there's her sister Martha Dallas, and a cousin from the northeast, Stella Boston. Tyronne Comfort, Dunaway Funeral Home, Sig Steen; North, East, West and South; Summer, Winter, Fall and Spring; Lots of Weeks, Minnie Knights. Most patriotic is U.D. Peoples.

The End

Acknowledgements

SAM AULD — My old and valued friend — his steadfast loyalty and vivid memory have helped me validate Bill's engineering history. He was always there for me throughout the years, and thanks to his meticulous notes, has helped me immeasurably as I've searched for accuracy in writing this book.

HANK BEAIRD — He shared his wonderful, impressive, and funny memories of Bill during their years of flying together in the development of Learjet, and of the years he worked with me, as test pilot for Lear Fan.

KAREN BOLDRA (SPECIAL K!) — She left her home in Atlanta and came to Reno to tackle the great yeoman's job of assembling the first rough draft from the mountains of Lear archives and Olsen and Johnson history. Thank you, Karen.

JERRY DELLA — It doesn't work without her. She picks up the pieces, puts out the fires, keeps track of cash flow, and in a thousand different ways helps me to put one foot ahead of the other!

VICKI DEVINES — I owe her a debt of gratitude you can't believe. This girl spent long days that melted into years at the archives, and fed us priceless information with a quick phone call.

ROLLAN MELTON — My dear friend, he was one of the first people to get on my back about writing this book — and never let up!

STAN SEIDEN — He could remember what I'd forgotten about Daddy and Olsen and Johnson — and how we laughed, remembering!

JUNE SHIELDS — The first person who, years ago, started to record, interview, document, push and encourage. I salute you, June.

MICHAEL SION — This gifted young journalist's modern perspective contributed to the flow and clarity of many areas of the manuscript.

GERMAINE STOLL — There's no way to describe what I owe this wonderful friend — for all she did for us in Geneva, her warmth, her mothering of us all.

RICHARD TRACY — A steadfast friend who had classy notes to jog my memory.

TIFFANY VAN der STOKKER — What wonderful ability and sense of humor — she just kept right on typing and deserves a medal. We sure had fun working together on this monumental project.

LILLI LOCKE — My incredible secretary whose lovely voice on the telephone kept us all going in the right direction.

This First Edition of
Bill & Moya Lear
An Unforgettable Flight
is limited to 5000 copies.

The paper is Cougar Natural Text
and the type is Monotype Dante.

Designed by Susan Flake,
Herb Yellin and Jim Richards.

Typography by
Reno Typographers, Inc.

Printed by Ross Printing.

Binding by Mike Roswell.